St. Albert the Great

ALBERTVS MAGNVS EPISCOP' RATISPONE.
Nascitur Lauingæ Anno 1293.
Obyt Coloniæ Agrip. Aº 1382.
Magnus es, at major fieri dum ALBERTE, recusas
Dispeream, si quid majus hic orbis habet.
A 2.

ST. ALBERT

the Great

BY

THOMAS M. SCHWERTNER, O.P.,
S.T.Lr., LL.D.

MEDIATRIX PRESS

ISBN: 978-1-953746-04-7

Imprimi potest:
FR. STEPHANUS McDERMOTT, O.P.,
Prior Provincialis

Nihil obstat:
FR. GUILLELMUS OWENS, O.P.
FR. FRANCISCUS DOMINICUS McSHANE, O.P.

Imprimatur:
✠ SAMUEL A. STRITCH,
Archiepiscopus Milwaukiensis

Mediatrix Press
607 E. 6th Ave.
Post Falls, ID 83854

Table of Contents

PREFACE BY THE GENERAL EDITOR

SELDOM, in the wide range of biographical literature, does a subject present itself more illuminative and inspiring than the life of St. Albert the Great. It is of interest not alone for its own sake, but also for the light cast by it over a large portion of one of the world's most absorbing periods, the thirteenth century, with its prolific wealth of thought and enduring achievements. In this supreme epoch Albert the Great holds a unique position.

But what at first glance particularly attracts our attention in this great Saint and Doctor of the Church is his modernity. Although truly medieval, in as fine a sense as Dante and St. Francis, he none the less projects himself into our century and from many points of view might be considered a modern of the moderns.

We are living in a mechanized age, but mechanical invention and the designing of automatic devices were familiar tasks with him. In the popular imagination they even caused him to be regarded as endowed with magic powers.

Science, too, is looked upon as peculiarly the prerogative of our times. But scientific study and experimentation were favorite preoccupations with St. Albert. He was gifted with a keen instinct for scientific investigation and research. He was a born naturalist and experimentalist. Natural phenomena engaged his attention from early youth; he probed into their secrets and arrived at startlingly accurate conclusions. Laboratory research, no less, was congenial to him and from all sides he gathered details of medical facts for practical application.

Education, once more, is a passion with the men of our day. Most unreasonable claims are not seldom made in its regard. Albert was an expert pedagogue, a great schoolman, a guide and director in the most advanced problems of university development in that heyday of progressive university life. But more than all this, he himself undertook the herculean task of collating and interpreting the philosophic lore of the ages—Classical, Arabic, and Christian—gathering the vast masses of unrelated and scattered material, arranging and adapting it so that other hands might ultimately fit it in its proper place within the loftiest system of human thought. To all this the author vividly refers. How little more than pygmies, by the side of such a man, are not seldom the most noted of our modern educators!

But who shall take amiss the final conclusion of our author, when he counts it as the greatest of Albert's educational achievements that out of his own classroom went forth, to blaze his way across the world and through the far reaches of time, that shining luminary and brilliant genius in the realm of constructive thought, St. Thomas Aquinas? To that same fountain too—in the poet's words—other suns repaired, lesser luminaries, yet splendors of no mean magnitude, and in their urns drew golden light.

So we might continue, were there further need, to illustrate the closeness of Albert to our own times. And yet there was also a difference. More, perhaps, even than any other man of his own day, he avoided all overspecialization. Exaggerated as our statement may appear, he can best be said to have specialized not in one branch of learning or science, but rather in all.

True, it may be urged, that in consequence he did not reach that supreme excellence of constructive philosophic thought achieved by his own pupil, St. Thomas. But Thomas, as the author bids us to remember, built on the foundations and with the material of his pioneering forerunner, teacher, and best-beloved father, St. Albert. If Augustine cannot be thought of without Ambrose, neither should Thomas be mentioned without Albert. Such, indeed, is the beauty of the Divine plan, where each is to minister to each, that we may attain together to the perfection of the high ideal God has set for us, our ultimate possible likeness to the God-man, Christ Jesus.

It was for Albert the Great to follow precisely the course he did. In the highly developed university life of that thirteenth century—intellectually the keenest and most assertive the world has ever known to the present day—Albert so impressed the brilliant minds of his contemporaries with the unrivaled catholicity of his knowledge that they conferred on him a doctorate such as no other man ever received—not in one branch of learning only or another—but in all. With one consent they acclaimed him, and for all time he remains, the Universal Doctor!

I can here but adumbrate briefly what the author of the present volume so eloquently details in his successive chapters on this particular point.

Albert was equally illustrious as preacher and as teacher; as prelate of the Church and as Provincial of his Order; as reformer within the Fold of Christ and as valiant defender of his own religious brethren; as gifted statesman and no less successful diplomatist; as one of the world's most marvelous scholars and at the same time a leader among its pioneer experimentalists and investigators; as collator and interpreter of the wisdom of Greeks and Orientals, and withal path-breaking philosopher and luminous theologian; as author, no less, of innumerable writings, vast in extent and rich in content, that alone might have engaged far more than the lifetime of any ordinary man; as zealous pastor of souls, indefatigable in his labors, and as equally apostolic prelate on whom seemed to rest the care, not of his own faithful only, but of many churches; as mystic, drawn by the strong cords of love and refreshed by Divine intimacies, and as glorious saint of God, making himself all things to all men, that he might win them all for Christ. And last but not least, we must not forget to mention, as most characteristic of the man, his great and tender and most childlike devotion to Mary, Mother of God and Mother of men, whom from childhood to his declining years he venerated with an ardent affection, in whose praise his lips dropped sweetness and his words were lyric.

And now coming to the man himself we behold him, not tall in stature, but with atlantean breadth of shoulders, built to carry the immense burden that weighed upon him. His energy, his endurance, his ceaseless labors, his courage under difficulties, his fearlessness in defense of right and justice were qualities truly epic in him, yet which, if we cannot equal, we should at least strive to imitate. And here, precisely, is the great practical value of his life, that it should help to make our own more beautiful, apostolic, and heroic. Catholic Action should draw from him vital inspiration.

Taking him all in all, the Middle Ages only, and perhaps the thirteenth century alone, could have produced St. Albert the Great. But it is equally evident that our own epoch, and our present generation, seem particularly qualified to appreciate his spirit and achievements.

In presenting, then, the life of such a man we are doubly happy that we can do so through the mediation of one who is his own brother in religion, wearing the same habit of six hundred years ago, with the same zeal that once consumed the heart of Albert in the cause of God.

The glory of the sons of Dominic links, indeed, in one unbroken splendor, the thirteenth century with our own. The ideals of their Order remain the same in past and present. Its activities of yesterday are no less its pursuits of today. The spirit of its Founder has not been allowed to languish and burns as brightly in the latest of his children as in the earliest sprung from him. And so from the thirteenth century to the twentieth is no far cry for them.

As preacher, pastor, editor and writer of various volumes, the author has for years been well and widely known. His studies and activities have extended into many fields, broadening his interests and enabling him to cope with a task such as that which he has here successfully accomplished. It is my privilege, then, to lay before the reader, as a worthy tribute, the Life of Albert, canonized Saint and Doctor of the Church, whom all the ages have proclaimed, "the Great."

Joseph Husslein, S.J., Ph.D.

St. Louis University,
November 2, 1932

AUTHOR'S PREFACE

IF Albert the Great has received rather scant treatment and shabby consideration at the hands of English, and even English Catholic historians, the reason is not far to seek. It is because they, like scholars of every tongue, but only in a greater degree, have been handicapped by the very incomplete state and exploitation of Albertinian research, and by the unsatisfactory and inadequate presentation of Albertinian thought.

Naturally one would expect to find German scholars in the forefront of those who sought consistently to vindicate the memory and achievements of their own medieval fellow countryman. But as late as 1880 Henry Cardauns chided his own people for their chronic neglect of Albert's memory and their criminal indifference to Albert's greatness. This well-merited rebuke, coming from a scholar of established reputation, was well taken. From that day dates a veritable renaissance of historical interest and of research into the rich life and solid achievements of Albert, as also a resumption and prosecution of that popular cult which was not afraid to avow it would not be satisfied until it had received formal papal approval and liturgical consummation. This latter was obtained in a most striking and glorious manner on December 16, 1931, when Pope Pius XI, by his decretal bull, *In thesauris sapientiæ*, not only numbered Albert among the saints of God, but also accorded him the rare aureola of a Doctor of the Church. We may consequently expect the next decades of years to produce a vast literature on St. Albert. Not only is this hope founded on an eventual critical edition of his works, but also on the fact that the multiform activities of the man are now being studied and investigated by a corps of scholars who believe that their minute labors will prove of abiding value for a better understanding of the prehistory and early beginnings of the *philosophia perennis*, which the Church depends upon so largely to offset the assumptions and to meet the vagaries of the resurgent anti-intellectualist philosophy of our machine age.

This hopeful forecast and promise of a burgeoning Albertinian literature, while highly inspiriting to the student of medieval thought, is painfully discouraging to a biographer of Albert, for he knows that each month sees so much new light cast upon the life and activities of Albert that what he has written at the cost of much study and research becomes outmoded and antiquated before it has had so much as a chance to come from the press. As no historian presumes to exercise the prophetical office he must be patiently resigned to cope with the task of trying to summarize what has been published at the period when he himself sets to work. We are not afraid to confess that scarcely anything worth while in the published Albertinian literature has been overlooked by us or left out of sight in writing this work. But we are not rash enough to suppose that we have said the last word, that we have drawn the final conclusion, that we have opened up the ultimate possible vista to a better and fuller understanding and appreciation of the wondrously rich life and thought of Albert.

The difficulties confronting a biographer of Albert are appalling by reason of the many-sided activities of the man. Besides, not all the documents showing forth his labors have been discovered, interpreted, and fitted into the complex picture of the times in which he lived. Not all the works of Albert have as yet been published, nor have even all those mentioned in the old catalogs of his writings been ferreted out of archives and libraries. The authenticity of many works published over his name has not been finally determined or established. The chronology of his exterior activities, as also of his voluminous works, depends upon the erudition, dexterity, and critical powers of each respective and newly arrived investigator, and scarcely any two of them sit down together in perfect agreement. It is a source of great satisfaction—and we may say of justifiable pride—that quite independently, by our own researches and computations, we have arrived at the identical chronology (except in the one case of the date of Albert's ordination to the priesthood) of Father Fredegand Callaey, O.M.Cap., whose *Curriculum Vitae* proved satisfactory to the Roman Congregations concerned with the possibility, feasibility, and actuality of Albert's canonization and inclusion among the Doctors of the Church.

We have sought to paint briefly the prodigious exterior activity of Albert against a true background of the times in which he multiplied himself as no other contemporary churchman. We have not expatiated at length on the many acts of a social nature which ate in so mightily upon his time because these, in the aggregate, present activities of a single type. For while, undoubtedly, much local or regional history underlies each cold, formal, legal action in which Albert was engaged, it was manifestly impossible, without enlarging this work unduly, to dilate upon the peculiarities and particularities of each case. Without, therefore, consciously omitting to mention each instance, we have rather sought to draw composite pictures of the various categories of his varied activities. We have not incorporated the many legends which began clustering around Albert's name, even in his own lifetime, which luxuriated, as in the case of no other medieval man, during the first five decades after his death. Legends have been utilized only insofar as they cast light upon his character or upon the achievements (at least in the popular mind) of a man whose shadow Goethe seemed bent on resurrecting in his *Faust* and Edmond Rostand dreamed of evoking in *L'Automaton*, as a flat condemnation of the blatant protagonists of our own self-satisfied machine and industrial age. As regards the intellectual action of Albert, we have sought to place him in his true orbit of history without on that account undertaking the task of interpreting or evaluating his thought by the norms which his pupil Thomas Aquinas fixed and settled for the centuries to come. Albert's mind is impressive enough in its own right. And it detracts nothing from Thomas's greatness to keep forever in mind that he was signally favored by Providence in having had a professor of Albert's mental sweep, sympathy, and suggestiveness.

Albert's personality has emerged in new splendor and attractiveness since the day when Father Paul de Loe, O.P., in 1900, adjudicated in the *Analecta Bollandiana* (1900-1902) the sources and literature bearing upon the life and action of the great medieval schoolman. His intellectual eminence has been better appraised since the critical editions of some of his works by Wimmer, Jessen, and Stadler, which have inspired a large body of historians to investigate separate phases of his academic labors. His scientific importance has been vindicated by Pouchet and scores of others who took a hint from his epoch-making work. His name will shine with growing glory in the ages to come in proportion as scholars determine with greater accuracy the universal genius of which he was possessed and which he perfected by assiduous study and unflagging exercise.

In his lifetime he was called the Universal Doctor—and those

Catholic ages (proof against the mania for specialization so characteristic of our own times) meant by that honorific name and title to delineate a man whose intellectual interests did not proscribe social action, whose scholastic enthusiasm did not preclude active apostleship. He did make a synthesis of all preexisting knowledge in his voluminous works. But he made in actuality a still better synthesis in his own life. For he was at once priest, professor, preacher, poet; he found time to serve as provincial, bishop, papal legate, crusader, politician, pedagogical reformer, and sewer of the torn garments of Catholic social unity in Europe by advising kings, princes, and peoples to embrace the things of peace; he multiplied himself for the unborn ages by writing a library upon which the scholars of the centuries to come were royally to regale themselves, without always stopping to give his bounty mention or credit; he harmonized philosophy and theology without allowing the natural sciences to misprize themselves as mere servitors of the body; he showed men how to be scientific without feeling compelled to embrace atheism or espouse materialism. And the informing spirit of his universal activity and apostolate was the sanctity whereby he grew in ever more conscious sensitiveness to the Holy Spirit operating within his soul, all unseen, since that day when the regenerating waters of baptism had been poured upon his head in his own lovely native town of Lauingen. Albert was first and foremost a child of God. His chief business, as he took it to be, was to put on the Christ through charity. This combination of high mysticism with sane practicality, of fecund social action with pioneering intellectual investigation, of rare scientific temper with tender understanding of the popular heart was Albert's own method of interpreting the words which St. John puts down as characteristic of the Christ: "For their sakes I sanctify Myself" (John xvii. 19). This wedlock of the active and contemplative life gives unity to the universalist temper and character of Albert. Had he failed in sanctity he might some day have come to be looked upon as a mere superman, or if the ideals of an industrial age shall prevail, as a kind of robot glorified by the possession of a matchless brain.

Pope Pius XI has pointed out that the long delay in Albert's apotheosis has something providential about it. For the contemporary world, which seems to have forgotten the postulates of the spiritual in the bitter need of attending to the imperatives of the physical, needed a man whose whole life takes on consistency from his persistent effort and endeavor to make the things of sense and time subordinate and subservient to the things of the spirit and eternity. If Albert, by reason of the pressure of historical circumstances, had to wait six hundred and fifty years for the halo of sainthood it was, perhaps, because precisely our age needed the example of a man whose apostolic zeal extended itself to the mind as well as to the heart and hand. If Albert had to wait six hundred and fifty years for the crown of the Church's doctorate it was, perhaps, because our children, whom we have taught to use their hands for the multiplication of the comforts of the body, needed to be taught to use their brains as well for Godward thinking, both in their own behalf and, by a Christlike consecration, in favor of the commonweal. An earlier canonization would have been premature and consequently shorn of its historical significance and spiritual actuality. A later canonization would have been belated and thus cheated of its social impressiveness and religious immediacy.

We have drawn up a catalog of the sources and main works upon which we have based this biography. These original sources are quoted in abbreviated form in the footnotes which, to preserve the reader from distraction, are gathered at the end of the volume. We have quoted in full in the footnotes modern literary studies and monographs, based upon and growing out of the primary sources. And we entertain the belief that none will fail to see the reason why we have placed side by side in the closing chapter—which takes the form of an epilog—the estimate of Albert made by Blessed Humbert de Romans who knew the Saint in the flesh, and the decretal appraisement of Pope Pius XI who gathers together the hoarded conclusions of the Catholic ages on this colossal historical figure. Humbert's close-up gives us a glimpse of the attractive personality of the man as he appeared to those who had the best opportunity of seeing him at close range; Pius's verdict presents us, in historic perspective, with the majestic proportions of the scholar, social savior, and saint whom the ages have done themselves honor in acclaiming as the Great. Speaking with the authority of Peter and the tender solicitude of the common father of the faithful, the Sovereign Pontiff insists that Albert has precious lessons not only for the individual Christian of our age, whom his sane sanctity cannot but solicit to the higher roads of spirituality, but also for contemporary society, whom his sweet reasonableness cannot but steer into the haven of international peace and the port of interracial amity.

For those who are eager to learn from Albert practical lessons for everyday life, as also to experience the power of his intercession, I have published (Paulist Press, New York) *St. Albert the Great: Life-Sketch and Novena.*

THOMAS M. SCHWERTNER, O.P.

Washington, D. C.,
August 4, 1932.

SOURCES

The first critical study of the life and works of Albert was made by Echard and Quetif in the *Scriptores Ordinis Praedicatorum* (Paris: 1719), I, 162 ff. Father Paul de Loe, O.P., after a life of study, research, and publication of fugitive studies and *pieces*, published his findings and conclusions in the *Analecta Bollandiana* (1900-1902) under the title *De Vita et Scriptis B. Alberti Magni.* By this erudite study he opened the way and established the norms for all subsequent research into the original sources and the literature on Albert. This mass of writings was submitted to a searching examination by Franz Pelster, S.J., in *Kritische Studien zum Leben und zu den Schriften Alberts des Grossen* (Freiburg: 1920). An even more acute study in evaluating the studies of scholars on the sources and literature having reference to Albert's chronology was made by H. Scheeben, *Albert der Grosse. Zur Chronologie seines hebens* (Vechta: 1931). The same authority has dealt with the chronology of Albert's works in the *Revue Thomiste* (1931), 36-68, and in the *Archivum Fratrum Praedicatorum* (1932), 223-263. G. Meersemann, O.P., has envisaged all fundamental questions regarding the authorship, content, and tradition of Albert's published, unedited, authentic, and spurious works in his *Introductio ad Opera Omnia B. Alberti Magni* (Bruges: 1931). The *Revue Thomiste* (1931), 198-238, published an admirably arranged but incomplete bibliographical catalog of all Albertinian literature.

I.
Primary Sources

I. *Autobiographical:* Unlike most medieval authors Albert furnished much data of a personal kind, most of it having reference to his youth and his episcopal days. This can be found in *De Animalibus* (B. III, tr. 2, Chap. 6); *Meteorum* (B. I, tr. 1, Chap. 1); *De Mineralibus* (B. II, tr. 3, Chap. I; B. III, tr. i, Chap. 1); *De Causis et Proprietatibus Elementorum* (B. I, tr. 2, Chap. 3); *De Natura Locorum* (B. I, tr. 3, Chap. 2; B. I, tr. 3, Chap. 3, 7). In his *Commentary on St. Luke* there are reminiscences of his childhood told impersonally, and in the same work and in his *Commentary on St. John* there are distinct echoes of his episcopal days. His sermons are filled with thinly veiled autobiographical experiences and the prayers he attached to the sermons on the Sunday pericopes reveal his pious soul in many cases.

II. *Archival:* The instruments and acts of a documentary kind having reference to Albert are divided into three classes.

A. *Pontifical Acts: A. Potthast, Regesta Pontificum Romanorum (Berolino: 1875); T. Ripoll,* Bullarium Ordinis Praedicatorum *(Roma: 1729); B. de la Ronciere,* Registres d' Alexandre IV *(Paris: 1895); J. Guiraud,* Les Registres d' Urbain IV *(Paris: 1901); Jordan,* Registres de Clement IV *(Paris: 1894); J. Guiraud,* Registres de Gregoire X *(Paris: 1893); C. Rodenberg,* Epistolae saeculi XIII e Regestis Pontificum Romanorum Selectae *(Berolino: 1894).*

B. *Acts of Albert* as master of theology, provincial of Germany and Bishop of Ratisbon: Denifle, Chatelain, *Chartularium Universitatis Parisiensis* (Paris: 1889); extracts of his Acts as provincial are reproduced in the *Vita Alberti Magni* of Peter of Prussia (Antwerp: 1621), chapters 26, 27, and 31; in the municipal archives of Basle there is preserved the *Series Capitulorum Provincialium Teutoniae Ordinis Praedicatorum* (MS. E. III. 13); *Acta Capitulorum Generalium O. P.* (ed. Reichert), I, 1220-1303 (Roma: 1898); H. Finke, *Ungedruckte Dominikanerbriefe des XIII Jahrhunderts* (Paderborn: 1891); Aventinus (G. Thurmeier), a Bavarian chronicler who died in 1534, gathered many notices about Albert in his *Bairische Chronik* and his *Annales Ducum Boiariae*, published in his *Opera Omnia* (Munich: 1884), the former in Volume V, the latter in Volume III; L. Hochwalt, who lived in the fifteenth century, completed these notices in his *Catalogus Episcoporum Ratisbonensis* which A. Oeffle published in *Rerum Boicarum Scriptores* (Augusta: 1763) I; J. Janner, *Geschichte der Bischöfe von Regensburg* (Regensburg: 1884); T. Reid, *Codex chronologico—diplomaticus Episcopatus Ratisbonensis* (Ratisbon: 1816); *Monumenta Boica* (Augusta: 1763); C. de Lang, *Regesta sive Rerum autographa Boicarum* (Augusta: 1825).

C. *Municipal, Episcopal, and Monastic Acts of Albert* relative to his public life, especially after his resignation of the see of Ratisbon: T. Lacomblet, *Urkundenbuch für die Geschichte des Niederrheins* (Köln: 1846) II; A. Riedel, *Codex diplomaticus Brandeburgensis* (Berolino: 1838); R. Picken, *Monatschrift für Rheinisch—Westphälische Geschichte* (Trier: 1876); L. Ennen and G. Eckertz, *Quellen zur Geschichte der Stadt Köln* (Köln: 1863-1871) II,

III; H. Cardauns, *Regesten Conrads von Hochstaden*, in *Annalen des Historischen Vereins für den Niederrhein* (Köln: 1880 sq.) fasc. 35. The will and last testament of Albert, discovered by Schmeller, was published in *Münchener Gelehrten Anzeigen* (1850), 45 ff., and by J. Sighart, *Albertus Magnus* (Paderborn: 1857), 248 ff.

II.
Secondary Sources

A. *Literary Sources.* The first biographical account of Albert is found in the *Vita Fratrum Ordinis Praedicatorum*, written about 1260 by Gerard de Frachet on the command of the Master General of the Order, Blessed Humbert de Romans (ed. Reichert. Lovannii: 1896). Thomas of Cantimpre, who was a pupil of Albert at Cologne, gathered valuable data in his *Bonum Universale de Apibus* (ed. Colvenerio. Duaci: 1627). Important biographical facts regarding Albert's part in the foundation of the Convent of Dominican Nuns at Paradise were gathered by Henry of Osthoven in his *De Institutione Paradysi et humili ingressu sororum*, and published by J. S. Seibertz in *Quellen der Westphälischen Geschichte* (Arusberg: 1858) I; in the *Historia Ecclesiastica* of Ptolomey of Lucca, O.P., composed about 1300, and published by Muratori in *Rerum Italicarum Scriptores* (Mediolani: 1728) XI, col. 1150, and in part by Echard and Quetif in *Scriptores Ordinis Praedicatorum* (Paris: 1719) I, 162 ff; in the *Vita S. Thomae Aquinatis*, written by William Tocco about 1319 (*Acta Sanctorum.* Martii I, 660 ff.), and in the *Processus inquisitionis jactae super vita, conversatione et miraculis Fr. Thomae de Aquino* (*Acta Sanctorum.* Martii I, 706-712). About 1330 the Dominican chronicler, John of Cologne, wrote a short life of Albert in his *De Viris Illustribus ethnicis et christianis* which was edited by Leonard de Rubeis, O.P., at Venice, in 1750, and has been prefixed to the first volume of the Leonine edition of the works of St. Thomas Aquinas (Rome: 1882).

B. *Biographies:* The first complete biography of Albert was written about 1365 by Henry of Hereford in his *Liber de Rebus Memorialibus* (ed. A. Potthast. Goettingen: 1859). It contains a catalog of Albert's works at the end. It is possible that an older life of Albert, hailing from Cologne and quite independent of the life in the Process of St. Thomas, and which is preserved in Codex 939 of the Bayrisches National Museum at Munich, served Henry as a model.

In 1414, Louis of Vallodolid, O.P., professor at St. James, Paris, composed a *Vita Domni et Magistri Alberti Magni*, based upon the *Vitae Fratrum* of Gerard de Frachet, the *Bonum Universale* of Thomas of Cantimpre and the *Legenda Sancti Thomae* of Bernard Gui, who depends almost entirely on Stephen Salignae, Ptolomey of Lucca, and William Tocco. Louis is the first to mention many edifying details, miracles, the erection of a chapel at Lauingen, preservation of the body of Albert, and Pope John XXII's eagerness to canonize Albert at the time of Thomas's apotheosis. This biography was first published in *Catalogus Codicum Hagiographicorum Bib. Bruxelliensis* (Bruxelles: 1889) II, 95 ff.

In 1483 an anonymous author of Cologne composed a short life, *Vita brevis et compendiosa*, generally called *Legenda Coloniensis*, and edited in part by de Loe in *Analecta Bollandiana* (1900), 272 ff. It is a résumé of everything that had so far been written about Albert. He laid under contribution a chronicle of Ratisbon, so far undiscovered, which gave some new facts about Albert's episcopal career, and a local Cologne chronicle giving particulars about the exhumation of the body of St. Cordula, which Albert conducted.

About 1486, Peter of Prussia, O.P., undertook the composition of the first critical life for the purpose (1) of arranging in chronological order the true facts in the life of Albert, (2) of defending him against the charge of having practised magic, and (3) of establishing his sanctity. It is the most complete medieval biographical source for Albert's life, though its authority is somewhat impaired by the evident desire of the author to make manifest the holiness of Albert. For this purpose, Peter used apocryphal legends as, for instance, the one (Chapter 53) in which Albert is said to have liberated six thousand souls from purgatory on his death. It was first published at Cologne in 1487 and reprinted in 1621 at Anvers.

Rudolf of Nijmegen, about 1488, wrote his *Legenda literalis de Alberto Magno*, utilizing the biographical and edifying data of Peter of Prussia, and omitting all polemical elements. From a source which has not yet been discovered he borrowed some welcome facts. It was published at Cologne in 1490, and reprinted in 1928 by H. Scheeben, who wrote a valuable preface.

C. *Modern Lives:* J. Sighart, in 1857, published *Albertus Magnus* (Paderborn), which was soon translated into French, and into English by Dixon, with notable abridgements. With this biography a new impetus was given to the study of Albert's life. E. Michael, S.J., in his monumental *Geschichte des deutschen Volkes im Mittelalter* (Freiburg: 1903), III, wrote a masterly monograph which was completed by H. Wilms with his *Albert der Grosse* (München: 1930) and A. Puccetti *Sant Alberto Magno. Profilo Biografico* (Roma: 1932). The final and authoritative life, *Albertus Magnus* (Bonn am Rhein), laying under contribution the enormous Albertinian literature, and investigating every minutest point with the utmost care was published by Heribert Scheeben in 1932. M. Grabmann, in a series of German articles, translated into Italian and enlarged with the latest results of historical research, envisages the intellectual life and influence of Albert: *L'lnflusso di Alberto Magno sulla Vita Intellecttuale del Medio Evo* (Roma: 1931). Nor can his important article in the *Angelicum* (1929), 325- 351, be overlooked: *"Die Wissenschaftliche Mission Alberts des Grossen und die Entstehung des Christlichen Aristotelismus."* The tribute which art has paid to Albert appears clearly from Scheeben-Walz, *Iconographia Albertina* (Freiburg: 1932). Everything pertaining to the cult shown Albert during six centuries has been gathered together and arranged in an orderly fashion by A. M. Walz: *Esposizione e documentazione storica del culto tributo al B. Alberto Magno* (Rome: 1930; and a supplementary volume, Rome: 1931).

CHAPTER I

EARLY YEARS

IN the lazy little Suabian town of Lauingen on the Danube, not more than thirty leagues from Augsburg, Albert the Great began his colorful progress through the world during the closing decade of the twelfth century. Mists of popular legend hang about the circumstances and conditions of his early years as also about the honorable name by which posterity knows him.

The word-juggling Humanists, Vives and Neuman[1]—ignorant as most Humanists were of the popular lore of the people—suggest with too much glibness that the name *Magnus* is but the verbal contraction of Albert's family name de Grote. At a time when many family names were being constructed out of the provenance, occupation, physical or mental characteristics, or historical experiences of individuals, it was generally known that Albert sprang from the well-known family of the Bollstadt, of whom there is frequent mention in the annals of the times. Thus, for instance, there is a Rudolf, a Sigfried, a Hans Bollstadt in the thirteenth century, all of whom were in the service and employ of the Hohenstaufen though their relationship with Albert cannot be established. The male line died out in 1607.

Others suggest that the name had reference to Albert's physical stature as was the case with Albert I, Duke of Braunschweig, who was called *Magnus*, or "the Fat," to distinguish him from his son Albert II, *Pigmus*, or "the Small." Now, were this the case with Albert, his contemporaries would have called attention to it. But the opposite is just the case. According to the most reliable authorities of the time he was rather small of stature. Thus, John Meyer, who reproduces the *Legenda Coloniensis* written within thirty years of his death, remarks that he was "the great Albert, great in his knowledge, small in his person."[2]

Sometimes his rather diminutive size is played up for rhetorical

---

[1] Fabriccius, *Bibliotheca Latinae Mediae et Infimae Aetatis.* (Hamburg: 1734), I, 113.

[2] J. Meyer, *Liber de Viris Illustribus Ord. Praed.* (ed. de Loe. Berolini: 1918), 12, 40.

effects, as when Peter of Prussia remarks that,[3] at an audience, the Pope bade him to stand up as he thought he was upon his knees. Rudolf of Nijmegen[4] says that he had a striking figure without making any particular reference to his height. Thomas of Cantimpre,[5] Albert's pupil, repeats the statement of the Augustinian Provost, Gavilus, that Albert was distinguishable for nothing so much as a mole on his right eyelid.

The Dominican Master General, Humbert de Romans, speaks of "the gigantic shoulders upon which he had carried so long the yoke of the Order." Rudolf also mentions his giant shoulders.[6] The same appears from the depositions made after the canonical inspection of his relics at Cologne on November 12, 1857.[7]

That Albert was a man of medium height, broad shoulders and great powers of physical endurance, would seem to have been due to his ancestry. For the Suabians, from their earliest appearance on the stage of history, were ever twitted by their taller neighbors for their mediocre stature, their large feet, great shock of wiry, auburn hair, big shoulders, and big heart—a common characterization which holds good to this very day. Besides, he sprang from a stock that needed to be strong in order to retain their place in the employ of the Emperor Barbarossa, who was careful to surround himself with men of great endurance.

It is plain, therefore, that Albert was not called "the Great" during his lifetime for any reason of physical size. He was generally spoken of as "Albert the Teuton" or "Albert of Cologne" which latter appellation he himself sometimes affected because of his great love for the German metropolis. At Paris he passed as "Albert the Master" or "Albert the Theologian." After his resignation of the episcopacy he was called "Lord Brother Albert." In 1260 Gerard de Frachet, in his *Lives of the Brethren*, speaks of him as a "man of great repute and sanctity, distinguished for his knowledge of natural sciences, provincial of the

---

3 Petrus de Prussia, *Legenda Alberti Magni* (Coloniae: 1486), 320.

4 Rodolphus de Novimagio, *Legenda litteralis Alberti Magni* (ed. Scheeben. Coloniae: 1928), 42.

5 Thomas Camimpranus, *Bonum Universale de Apibus* (Duaci: 1627), 143.

6 Rodolphus de Novimagio, *op. cit.*, 43.

7 H. Goblet, Der sel. Albertus Magnus und die Geschichte seiner Reliquien *(Köln:* 1880), 97.

German province, Brother Albert, the German, Master of Theology."[8] And Ulrich of Strassburg, his favorite pupil, says that because of his learning he might be considered "the most remarkable marvel of his age."[9] Cardinal Ehrle's contention[10] that the name *Magnus* was first used among the people and not in the schools of the thirteenth and fourteenth centuries has been disproved by Monsignor Martin Grabmann[11] who shows conclusively that the title first appears about 1343 in the *Liber Certarum Historiarum* of John of Vitry. That the learned world had contributed its share in giving this title currency is shown from the *Pugio Fidei* of Raymond Martin[12] which, in Albert's lifetime, called him *Magnus philosophus*, and from the custom of calling and citing Albert by name even before his death. This was one of the grievances of Roger Bacon against Albert. By the early fourteenth century the appellation was common among students as appears from the marginal note to a manuscript *Commentary on Peter Lombard* where he is styled *Albertus Magnus.*[13]

Perhaps the social station of Albert had something to do with the name he subsequently obtained. For he moved in circles whose every member was looked up to with awe and respect by the common people of the day. His parents belonged to the inferior nobility, called the *militares*, not necessarily because they bore arms but rather because they were charged with representing the emperor's authority in the town. It is not clear, nor perhaps ever will be, whether his father was

---

[8] Gerardus de Fracheto, *Vitae Fratrum* (ed. Reichert. Lovanii: 1896), 187.

[9] Petrus de Prussia, *op. cit.*, 260.

[10] F. Ehrle, Die Ehrentitel der scholastischen Lehrer des Mittelalters (München: 1914), 7.

[11] M. Grabmann, L'influsso di Alberto Magno sulla Vita Intellettuale del Medio Evo (Roma: 1931), 30.

[12] Raymundus Martin, *Pugio Fidei* (Parisiis: 1651), 445.

[13] F. Pelster, "*Die Ehrentitel der scholastischen Lehrer des Mittelaltcrs,*" in *Theologische Quartalschrift (1922), 43.* George Schneider says (*Handbuch der Bibliographie*, Leipzig: 1930, 454-455): "*Nun gibt es noch Pseudonyme im weiteren Sinne. Viele mittelalterliche Namen sind es zwar nicht der Absicht, aber der Wirkung nach. Es liegt in der Eigenart der Beinamen, die die zahllosen gleichlautenden persönlichen,* also *die Taufnamen unterscheiden sollen, und aus Eigenschaften, Würden und Herkunft abgeleitet werden. Der Träger selbst schreibt sie willkürlich; der Abschreiber fährt erst recht ungenau. Schriftsteller und Publikum ersetzen ausserdem ohne viel Bedenken die alten Beinamen durch neue. Die Persönlichkeiten werden dadurch oft so unkenntlich gemacht, als ob sie wirklich Pseudonyme führten. Die Beinamen Grotus, Magnus, Bolstadius, de Colonia, Ratisbonensis, Lavingensis, Teutonicus bezeichnen alle denselben Albert den Grossen.*"

a chevalier or an officer of the Royal Court of the Hohenstaufen. At any rate, the family possessed a stately palace, the site of which is still pointed out in a corner of the market place of Lauingen, in the diocese of Augsburg, on the banks of the Upper Danube in Suabia. Then Lauingen was directly under the rule of the Emperor, passing over to Bavaria in 1270 under Henry of Bavaria. It appeared as a hamlet as early as the days of Arnulf in 890. Even from Roman days it had been frequented as a bathing resort by the Roman nobles of the castle of Faimingen near by. With the growing importance of the place, Lauingen, in 1307, under Duke Henry the Strong, obtained the rights and freedom of an imperial city.

In this lovely spot Albert's father represented the Emperor to the complete satisfaction of the people. Owing to the medieval disregard for intimate personal matters it is impossible to determine with absolute certainty the day and date of Albert's birth. Many reputable historians put it in the year 1193, basing their computation on the statement that Albert died in 1280 at the age of eighty-seven years. Other historians, basing their contention on the statement that he entered the Dominican Order as a lad of sixteen years assign the year 1206 for his birth.[14] That he was born at Lauingen and not at the family manor in Bollstadt, about two leagues away as some contend, is abundantly plain from the seal he used before his consecration as bishop: *Sigillum Fratris Alberti de Lauing, O.P.*[15]

We know for a certainty that he had a younger brother, Henry, who became a Dominican, and acted as prior of Würzburg when Albert made his last testament, and who was included among his executors. Because he made a bequest in his will to the Dominican convent of nuns at Gotteszell, near Gmund, in Suabia, a local tradition has persisted that he had a sister living there. For the same reason another sister was included among the nuns of the Convent of St. Catherine at Augsburg, established in 1250.

Nothing has come down to us about the early years of Albert save

---

[14] F. Pelster, Kritische Studien zum Leben und zu den Schriften Alberts des Grossen (Freiburg: 1920), 34-53; P. Mandonnet, "*La date de Naissance d'Albert le Grand,*" in *Revue Thomiste (1931), 9-33.*

[15] Pfeiffer and Platz, Kurze Geschichte der Stadt Lauingen und des sel. Albertus Magnus (Donauwörth: 1881), 80-81; C. Weller, "Die staufischen Stadtgründungen," *in* Württembergische Vierteljahr-Hefte für Landesgeschichte (1931), fasc. 3, 4.

that he had pious parents. In those days of faith mothers gave all their time and care to the religious education of their children and we may assume that the lad was carefully instructed in the rudiments of his religion.

Many allusions to the happy and blessed estate of childhood, its innocent joys, its petty worries and omnipresent dangers; to the reciprocal duties of parents and children and the compensations flowing from a faithful observance of them, can be found scattered with a lavish hand throughout his many works, but especially his *Commentary on St. Luke.*[16] All these, perhaps, may be but distant echoes or reminiscences of the care-free days of his youth. Perhaps, too, in the dark hours of his reforming zeal, as Bishop of Ratisbon, he compensated his heart and recouped his spirit by memories of his parents, who had sought to instill into his unfolding mind and receptive heart lessons of piety and purity, obedience and respect for elders—in a word, all those elemental Christian virtues about which he discoursed so engagingly, even naïvely, in his works up to the very last.

This respect for youth, the *maxima reverentia pueris*, imparts a peculiar warmth and perennial buoyancy to the words of a man whom not even his wide experience with a calculating world could disenchant or rob of his love for home and its tender memories, for the young and their golden dreams.

The only positive data, however, the earliest chronicles vouchsafe us about his early education, is the statement that after a careful instruction at home he was educated in a way befitting his social rank. Whether it was at the hands of the chaplain of his father's manor or by the monks of a monastery near by, is unknown. As there were no elementary public schools in that day the children of the better families were, as a rule, handed over at a tender age to the monks, who taught in their own monastic establishments or under the eyes of the bishops, in schools attached to the cathedral.

But it would be a mistake to look upon the youthful Albert as either a solitary recluse or a priggish and aloof child. Far too beautiful around Lauingen was the great outdoors to leave his rich and fervid imagination unimpressed. The forests were filled with birds which the

[16] Opp. X., 242; 148; 237; 127; 334; 333.

lads of the town sought to bring down with their crude improvised weapons. But a child like Albert could count upon falcons and masters of the hunt in his outdoor expeditions, and he himself relates his own experience: "I went through the fields with dogs, the falcons flew on high, and when the birds scattered in the air they were assailed by the falcons and forced to come down to the earth. They were nearly half dead, so that one could catch them with the hands. After the hunt we gave a bird to each falcon."[17] On another occasion he describes a struggle between an eagle and a swan in this wise: "In my youth I and many of my companions were looking on an eagle fighting with a swan. Both rose so high in the air as to become almost invisible to us; and after about two hours, during which we were watching, they descended. The eagle was perched upon the swan and overcame it; but one of my companions running up seized the swan, whereupon the eagle flew away."[18] He also speaks about the migration of wild geese and how, in their flight, they follow the wind currents. Another time he tells of some bird hunter who came across an old blind pigeon in a deep forest. Two young doves came to the assistance of the old bird at the approach of the hunters and carried it off to safety.[19] From the hunters in their bright blouses and cocked hats, with their easy manners and self-assurance, Albert as a boy gathered much first-hand information about bird life which he forthwith put to a practical test. There is a kind of hushed wistfulness in his recounting of these boyhood experiences, years later, in his books.

But he loved the water, too, so near at hand, in the rushing Danube, which of all rivers of the earth changes color most and wears a really ominous green look for twenty-four hours before a storm. Thither from the fastnesses of Hungary, in long spearlike boats, had come, and were still coming daily, the dour-faced barbarians who infested his native land. These incursions rendered necessary those many fortresses on land and along the river banks which were for Albert a source of continual wonder and endless exploration. He watched the invaders ply their trade of fishing and was able later to recount with fidelity the course the fishes took in the waters of the Danube. Perhaps other

[17] Opp. XI, 444.
[18] Opp. XI, 453
[19] Opp. XI, 383.

healthy lads joined him in fishing in the small grottoes along the shores of the river where, as he tells us, the fish were so plentiful that they could be caught with the hands. But these beautiful days of youth soon ended. As he showed no interest in a military career and experienced no desire to follow in the footsteps of his father, in the Emperor's service, it was necessary for him to look about for a higher education. Since no notable schools of higher education existed at that time in Germany, he was compelled to consider the merits of some of the well-established schools of Christendom which then welcomed students—especially youths of noble rank—from foreign countries.

So in the first flush of his manhood Albert determined to leave the fatherland he loved so well, whose beauties had ravished his eager and alert mind, for a long, toilsome, and dangerous journey to Italy. On the way he probably stopped at Paris: gay, polite, cynical, pardoning all moral recklessness so long as it offended not against courtesy and chivalry. By foot he pushed on to Venice, sitting proudly on her artificial throne, with glittering skirts proudly gathered up about her in disdain of all the world, except such part only of it as would traffic with her to its own financial disadvantage. Pensive, wistful, cosmopolitan, she was the one city of Italy which would not hesitate to scandalize all Christendom by going out of her way to flatter the Moor nor blushed to drive her bargains with the Jews. Paris must have appealed mightily to the buoyant, effervescent spirit of Albert, but Venice responded to that melancholy strain which courses in the veins of every German.

But what induced Albert, a strong, engaging young man of twenty, to cross the Alps and turn to Padua? Why did he not tarry in Paris? in Bologna?

It is about the year 1217. Why should he seek out Padua for higher education when its university was not yet in existence? For we know that it was only in 1222 that a band of fractious Bolognese students, who were dissatisfied with the quality and method of teaching at their university, with the arrogance of the professors and the meddlesomeness of the *podesta,* or city magistrate, acceded to the inducements of the Paduan people to migrate in a body, nearly four thousand strong, to the golden city on the Bacchiglione.

Many answers, all unsatisfactory, have been given. The latest and most learned historian suggests that the death of his father may have turned Albert's mind toward an uncle who, living in state at Padua, acted as a trusted agent of the Emperor.[20] Perhaps, it was a dying father's wish to see a son, on whom he had set high hopes, in the safe-keeping of an elderly and worldly-wise man. He would not only keep the youth from the free and lascivious life of the students, but also introduce him to influential persons and present him at advantageous places.

Even if Padua's school could not glory in a world-wide renown, it was a fact that, after the treaty of peace signed at Constance in 1183 between the clergy and the Hohenstaufen, education was making rapid and creditable progress there, with special insistence upon and interest in the arts and natural sciences. The Paduans were shrewd enough to know that their schools could not compete in the teaching of law with the University of Bologna or in theology with Paris. Hence, they focussed their attention and efforts on the arts (including as these did philosophy) and the sciences, embracing the study and practise of medicine. This latter science became later the special care of the University of Salerno.

Strong, robust, quick-footed, Albert appeared betimes in the narrow cobbled streets of Padua, or in the piazza before the cathedral which was in the process of construction, wearing a bright coat of silk, a sword at his side, a cap with a gay, waving plume on his head. He was good to look upon with his firm, solid cheeks, into which some of the russet color of sunshine had stolen, and with his bright eyes that had never looked upon forbidden sights and therefore did not droop with shame. He soon made friends with the other students, for he was by nature friendly, sociable, and communicative, while his inquisitive search for knowledge extended in all directions. He was ever ready to discuss the lectures of the professor with his fellows and just as much prepared to glean from his masters the latest opinions in the academic world as well as any bits of knowledge gathered laboriously from precious manuscripts. For many days together he exchanged experiences with everyone he met about the great earthquake in 1222, which wrought so much havoc all over Lombardy.[21] Later on, in his books, he will seek to give the reasons for this catastrophe as did most

---

[20] H. Scheeben, Albert der Grosse. Zur Chronologik seines Lebens (Vechta: 1931), 13.

[21] *Meteor.*, Opp. IV, 626.

of the chroniclers of the day. On holidays he and his companions crossed the broad plains surrounding Padua in all directions to look for curiosities of nature. Thus in later years he recalled how during his student days he had seen a well which after having remained shut up for a long time, emitted poisonous fumes so freely that two men were asphyxiated on the spot. A third man looking into the well was overcome by the gases and lay unconscious on the ground for two hours.[22] Or again, he rode out on horseback to some of the cities near by. He writes later on:

"When I was at Venice, being still a youth, they were sawing stones for the repair of one of the churches, and it chanced that in one of these blocks there appeared the figure of a head, as of a king, crowned, with a long beard. The countenance had no other defect, save that the forehead was too high, ascending toward the head. All of us who examined it were satisfied that it was the work of nature. And I, being questioned as to the cause of the disproportioned forehead, replied that this stone had been coagulated by the action of the vapor, and that by means of a more powerful heat without order or measure."[23]

Who will not say that, in spite of a certain obscurity in his terminology, the young student already manifested some understanding of those phenomena which present-day geologists explain as the result of volcanic heat and the action of vapor? As Albert blandly confessed, his fellow students turned to him for explanations of such natural phenomena as they chanced to come upon in their exploratory excursions. Thus, particularly, he made them gape in wonder at his explanations of the effects of vapor on roses, the idiosyncrasies of fishes, the peculiarities of animals and stars, together with a dozen other subjects in which medieval man was deeply interested. To his fellow students he seemed a youth interested in everything. Is it any wonder, then, that he was able to shine as a brilliant conversationalist?

He was at ease, too, with the townspeople who, in a school like Padua, were not forbidden, as in the big university centers of the world, from holding converse with the foreign students. If he freely lavished his knowledge and observations it was not for empty display,

---

[22] Meteor., *ibid.*

[23] *Mineral.*, Opp. V, 48.

but rather as a means of inviting the confidences of those who possessed riches which he, coming from a backwater stretch of the world, had had no opportunity of laying hands upon. But with the simple country yokels, who, just because their eyes had not been dazzled with the sights of city life, were close observers of the mysteries and marvels of nature, he was the very soul of affability. He beguiled them by his wonderful stories (perhaps, with a good-natured smile up his sleeve) into revealing everything they had observed in their close communion with nature. He shall keep up this winsome attitude toward his fellows all his life, being in this the genial Suabian from the Danube country.

If Albert at this time had not yet read the *Eruditio Didascaliae* of his fellow countryman, Hugh of St. Victor, who had died just about half a century before, at Halberstadt's convent, Hammersleben, he nevertheless already exemplified in his life, and later would show forth in his academic labors, the wisdom of that great pedagogue's words: "Some things are worth knowing on their own account; but others, although apparently offering no return for our trouble, should not be neglected, because without them the former cannot be thoroughly mastered. Learn everything; you will afterwards discover that nothing is superfluous; limited knowledge affords no enjoyment."[24]

Now, ever since the days of the Greeks and Romans, and the analogous forerunners in the educational systems of the Orientals, the arts which Albert had come to Padua to master had been approached over a sevenfold route. The journey took anywhere from six to fourteen years, depending upon the excellence of the masters and the application of the student. There were, first, the studies that fitted a man to think—grammar, rhetoric, dialectics; and secondly, the sciences of language—oratory and logic, generally spoken of as the *trivium* or *triviales* because, as Hugh of St. Victor remarked, they were considered the well-beaten ground of three roads, or the crossroads, open to all. Then there were the mathematico-physical studies—arithmetic, geometry, astronomy, and music, called the *quadrivium* or fourfold road. Together, these seven branches of study were intended to fit a man for the pursuit of science in the strict sense of the term: namely, the combination of philosophy and theology, which at the time was spoken

[24] *Didascalium*, VI, 3.

of as Scholasticism.

That constant application to the study of pagan authors might not work havoc, at a most impressionable period of life, with the students' souls, the Christian masters were careful to attach a mystical and symbolical meaning to the seven arts or departments of studies. These recalled the Seven Gifts of the Holy Ghost, or the Seven Words on the Cross, or the Seven Petitions of the Our Father, or the Seven Virtues, or the Seven Pillars of Wisdom, according to the tastes of the master or the preference of the pupils. Scarcely a week passed without some outspoken reference to this symbolical acceptation of the branches of learning. This constant overshadowing nearness of the spiritual kept many a student from imbibing, with his pagan classics, poisonous ideals of life.

Snares in plenty were indeed spread for the students' feet in populous centers, far from home, without supervision by interested friends. Life was young, the city was gay, and wine made the blood boil and the brain burn. But the constant association of the most intimate truths of the faith with the most mundane of secular affairs and pursuits saved the Christian conscience from being utterly smothered in the hot air of the pagan classics. A student might momentarily forget or shelve his religion; he could not permanently disregard or disown it.

Now Albert did not need, though no doubt he always welcomed, such reminders of life's first concern and business. All the chroniclers are one in saying that in the midst of the giddy life of the student world he retained the poise and strength of character to practise his faith openly and intensely. He was found at the soul-touching services in church on the appointed days, and when these were carried out on a superb stage at the church of Santa Justina, it seemed for all the world as if the skies had opened and he were in attendance at the ritual of heaven. Oftentimes he worshiped in such venerable churches as St. Daniel, St. Nicholas, or St. Mary Magdalen, each one of which had beauties all its own. He was a great lover of fine architecture and had been made so through his early interest in the fortresses of his native Suabia. Hence, he must have paused many a time to gaze in wonderment on the bridges and ramparts of Padua, constructed with great care and expense to withstand the incursions of the imperial armies which, like waves on the seashore, were constantly pouring over this key city of Lombardy. He watched the Communal Palace rise before his eyes, a dream of beauty in marble. But what must have fascinated him most was the building of the new cathedral, which was completed in 1224 and gave unmistakable signs of Oriental architectural influences. For this corner of the world, indeed, Albert had a special regard, because it had cradled his mental master, Aristotle. Did he who later on examined so closely the mortar and stones of the Cologne cathedral's foundations learn something of the building arts from the Italian masons who then, as now, were probably the most loquacious of Italian craftsmen?

For some reason, at first unaccountable, led on perhaps by mere curiosity or gossip, he repaired oftenest to the church of the Dominicans, who had come to Padua in 1217 and immediately made their presence felt in the university world by preaching in their own poor chapel located in one of the outlying quarters of the city. Here one was always sure of meeting learned men who, somehow, had not forgotten their humanity in the pursuit of learning. They confessed frankly to a special love for the student body. And they preached in a new way that was highly acceptable to the students—not long, dry-as-dust sermons, held together with little of the cement of philosophy and constructed out of large boulders of patristic lore, but instead, living discourses, where the head was not cheated at the expense of the heart, nor the heart was left to feed itself as best it might on the tough meat of pure reasoning. World travelers, many of them, these Friars moved about with eyes open to every advantage that might be turned to the service of the truth and Christ. And their sermons were like nothing so much as a clarion call to arms for Christ, the Captain of Souls, whose interests were being challenged by the new learning on which the students set so much store, and by the new freedom which meant, for most of them, fresh opportunities of indulging the flesh. Then, too, one was nearly always sure of hearing some strange preacher who, in passing by, had been prevailed upon by the brethren to tarry long enough in the city to address the students who cared to hear. Surely, Santa Maria delle Grazie was a place of delicious surprises, all the more sought out by many youths whose cup of desire was not filled up by lectures in the classrooms nor, it seemed, liable to be filled by anything, anywhere, in the material world—just then.

CHAPTER II

THE GREAT DECISION

NOW, there was much hubbub in the university world of Padua in 1228. The arrival of the General of the Dominicans drew attention once more to these new-fashioned, white-clad Friars, whose government and manner of living were frankly democratic and whose preferences were all for the new liberty which came in with the rise of the Communes and, having asserted itself in the political and economic worlds, was fast carrying off the day in the universities. This stranger, too, spoke the new language of the day and showed forth in his converse with others that good comradeship without which democracy is either a menace or a mockery. No wonder the students flocked to hear Jordan of Saxony,[1] for the memory of what had happened on several of his former visits to Padua had not faded from the minds of the older students nor was a knowledge of it withheld from the notice of the newcomers.

He was gaunt, but never tired; dusty from much walking over country roads, but fresh as dew in the interest he showed in the very least of the students; stern with himself, but always smiling with others; a good companion; a lover of dogs and animals in general; a born improviser in his sermons and quick at that form of repartee popular among students; a good singer, with an accurate and true, though booming, voice; a sworn enemy of those shallow men who tried to cover over their superficiality with a show of stern regard for the majesty of the written law; a former professor at Paris whom his students remembered for his competency but madly loved for his understanding spirit; a scientist who wrote mathematical treatises which a literary pirate and plagiarist was to publish three hundred years later as his own, much to the astonishment of the men of that day; a friend unexcelled, whose letters to Blessed Diana d'Andalo, who suffered several broken ribs at the hands of her father when he tried to drag her from the convent at Bologna, are the finest specimens of their

[1] M. Aron, *Un Animateur de la Jeunesse au XIII e siècle* (Paris: 1931), 60, 174.

kind in medieval times; a gentle father who rebuked a superior for chiding a crowd of students giggling during prayer hour over the creaking backs and cracked voices of the old monks; a humorist who called upon the brethren to rejoice with him when, having lost his right eye, he declared he had been mercifully delivered from one snare of his soul—in a word, here was just the kind of man for whom young, bubbling students would cancel all their engagements and whom they would go out of their way to see and hear, an ideal man, who was soon discovered to be better than the ideal itself and who improved upon acquaintance. No wonder he has been called the siren of souls; for just because men forgot to lock up their sons—as mothers did their daughters at Milan when St. Ambrose preached on virginity—Jordan never preached to the university students without forthwith leading a crowd of them away to the convents of his Order. The announcement of his coming to a city was the signal for the monastic tailor to sit up day and night making habits. It is on record that white wool could not be brought fast enough from England, where the cloth of most medieval habits was made, or in sufficient quantity from the Humiliati, or wool weavers of Lombardy, to supply the need. It was consequently necessary to use colored materials as a makeshift in the emergency. And Jordan drew the greatest fun of his life out of these corporate conversions, as he never tired of describing them deliciously and just a bit wryly, in his letters to Blessed Diana.

Because there was such an abundance of volunteers, Jordan could afford to be very exacting and discriminating in his choice. Europe had learned the mistake of taking unfit candidates for the priesthood after the Black Death of the year 1000, when the ranks of the clergy had been cut down more than half, thus necessitating the admittance of men for whom the sanctuary was rather a career than a consecration. Jordan used all his native powers of shrewdness and gave free play to his uncanny psychological insight when dealing with these men who offered themselves to him. And he seldom made a mistake. It was he who with a sweeping gesture of welcome threw open the convent portals to Hugh of St. Cher, who, later on, gave the world the first Biblical concordance, established the first professedly Biblical school and, as cardinal, pacified the northern countries that were rebellious toward the Holy See. He did the same for Blessed Humbert de Romans, who, as general of the Order, elaborated its distinctive liturgy;

stabilized its spirit for the ages to come in his *Commentary on the Rule of St. Augustine* on which the Dominican rule is based; aroused Europe to go on a crusade against the Turks and, as a fruit of this recruiting work, left behind a book of stories and jokes for preachers. Again he welcomed St. Raymond Penyafort, who codified the entire canon law of the Church for Gregory IX in the incredibly short period of three years; became General of the Order; organized missions among the Arabs, Jews, and Mohammedans of Spain; established the first chairs of Oriental languages in Dominican schools, which innovation served as a hint to the Council of Vienne in 1330 to order such studies in the universities of Paris, Bologna, Oxford, and Montpellier; bequeathed posterity a book of moral theology from which the casuistic method of teaching this branch of ecclesiastical learning was elaborated. Or, again, he prevailed upon Vincent of Beauvais to enter the Order in which he distinguished himself by acting as the instructor of the sons of St. Louis IX, for whom he wrote the *Speculum Majus*, an encyclopedia embracing all the knowledge of his time. These are only four out of more than a thousand youths whom Jordan won for the Order during the fifteen years of his generalship from 1221 to 1236. Need we wonder that Padua was on tiptoe when word came during the summer of 1228 that he was about to march into the city over the rough, basalt-covered road, through the beautifully carved stone gate on the west side of the city?

Albert was certain to be among those who turned their footsteps to the Dominican convent where Jordan established the base of his operations during his assault upon the academic world of Padua. He had seen this wonderful charmer of souls on at least one of his former visits, probably the one when he had led away forty-three students to the convent as the trophy of his zeal. But that was far back in 1223. Much water had coursed under the bridge over which Albert was as yet afraid to pass to the haven of peace, as every monastery was then considered. He had had time to think these many months. His heart was unspeakably sad. Many of those who had entered the schools with him had made the great decision, had brought the irrevocable sacrifice. Others, again, had returned to their own homes and countries to carve out a future for themselves. He knew for a certainty that he had no attraction for a military career which just then, in the high noon of the crusaders' ardor, was open to men of courage and endurance. He cared not a fig to replace those of his forebears in the service of the Emperor who, since he had left Lauingen these many years, had rendered an account of their lives to the King of kings. Neither could he remain forever at Padua, especially so as he did not care to make haste to take his bachelor's or master's degrees—a failure or indifference for which later on Roger Bacon would twit him in the most personally abusive and vitriolic words.[2] There was little use to consult the professors, who for an easily explainable reason took little concern in students about to leave Padua. The necessity of doing something with himself, of choosing a career in life, gnawed at his mind. Perhaps, his college chums noticed that he was preoccupied, worried, restless, loath to join as of old in scientific excursions or recreational hikes across the country. Did they do him the injustice of thinking that love, licit or illicit, had stolen away the peace of his heart and made him suddenly indifferent about taking his degrees? There seemed to be for him no balm in Gilead. Was there, the students asked one another, was there some cryptic explanation for the frequency of his visits to the churches of the city? It was the bitterest battle Albert had been called upon so far to fight. Its pain was all the more exquisite and poignant because the struggle was all within.

The whole story of what happened during this dark night of the soul is told swiftly and simply by Brother Gerard de Frachet, whom Humbert de Romans had commissioned to write the histories of those among the brethren who had cast glory on the Order in the first half century of its existence. The story runs thus:

> "A certain brother, a man of good name and excellent station in the Order, when as a young man he was studying at Padua, had conceived a half-formed wish to join the Order through the advice of the brethren and the preaching of Master Jordan. But the youth's uncle who lived in the place refused permission. Hence, he forced him to swear that for a certain period he would not go to the house of the brethren. After this time had expired, however, coming frequently to the brethren, he resolved to join. But fear lest he should leave made him vacillate very much. One night he saw in his dreams that he had entered the Order and left after a short time.

[2] Rogeri Bacon, *Opera quaedam hactenus inedita* (ed. Brewer. London: 1859), I, 327.

Waking up he was rejoiced that he had not entered, saying in his heart: 'Now I see that that would have happened which I feared would happen had I entered.' Now that same day, while listening to a sermon of Master Jordan, who, in speaking about the temptations of the devil, remarked how he subtly deceived the unwary, said: 'There are those who propose to leave the world and enter the Order but are frightened off by the devil who suggests to them in their dreams that they will enter but not persevere. And hence they go driving about alone in red garments, or with others, only to find that fears about entering the Order disturb them, or, if they actually have entered, are so horrified that they upset themselves.' Then the young man, greatly wondering, approached him saying: 'Master, who hath revealed my heart to thee?' And he explained to him all his thoughts and dreams. Then the Master, having conceived a great and firm confidence in God, comforted him against such temptations. He hearing these words was completely changed and, casting aside his fears, entered the Order. The brother himself frequently narrated this."

The manuscripts of Berlin and Leipzig add that "Brother Albert, narrating this, said that the memory of the promise of that holy man had been a powerful remedy for him against the temptations he had in the Order either from the devil or the world."[3]

Though Gerard de Frachet does not assign a definite date for this occurrence, the best historians today are agreed upon the year 1229.[4]

As was Jordan's custom, he immediately saw to it that Albert, laying aside his rich student's robes, was clothed in the heavy white wool of the Order. The novice entered upon his period of test and trial. He was up at midnight to join in the recitation of the Divine Office. The hours of the day were punctuated by the official prayers of the Church. Early at night the brethren gathered to thank God for the

---

[3] de Fracheto, *Vitae*, 187-188.

[4] H. Scheeben, *Chronologie*, 8-15. The chronology for the early years of Albert's life is a hopeless muddle: Mandonnet in *Revue Thomiste* (1931) 9—32; Pelster, *Kritische Studien*, 52-58; E. Vacant, *Dictionnaire de Théologie Catholique*, art. "*Albert le Grand.*" Through independent research we have arrived at the same chronological results as Fredegand Callaey, O.M.Cap., in his *Curriculum Vitae* for the Canonization *Votum: Analecta Ord. Praed.* (1932), 475-530.

blessings of the day and to commend themselves for the night to the tender keeping of the Blessed Mother of God in the *Salve Regina*, which Jordan had ordered to be sung as the brethren filed through the church to bed. Abstinence from meat was perpetual and, as if this were not sufficient affliction of the flesh, there was a strict second fast of forty days besides the Lenten season prescribed for the Church Universal. Though we do not know Albert's master of the spiritual life and initiator into Dominican customs, he must have been a man of great sanctity else he would never have held his post in those days of primitive fervor under Jordan whose fleetness of foot was such that he inspected nearly all the convents between Paris and Bologna each year. For it was his wont to preach during Lent in Paris and during Advent in Bologna. The stripplings he had transplanted from the world into "the garden closed in" of the Order were, for various reasons easy to divine, the objects of his special care and solicitude. Whatever temptations Albert may have been forced to undergo during this period were dispelled by the promise Jordan had given him when he had made the great exchange.

It is difficult to say, in view of the conflicting statements of the early biographers,[5] where Albert passed his novitiate days. While it is almost certain that he received the habit at Padua, the majority of writers agree on Bologna as the place of his first experience of Dominican life. And, surely, no spot better fitted to fire novices with the high dreams and ideals of St. Dominic, could well be imagined. For this city had been the theater of his great activity, and here, at St. Nicholas, tired out in body from much labor and wrestling, he had resigned his pure soul to God. The very corridors of the convent remained murmurous of his great zeal for souls, even as a shell reverberates the roar of the sea. Here too, his body rested, not as yet in the magnificent *Arca* of another day, but in the love of those who called him father.

There is great diversity of opinion as to where Albert made his theological studies, since having studied philosophy at the University of Padua, he was deemed ready to enter upon this difficult way to new quarries of riches. Andrew Gloria, who is generally very reliable, contends that he remained in Bologna after his novitiate, attending

---

[5] H. Scheeben, *op. cit.*, 8-15.

lectures in the university just a stone's throw from the convent.[6] Others maintain, though without any documentary proof, that he was sent to Paris, since the best school of theology would seem to have been the fit place for one who enjoyed an enviable name in the arts. Rudolf of Nijmegen would have it that he studied theology in Cologne.[7] In favor of this it is urged that, being a son of the German Province by his religious profession, Albert would naturally receive his theological formation among his own. Whatever the truth may be, we are certain that he passed these years in serious application to his studies. Since the curriculum of studies among the Dominicans had not as yet been finally fixed—a task to which he later on would lend a hand—it is permissible to conclude that he followed the course obtaining in the theological schools. Of one thing we may be certain, that the education imparted was of a superior kind, with a strongly marked bent for practical use and instant application to the preaching of the Word. There are no indications about his professors.[8]

No record of the date and place of Albert's ordination to the priesthood has come down to us, but it must have been at the completion of his theological studies, about the year 1233. Six years had passed rapidly in the pursuit of a knowledge of theology. They must have been happy years, alone with God, since no jarring note of earthly interests or occupations spoiled the soundless symphony. Rudolf gives us a clue to the peace and contentment of this period of Albert's life, a true index to the spirit with which he studied: "Albert bore a true love of wisdom, even in his outward appearance, and strove by every means in his power to plant in the garden of his soul what is sweeter far than honey—the flowers of every virtue. His superiors, being desirous to reward him for his labors which placed him at the head of the brethren, promoted him to the rank of lector and sent him to Cologne, the famous metropolis of Germany."[9]

---

[6] Andrea Gloria, "*Quot annos et in quibus Italiae urbibus Albertus Magnus moratus est,*" in *Atti del Reale Instituto Veneto (Venezia: 1880), 1025-1050.*

[7] *Rodolphus,* Legenda, 12-13.

[8] *Ibid.*

[9] *Ibid.*

CHAPTER III

DOCTOR AND PEDAGOGUE

ALBERT must have taken it as a mark of heaven's will that, immediately following his ordination, teaching was given him as a life's work. He might, in fact, be well satisfied with the choice of his superiors, for in those days a teacher was a man of power and influence. But while there were many teachers in Christendom there were few pedagogues in the original meaning of the term. He meant to be one in the true sense of the word. Hence he would instruct others unto justice, inflaming them with an ardent zeal to put an end, by the rays of learning, human and divine, to the darkness that was then befogging so many minds. His natural gifts, which he could not have ignored or explained away save through some clever trick of false humility and self-deception, gave him guarantee enough that with God's grace he would do something worthy of the habit he wore.

Now, learning at that time, in Germany, had sunk to a very low ebb because of the almost chronic condition of war. The young men who were not bearing arms were necessarily engaged in working the fields. With a clergy poorly instructed in divine learning we cannot be surprised if the morals of the people decayed in a frightful way. Hence, the bishops welcomed the coming of men who opened a school of theology, frequently of philosophy, wherever they settled. For it was a fast rule in the Dominican Order that in each convent a school be established at which not only all the brethren, from the Prior down, were obliged to attend daily, but where the secular clergy and the laity were free to come. In some places the bishops ordered all the clergy of the city to attend the Dominican schools, and cases are not unknown where the head of the diocese himself set the example. Professors for the convents, now opening rapidly, were greatly needed. Nor were the Friars prepared to risk their good name and ruin their prestige by installing second-rate teachers the like of whom might be found in practically every center. If they were invited to teach, their teaching must needs be the best in the environs. Because they lived up jealously to this rule, there need be no wonder that new convents of the Order were sought by practically every bishop of Europe.

It was in 1221 that Jordan had sent from Paris to Cologne Brother Henry, who had joined the Order with him and together with him had received the bachelor's degree. The Friars established themselves in the Stolkgasse (*Vicus Stolkorum*) not far from the cathedral. The site today is called *An den Dominikanern*, and is occupied by the federal post office. There was situated here a small lodging house for pilgrims which was easily turned to monastic uses. Attached was a mean chapel dedicated to St. Mary Magdalen. As was their wont, the Friars began at once to preach, and as happened everywhere, people flocked to hear them, for they had an undoubted message to deliver which preachers of the day had utterly failed to convey. As soon, however, as the people gathered around the rude pulpit in goodly numbers the local clergy, stung not by remorse for their own negligence but by envy of the newcomers, hastened with complaints to Archbishop Engelbert. But the latter gently retorted: "So long as we see nothing but good in the Friars we will let them work." The opponents then fell back upon the dire prophecies of St. Hildegarde, who had foretold the coming of a new kind of monks in white garbs who would place the clergy in danger and the city under oppression. That the fat incomes of the clergy were in danger accounted in great measure for their sudden sensitiveness of soul. Engelbert, intrepid warrior that he was, simply replied: "If this prediction is from God it is only right that it be fulfilled." The Friars, unperturbed, but not unmolested by the petty persecutions of the outdistanced clerics, kept on preaching.

Chief and most sought after was Brother Henry who knew the faults of his own people and the best avenues of approach to their hearts. Besides he had a polish and finish, acquired in the schools of Paris, that made his words well-nigh irresistible, especially to a people that could not but be conscious of its own cultural inferiority.[1]

On the death of this great preacher Brother Leo carried on the work which had been so solidly established. The people, however, were still broken-hearted over the loss of Henry, and for all his gifts of teaching and powers of persuasion Leo was no match for him. The clergy,

---

[1] Guillelmus de Tocco, *Vita Scti. Thomae Aquinatis, Acta Sanctorum.* (Antwerpiae: 1668), Martii I, 662.

thinking to find in the removal of Henry a golden opportunity for a renewed and more bitter attack on the Friars, stooped to methods which can be explained only on the ground of blind hatred. At this providential moment Albert arrived.

The new teacher, a German to his finger tips, was delighted, no doubt, to be back in his native land once more. He was the equal in learning of any of his adversaries, still burning with the fervor of his ordination, and aglow to ascend the professor's chair. While we find no reference to the subjects of his lectures, an old biographer says that he taught the liberal arts, explained the books of Aristotle on *Logic, Ethics,* and *Physics,* some portions of the Holy Scriptures and the *Sentences* of Peter Lombard. Students were not lacking, if we may take the word of Thomas of Cantimpre who received the habit in 1232 and prided himself on having heard Albert at Cologne.

The superiors of the Order knew the magic attaching to Albert's name in the popular imagination. They were wise enough to profit from it for the good of religion. Men of smaller vision would have left him undisturbed at Cologne to solidify the educational work he was carrying through with such signal success. But the foundation of a convent at Hildesheim had been ordered by the Chapter of 1233. Bishop Conrad II (1221-1249), who invited the Dominicans to his episcopal city, had been a student and professor at Paris, and on returning to his native dioceses had had more than one occasion of lamenting the low standard of ecclesiastical learning. With few of his own clergy to fall back upon as a nucleus for a seminary, he welcomed the opportunity of making room for these new Friars who, wherever they settled, opened schools of sacred science to which the secular clergy were gladly admitted. He laid down only one condition for the entrance of the Dominicans in his diocese, namely, that they forthwith open a school, man it with able professors, and keep it at the highest notch of scholastic efficiency. Is it any wonder that the Friars, anxious to make advantageous foundations, chose, as if by universal consent, Albert for the organizer of studies?[2] How long he stayed at Hildesheim is not known. That he made a good impression upon the bishop and the clergy and displayed great apostolic zeal among the people is the

---

[2] Henricus de Horvardo, *Chronicon* (ed. Potthast, Gottinagae: 1859), 201; A. M. Walz: "*Albert der Grosse als Lector Coloniensis,*" in *Angelicum* (1932), 147-167.

general verdict of all the chronicles. About the only reference to this period of Albert's activity is the account he gives of having seen a comet which was recorded as far off as China.[3]

It was for the same purpose of opening a school under the best auspices that Albert was sent to Freiburg in 1235.[4] Even if we had no assurance that he had arranged the initial matters at Hildesheim to the satisfaction of all, his early transfer to Freiburg for an identical purpose would be sufficient guarantee of his success. Here, again, his stay was very brief. But it must have been meteoric, for the legend-weavers were soon engaged in the merry business of linking up his name with the beautiful stone bridge which was thrown across the Rhine just at that time.

There is absolutely no documentary proof that he had anything to do with this enterprise, unless it may have been to manifest an interest in the work and the workmen. That Albert was interested in bridge building might indeed readily be assumed as in accord with his broad intellectual enthusiasm. It is in tune with his concern about everything that would be of advantage to the people—and, surely, bridges were such undertakings, as witness the work of St. Benet at Avignon and his Fratres Pontifices. There are those who hold that Thomas Aquinas, who had little aptitude for mechanics or engineering, was led to begin a treatise on bridge-building at the suggestion and instigation of Albert. Now, as Albert had just come from Cologne, where he had had Thomas as a pupil, it is easy to understand why his name was associated with the Freiburg bridge. At all events, the heroic statue in stone on the Freiburg Schwabenbrücke bears witness at least to Albert's presence at that time in this most beautiful city of the Black Forest.

After a short stay at Freiburg, Albert was ordered to Strasburg, where the Dominicans had settled in 1223, on condition that they conduct a school of theology.[5] Bishop Henry II, of Beringen, had no reason to regret the coming of the Friars. But the professors of the city were not pleased to see their schools suddenly deserted. It became the fashion to go in flocks to the Dominican lectures. The small church,

3 Opp. IV, 504; de Loe in *Analecta Bollandiana* (1900), 118.

4 F. Pelster, Kritische Studien, 84.

5 L. Pfleger, Archiv für elsässische Kirchengeschichte (1930), 1-18.

too, was soon overcrowded. The people, indeed, were so much satisfied with the sermons of the Friars, that it became necessary to build a larger church. Here, again, Albert is credited with having played a preponderating part in drawing up the plans of the church, though there is absolutely no documentary proof to that effect. Other legends attached his name to the initial work in the building of the cathedral. Though the documents have nothing to say on the subject, it is nonetheless significant that Albert's statue appears conspicuously on the famous clock of "The Twelve Apostles." It is a relief to be able to escape, at this stage, from the chronological confusion of the previous period to find Albert at Ratisbon for two consecutive years.[6] This city was highly favored by the Hohenstaufen Emperors who, because they liked to tarry in this pleasant spot, found means of enriching the city with fine churches and schools from a treasury that was nearly always depleted from the drain of war. It was a common saying of the day that the Ratisbon schools were better attended than any in the Empire. We may legitimately conclude from this that the professors were eminent teachers. And we may go a step further in concluding that when the Dominicans arrived in 1218 they were conscious of the necessity of providing professors who could not only hold their own but also compete with and excel the masters who had given the city its fair academic reputation. This was all the more necessary as the convent was in an out-of-the-way place and a powerful magnet was needed to attract the students to the outskirts of the city. Undoubtedly, this fact had something to do with Albert's call to Ratisbon.

Perhaps, too, it had something to do with his comparatively long stay here. That the Dominican school was frequented appears from the large hall built for the accommodation of the crowds. While it is true that the building shown today as Albert's classroom dates from a much later time and cannot by any possible chance be the one which echoed to his voice, still we know that the site is the same and the dimensions of the building are identical. And any professor might well feel flattered who could fill a spacious hall such as the Ratisbon classroom.

With very sparse documents at our command to reconstruct these years, we are forced to conclude that Albert taught Aristotle during this period of his professorial career. Thus he explained grammar,

[6] H. Scheeben, *Chronologie*, 17-33.

mathematics, and astronomy. He discoursed on logic and physics which then embraced the natural sciences. He carried his pupils aloft with him into the rarified air of metaphysics. Evidently, the students were elated with his teachings, for a crop of legends still persist which have reference to these years. So high was his repute for a knowledge of the secrets of nature that men now began to credit him with powers of magic. Such was the penalty a great teacher must have been prepared to pay for his eminence.

But his converse in the convent was without question exemplary, for his brethren elected him once, probably twice, to represent them as delegate at the provincial assemblies or chapters. They knew for a certainty that he would voice their wishes and defend their ideals. They reposed confidence in him.

Thus he was present at the General Chapter of Bologna, held in 1238. It was an especially important one, since a successor to Jordan of Saxony, who had been lost in a shipwreck on the way to the Holy Land, was here to be chosen. The French delegates were in favor of Hugh of St. Cher; the German-speaking delegates agreed upon Albert. His election, they knew, would guarantee a continuance of the forward-looking policies of Jordan at a very critical time. The ballots were cast. They were found to be equally divided between Hugh and Albert. Another ballot was cast and the choice fell upon Raymond of Penyafort. From the chroniclers it can be gathered that there had been a preliminary consultation during which Albert withdrew his name. There was no prohibition against such a preliminary discussion of candidates. With Friars from so many countries of the world in attendance it was the part of prudence to make precisely such provisions which, in this case, saved Albert for the classroom.

But he did busy himself at this Chapter with the regimen of the schools, as may be gathered from the large list of academic enactments which, if they do not bear the name of Albert, are all aglow with his spirit and eloquent of the ideals which he had made his own. About this time the suggestion arose about sending Albert to Paris for his doctor's cap. His teaching career had been distinguished enough to give grounds for reasonable hope that he, the first German contender for the doctor's honor, would bear the ordeal creditably to himself and his province. The Germans, at the time, were being twitted for their academic backwardness. Albert had tried to remove the stigma in various convents of his native province. Now, at Paris, he would have the chance to show the scholars of the north that something good could come from beyond the Rhine. From a careful comparison of the documents it can be computed that Albert set out on foot for Paris some time in the year 1234.

What were the thoughts running through his mind as, footsore and weary, he trudged the streets of Paris, then the metropolis of the world? Its population of one hundred thousand was augmented at this time by about twenty thousand students from all parts of the world. Did he make comparisons of this city with his own Cologne for the purpose of assuring himself that he would feel at home in this strange land? What topics did he discuss with the companion who walked by his side? Did they map out for themselves just how they would spend their time in order to draw most advantage from their stay in Paris, as had been insisted upon by the General, John the Teuton?

And who were all these monks hurrying to and fro, at six o'clock in the morning, while the convent bells were calling the brethren to Prime, the liturgical morning prayer of the religious communities? Why were these men abroad in the streets, while their fellows were hurrying to choir? And who were those noisy students, unsteady of foot?—oh, yes, none other than the Cornifici who, in the taverns and wine shops had argued all night over their lessons or else had kept a more devious rendezvous. Did those smears of light on the tiny lancet windows show the garret places of students who were paying a bitter price for learning? These and dozens of other questions must have teased the minds of the two wayfarers from Germany. On this island in the Seine, where clustered together the conglomeration of buildings called the University, might be witnessed all the bustle of a kingdom where men were anxious to play a part, the excitement of a public mart where men were bent on purchasing their desired goods. One thing was certain not to have escaped the newcomers—the air was charged with an all-consuming desire for learning and no more electric spot could be pointed out than the convent of St. James whither they were bending their footsteps. Would they find a cell in a building which was literally bursting with Friars, come from all parts of Europe to make their mark or win their spurs?

We see Albert enter the classroom with a copy of the Scriptures, of

Aristotle, of the Lombard.[7] No other work was permitted to the young professor who, on a lower bench than the presiding master, was expounding the Scriptures either in the literal, allegorical, or moral sense, or was unraveling the intricacies of Aristotle to students who, though eager to excel in dialectic skill, could not always follow the subtleties of the Master.

We do not know under what masters Albert lectured, but they surely were eminent men in their day or else they would not have found a place there. He answered good-naturedly the questions propounded by the students, for he was the soul of patience and long-suffering. But he was unbending in the matter of taking notes, and the students soon learned the reason why. For in the weekly review of topics discussed in class one needed to know every inch of the ground that had been covered; in the monthly disputations in each classroom, at which the lector, or assistant professor, urged objections against the thesis of the student, one needed a long memory and ready wit; in the semiannual ordeals in public, when any student in the audience might be called upon to object to the thesis which the bachelor or licentiate was defending, one needed to have a tight grip on the subject. In such exciting ways was the interest of the students maintained, their application to study fixed, and the young professor kept at the highest degree of efficiency. So the students, sitting on the rough, wooden deal benches, ranged around the wall, or in case these did not suffice, squatting uncomfortably and undignified on bundles of straw placed on the stone floor—whence the name of the street adjoining the Dominican convent, rue du Fouarre—performed the physical feat of jotting down notes as best they could. It was a luxury to be able to take notes, for writing materials were scarce and precious. Hence, notes were passed around, especially notes taken down by quick writers or by those who, in their anxiety not to miss a word, had invented a rude kind of shorthand. On the road to and from school the students repeated these notes for memory's sake. Mental gymnastics, in the form of jingling verses, were used frequently.

Under such circumstances Albert communicated to his students his

---

[7] H. Denifle, Chartularium Universitatis Parisiensis (Parisiis: 1889), I, n. 200; H. Denifle, "*Quel livre serait de base à l'enseignement des maîtres en théologie dans l'Université de Paris,*" in *Revue Thomiste (1894), 149-161.*

vast knowledge of the Scriptures, of Aristotle, and the Lombard, as can be seen from the commentaries on these books which he composed at that time. Because of his excellence in teaching, the unmistakable evidence of his erudition and the experience previously attained by him in the manner of conducting class after the tried and approved scholastic fashion, he passed much quicker than his contemporaries through the required stages of his teaching career. He was betimes made bachelor and licentiate and some time before the opening of the year 1245 received the doctor's cap.

Thomas of Cantimpre,[8] with his quick, sharp ear for the gossip of the town, reports that the devil appeared to Albert at Paris in the form of a fellow religious to dissuade him from study. Albert was said to have driven him away by the sign of the cross. Now it is just possible that Albert did meet with brethren during his Paris days who tried to wean him from his predilection for philosophy and the natural sciences. There was, even at St. James, at this time, a rather marked antipathy toward these scientific studies for the reason that they were looked upon as a new departure in method and were supposed to contain many pitfalls because of the vitiated texts of Aristotle. But without more positive proof than these idle reports of the masses we need not see in Cantimpre's remark a reference to a visible apparition of the devil. The truth of the matter would seem to be that a brother, in a spirit of true fraternal charity, warned Albert of the dangers he was running in preconizing Aristotle and his methods. And this, no doubt, only confirmed Albert in his determination, taken at Paris, to press the Stagirite into the service of the truth.

Albert's free hours were filled with interests far more engaging than the supposed visits of malign spirits from the other world. Shortly after his arrival—and the incident itself helps us to establish the date of his coming to Paris—Albert was visited by one of the two sons of Ferdinand III, King of Castile, Philip and Sancho, who though canons of the Cathedral of Toledo, were pursuing higher studies at the university. If the young prince sought out Albert among the hundreds of professors in Paris, it must evidently have been because his reputation had soon got abroad as a profound searcher into the phenomena of nature. Later on, recalling these days, Albert writes:

---

[8] *Thomas Cantimpranus, Bonum Universale, Lib. II,* Chap. 57, No. 18.

"When I was in Paris, among the doctors and in the Order (*de grege*) of St. Dominic, the son of the King of Castile came thither to prosecute his studies. The Prince's cooks having one day bought some fish, discovered one among them which is called in Latin *peccet*, but more commonly *pleiss*, and which was very large. Opening it, they found in the stomach a big oyster shell, which His Highness sent to me in token of friendship. This shell bore on the concave and smooth side the print of three reptiles with their heads erect, and so perfectly shaped that the eyes, despite their smallness, were quite perceptible. On the outer side were ten serpents bound together by the neck, but separated at the head and the rest of the body. It was easy to see on each of those prints the opening of the mouth and the tail of those animals. For a long time I possessed this precious shell; many persons saw and examined it. At length I sent it as a present to one of my friends in Germany."[9]

Now if Albert, so soon upon his arrival in Paris, attracted eyes upon himself it may in some measure be due to the deliberate efforts of the General, John the Teuton, who lost no opportunity to put his protégé in the most propitious light. Cantimpre, with his flair for news, reports[10] that during the stay of John the Teuton in Paris Albert joined in a public disputation, before the bishop, on the supposed abduction of the daughter of the Count of Schwanenberg by the devil. The city was in a state of high excitement and the most fantastic tales were invented and bandied about. With a shrewd eye toward justifying the presence of the Friars in the city, and more especially Albert in the university, the General engineered matters in such wise that the German professor was among those who sat as judges on the bench with the bishop.

On another occasion Albert was called in to serve on a Commission convened for the purpose of judging the fate of the Talmud, which was being freely circulated by the Jews, of whom there were hundreds in Paris. Besides Albert, there sat on the jury William, the Bishop of Paris, the Abbot of St. Victor, the dignitaries and professors of the university, and the two Dominicans who taught with him in the schools, John Pugensasimum, and Stephen of Autun. The condemnation was first read aloud from the steps of the cathedral and immediately after from

---

[9] *Opp.* V, 49.

[10] Thomas Cantimpranus, *ibid.*

the main square where the hangman's scaffold was reared when required. After that, copies of the condemnation were nailed to the doors of the principal churches and municipal buildings. In the big university square the book was solemnly burned in the presence of the people. The condemnation reads:

"The Jewish Rabbins having sent to us, invested with apostolic authority, some of their books entitled the Talmud, we have caused them to be examined by competent persons, experienced in such matters, fearing God and zealous for the Faith. Since we have discovered them to be full of innumerable errors, abuses, blasphemies, and impieties which can neither be read nor heard without exciting scandal, and as the said books cannot be tolerated without prejudice to the Christian Faith, we hereby declare, in accordance with the advice of the learned men whom we have consulted to this effect, that they cannot be suffered to exist in any shape or be returned to the Israelite doctors, and we condemn them by this present sentence. As to other works of this nature which the Rabbins have not yet delivered to us, despite our frequent remonstrances, or which we have not yet been able sufficiently to examine, we shall judge of them as time and opportunity shall enable us, and pronounce on them according to justice."[11]

We do not need the statement of Henry of Hereford[12] to assure us that, owing to the excellence of Albert's teaching, the systematic advertising of his influence, and the regard in which he was held by the influential men of the city, vast crowds of students gathered to hear him. A memory of this leadership lies at the bottom of the unfounded legend dating from two centuries later that because of the throng of students he was forced to lecture in one of the public squares, which came to be called the Place Maubert.[13] This name is supposed to be a contraction of the words "Place du Maitre Albert."

Shortly after Albert's death, however, certain verses became current in Paris and were quoted, with variations, for nearly two hundred years by every biographer:

---

[11] H. Denifle, *Chartularium*. I, 209, No. 178; L. I. Newman, *Jewish Influence on Christian Reform Movements* (New York: 1925), III, 318-319, 343-344.

[12] Henricus de Horvardo, *op. cit.*, 201.

[13] Echard et Quetif, *Scriptores Ord. Praed.* (Parisiis: 1719), I. 166.

"Cunctis luxisti, scriptis praeclaris fuisti
Mundo luxisti, quia totum scibile scisti!"[14]

Thus even his contemporaries were lost in wonderment over the extent of Albert's knowledge.

Naturally he bred a large offspring of eminent professors.[15] There was Blessed Ambrose Sansedonius, one of the most renowned preachers of his day, who grappled at close grips with one of the social questions of the age. So relentlessly did he hound the usurers, or gouging bankers of his time, that his life was in constant danger. But he needed not the assassin's dagger to rid him of life, for he occasioned his death by preaching with such vehemence that he burst a blood vessel. Then, too, there was Francigenus, who passed from Albert's hands to several important academic posts in the Order, continually multiplying his output of books. Again there was Denis of Viterbo who had no equal as a preacher in his native province.

His brethren in Germany, meanwhile, were following with closest attention the victories Albert was reporting in the intellectual center of the world. He had not belied their hopes and expectations. The professors he had helped to form before leaving for Paris had maintained his high educational ideals in the German schools, where a chosen race of eager pupils was being reared. There was immediate need of supplying them at home with the advantages which else they could not have enjoyed unless they went to Paris. With the rapid expansion of the Order in Germany, economic reasons forbade sending a large contingent of students abroad. Moreover, the secular clergy, and even bishops, were anxious for a seat of superior learning to be established at home, where they might combine study with their regular duties. Laymen, too, clamored for the fresh springs of learning. Instinctively eyes turned to Paris where Albert had just finished the prescribed three-year course of teaching. Soon he would be permitted to turn his footsteps in the direction of his native land.

---

[14] H. Scheeben, *Chronologie*, 23.

[15] H. Scheeben, "*De Alberti Magni Discipulis,*" in *Alberto Magno. Atti della Settimana Albertina (Roma: 1932), 179-213.*

Chapter IV

EDUCATOR FOR THE AGES

SHORTLY after the close of the scholastic year of the university, on June 27, 1248, Albert bade farewell to Paris. Did he carry with him the many priceless manuscripts which St. Louis IX had given him as a gift? We may take it for granted that, if for no other reason than as a souvenir of a highly prized friendship, he did not leave them behind him at St. James, which was as well equipped with priceless works as any library in Paris.

Along the way he had ample time to ponder the reason of his recall to Cologne. Two Chapters of the Order had demanded that four Dominican universities be erected in as many countries—at Bologna for Lombardy, at Oxford for England, at Montpellier for France, and at Cologne for Germany. Since the Chapter of 1248 had taken up the matter once more, confirming what had been decreed by the way of an *inchoatio*, as it was called, this demand for the new *studia solemnia* became part of the authentic law of the Order.[1]

Now this does not mean that the German province had been without schools or possessed only schools of an inferior kind. What the Order called for was the establishment of houses of higher studies modeled as nearly as possible and feasible on St. James of Paris which, largely because of its proximity to the university, had from the first, taken a unique place in the educational scheme of the Order. This would obviate the need of sending students to Paris, where it was next to impossible to find accommodations for the Friars coming from all over Europe.

Did Albert revolve in his mind how best to institute the *studium*? It is not surmising too much if we assume that as he vigorously marched along—for he was so rapid a pedestrian that he not merely attracted attention but was often showered with good-natured banter—he planned just what Parisian pedagogical features should be introduced at Cologne and what innovations would prove of decided advantage.

[1] *Acta Capitulorum Generalium Ord. Praed. (ed. Reichert, 1898), 41.*

It is probable that he arrived in Cologne in time for the corner-stone laying of the cathedral, on August 15, 1248.[2] Albert tells us that he had seen and examined the precious shrine of the Three Kings in which their bones, brought from Milan, were preserved. He likewise describes for us his minute examination of the foundations of the cathedral and the many interesting archeological remains that came to light during the excavations.[3] He had nothing to do, however, with drawing up the plans of the cathedral, as legend would have it and as art has pictured him. Yet this does not mean that with his keen interest in architecture he abstained altogether from converse with the architects and the workmen. Of the latter, each one in those days was a skilled master craftsman. Albert discloses in too many places of his written works and sermons a practical familiarity with the building arts for us to imagine that he acquired his expertness from books alone.

On Epiphany Day, January 6,1249, we find the Dominican convent in the Stolkgasse alive with interest.[4] King William of Holland, who had just been crowned in November, after the victory at Aix-la-Chapelle, was coming to pay Albert a visit. Grateful for his election to the Empire two years before, the monarch was now coming to Cologne to venerate the relics of the Magi and bestow gifts for the reconstruction of the cathedral, partially destroyed by fire. The train of knights and courtiers were entertained in the convent courtyard. The king went up to Albert's cell. What transpired Albert never revealed. Did he give the young and inexperienced king sage advice about the conduct of the realm and the prosecution of the crusades against the Mohammedans? Did he warn him against the chicanery of so many fawning courtiers who were panting for royal favor? That William was satisfied with the purpose of his visit is plain from his generosity to the Dominican Convent of Utrecht which, till then a mean and miserable place, was soon transformed into an abode conducive to study and prayer.

---

2 *H. Cardauns,* Konrad von Hochstaden, Erzbischof von Köln (Köln: 1880), 147.

3 *Opp.* V, 50.

4 de Loe, *Analecta Bollandiana* (1900), 263; XX, 281; de Loe, *Annalen des Historischen Vereins für den Niederrhein*, LXXIV, 188 sq.; Bohmer (*Fontes Rerum Germanicarum*, Stuttgart, 1843, II, 438) gives the *Chronicon de Episcopis Ultrajectinis* (1346); Ennen, *Quellen zur Geschichte der Stadt Köln* (Köln: 1865), I, 23, adds a great many details. E. Ebert gives an enlarged version in poetry in Schoppner's Bayrisches Sagenbuch.

It was natural that the people should be wrought up over the royal visit. But they were sorely disappointed that no particulars had filtered down to them either from Albert or from any of the brethren about what had transpired there. Hence, the popular imagination began to spin a web of legend which, while it contains no strand of truth, still bears witness to the high esteem entertained of Albert's knowledge. To the medieval man knowledge was power, not in our modern academic fashion, not as a mere shibboleth or advertising slogan, but in a really personal way. If Albert knew so much about the secrets of nature men deemed it was but to be expected that he knew practically all other secrets.

So in the fervid minds of the people the cold biting day of that visit is suddenly turned into balmy spring, with only gentle zephyrs blowing. The dead, dank shrubs and trees begin to blossom with Maytime luxuriance. The far-flung corners of the world leap to this cloister garth, suddenly transformed into a veritable conservatory of the most exotic plants and flowers. The bare trees, stretching out their arms to heaven in mute protest against the wintry death, begin to sag under the weight of fresh luscious fruits. Birds have come back in the twinkle of an eye; butterflies more radiant than a dream dazzle the eyes; fountains with the force of geysers leap into the air to catch the kiss of the sun and spread themselves in mad joy in gossamer veils of dancing color. At a table, in the center of the garden, two handsome youths, like Greek gods strayed into an alien land and home, serve the king with food which only a minute ransacking of the world could have brought together. And then quick as a flash the scene of beauty disappears at a sign from Albert!

That there is the exaggeration of a youthful people in this tale of magic may be easily and readily admitted. That Albert was familiar with many mechanical devices in olden times, such as the revolving stage at Rome in the time of Nero, the statue of Minerva made by Daedalus which walked and emitted sounds, and that he gave explanations of what must have been looked upon by his contemporaries as magic—explanations which may be regarded as refreshingly modern today—is familiar to all who have read his works.[5] His *barbiton*, or walking and talking statue, which he described in

[5] Opp. *De Anima.*

detail, would be the commonest of toys today. Authors at various times have essayed to give an explanation of this story. Perhaps Albert did have a conservatory in which flowers grew, something like the Adonis Gardens of the ancient Greeks which were nothing else than pots in which lettuce and wheat were forced in summer, or the Hypocausts of the Romans' Baths. Perhaps he had more than a passing idea of steam—his *sufflator*, or blower, Albert thus describes:

> "Take a solid earthen vessel provided with an opening at the top and bottom, and standing on feet. Fill it with water and place it near the fire. The steam is then generated in the vessel and steadily increases in proportion to the heat of the fire until, escaping with violence through one of the openings, it shoots the water far off on to the surrounding objects. If it escapes through the bottom of the vessel, it discharges sparks, burning coal, and hot ashes to a considerable distance. This sort of vessel is usually called *sufflator* (blower), and is ordinarily shaped like a man who is blowing."[6]

Did not his Dominican brothers in Greenland about this time, pipe hot water from the geysers to their convent of St. Thomas in Gardar to heat the rooms and grow vegetables? Perhaps these pioneers in steam borrowed their ideas from Albert's book on *Meteorology*. Whether there is any explanation or none at all of the story little affects the intellectual eminence of Albert. As the legend seems to have sprung up at the very time of the king's visit it could not but enhance the reputation of the man who had been called from Paris for the express purpose of getting under way an institute of higher studies. Now, since the natural sciences were an integral part of philosophy as it was then taught, we need not wonder that Albert and the brethren were anxious to see the Cologne *studium* begin under the best auspices. With such a popular story made to order by the people, Albert and his brethren did not have to resort to an elaborate campaign of advertising the new school. The people did it gratis and with as much innocent pleasure for themselves as advantage for the Friars. If Albert never showed himself so much a thoroughbred German as in his preoccupation with mechanics, and if the people who hawked the legend about ran true to

[6] *Meteor.*, Opp. IV., 100.

the German penchant for toys—and, incidentally, in our own day, for airplanes, zeppelins, and a score of other devices—none suffered from the visit of King William of Holland to Cologne, least of all the new school.

By just what steps and stages the school developed has not been written down. By nature and temperament Albert was far removed from the smashing radical, the ruthless innovator. If he had a weakness it was not in the line of destruction. His was rather a constructive, perhaps even a syncretist or eclectic temper. He was so much the good-natured German that he felt he could make the most awkward things do service for him. Hence, whatever good there was in the curriculum which he found at home when he returned to Cologne, Albert perfected and rounded out according to the best traditions of Paris—and, perhaps, even of Padua. Aristotle had never felt so much at home in Germany before. The Lombard was received with greater honor at Cologne than in his native Ravenna, and Denis the Areopagite, was more sympathetically interpreted here than in Paris. On all these texts Albert lectured with learning and originality. Much of his work was a bland paraphrasing of Aristotle—but, then, was Albert not trying to make the Greek acceptable to the German? Much of his commentary on the Lombard was merely the reduction of involved sentences into easily understood Latin, or perhaps even German—but was Albert not tearing away the verbal robes in order to expose the palpitating body of truth to men with a native bent for the practical and useful? Much of his commentary on the pseudo-Areopagite was only a patient unraveling of cryptic sentences to get at a possible meaning—but was not Albert seeking to provide his own people, yearning for mysticism, with a mystical speculation that did not carry in it the germs of pantheism?

Albert knew that impersonal teaching was a snare. He had been in the university world long enough to realize that a living man must be behind the lessons and lectures. The professor must be on more than speaking terms with the authors he is explaining. Hence Rudolf of Nijmegen tells us that Albert was always reading, studying, and meditating. He pushed his way into the innermost sanctuary of the minds of his authors and sat down there, as it were, to observe the operation of their mental processes and the conditions under which they best worked. Thus having seen everything for himself and tested his findings in the light of infallible Catholic truth, he began to lecture on the things with which his mind and heart were full.

How well Albert prepared his lectures and how even his sleeping hours were obsessed with the ambition to get at the true meaning of an author is well borne out by the dream which both Peter of Prussia and Rudolf of Nijmegen, basing their statements on the *Legenda Prima*, written about 1300, report:

> "When the Master was expounding the works of Denis, and had completed the book on the *Divine Hierarchy*, his courage failed him at sight of the difficulties which the rest of the work contained. He resolved, as St. Jerome before him did in regard to the book of Daniel, to put aside the work, and leave it unfinished, when the faithful Master, who permits not the laborers of His vineyard to be tried beyond their strength, sent to him, in his sleep, the Apostle St. Paul, who encouraged him to renewed ardor. The manner in which the preacher of the Gentiles appeared to Albert is thus related. A Religious, renowned for his learning and eminent virtues, whom many suppose to have been Thomas of Aquin, one day found a document in Albert's handwriting in which the following occurred: 'When I had completed with much toil the book on *The Celestial Hierarchy*, I began to explain the hierarchy of the Church. I got through the first chapter, on the Sacrament of Baptism, with much difficulty. But when I entered on the second courage failed me, and I despaired of being able to pursue it. Then after Matins I had a vision. I found myself in a church where St. Paul was celebrating Mass. Consoled beyond measure, I hoped that he would enlighten me as to the meaning of Denis the Areopagite. When the Apostle had said the *Agnus Dei*, a multitude of people entered the church; the Apostle calmly saluted them and inquired what it was they wanted. "Behold," they all exclaimed, "we have brought to you one who is possessed, whom we implore you to cure by freeing him from the devil." Having cast out Satan, St. Paul communicated this man with a particle of the consecrated Host. I offered my services at the ablution of the fingers, and, with fear, said, "Sir, I have long wished to be instructed in the mysterious subjects contained in the book of St. Denis, but especially on the grace of true sanctity." He answered me, with much kindness of manner, "Come with me after

Mass to the house of the Priest Aaron, which is on the other side of the river." I then followed the Apostle after Mass. When we reached the banks of the river, he without difficulty passed over. But it was otherwise with me, for I had scarce touched the water when it began to rise to such a degree as to render the passage impossible. The Apostle entered the house of Aaron, which he had pointed out to me; and while anxious as to how I should follow him, I suddenly woke. On reflection, I discovered the meaning of the dream. The first chapter explained by me treats, in effect, of the expulsion of Satan from the body of man by baptism, then his participation in the Sacrament of the Holy Eucharist. The following chapter leads him who receives the holy unction to the house of Aaron for it treats of the chrism with which bishops are consecrated. The deep waters increasing so suddenly arrested my pen; but the Apostle, through God's grace, rendered the passage easy to me. I then commenced to write again, and accomplished with God's help, what to my personal feebleness appeared impossible.' "[7]

So long and seriously had Albert pondered on the difficulties of this most difficult of theological books that, almost befuddled on the subject during his waking hours, his thoughts quite naturally leaped together through unconscious cerebration during his sleep. Such things happen to others as well who are not afraid to use their brains. Other portions of the dream are reproduced in the same chapter of Albert's *Commentary on the Ecclesiastical Hierarchy*, such, for instance, as the march toward the abode of the high priest, Aaron, and the obstacles that stood in his way.

When teaching was of such a high grade of excellence, when learning was imparted in such a personal and immediate way, it could only be a question of a short time until the Cologne school would forge to the very front rank. Students came in goodly numbers, without much urging, from the ranks of the clergy and nobility. For the benefit of the former, Albert organized a series of public lectures and disputes where everyone was free to air his own opinions and submit them to the acid test of general discussion. Bishops passing through Cologne

---

[7] Rodolphus de Novimagio, *Legenda*, 22-25; Peter of Prussia relates that he saw in Albert's own handwriting in his Commentary on the Pseudo-Dionysius the explanation of this dream.

came to the school to see for themselves what manner of teaching was being dispensed and how vast an enthusiasm for academic competency was engendered. Probably, to add prestige to the embryonic university, as also to fit his pupils for the business of dispatching public affairs as well, Albert kept in touch with the nobles of the town, which was the second most important one in the Empire. These did not deem it beneath their dignity to attend the classes where lessons in the best wisdom of ruling others were given. And the doors were not closed against those among the poor from the country round about who looked upon ignorance or even a mere simple rudimentary education as poverty of the worst sort. In this shrewd and far-seeing manner Albert established academic traditions at Cologne which, persevering after his death, made possible one hundred and forty years later the establishment of a full-fledged university, which needed not to hang its head in shame before any other school in Christendom.

Naturally the reputation of Albert drew the best minds to Cologne. When he had discovered for himself a lad of unusual powers, Albert would not spare himself in lavishing upon him the full riches of his knowledge that he himself had amassed so patiently and laboriously.

Thus, with keen eye, Albert soon discovered among his students at Cologne a kindred spirit who knew and appreciated the utilities and sanctities of genuine friendship. He was Ulrich of Strasburg, a bright, vivacious young man, who gave early promise of the theological eminence he would one day attain without, on that account, surrendering anything of that practical turn of mind which made him an admirable man of affairs and an ideal superior and leader. Frequently the two were seen walking together in the cloister, or through the streets of the city when business called Albert from his cell. Later on, Ulrich would accompany Albert as walking companion and secretary to the most far-flung sections of Germany, and the fragments of correspondence between them which still survive prove how implicit was the confidence of Ulrich in Albert's judgment.

But another friendship dated from these idyllic days of Albert. At the end of 1244 a young student of eighteen years, half German, half Sicilian, had been brought to Cologne by John of Wildhausen, the General of the Order, for the express purpose of getting him into a safe refuge, far away from his own people who had set their hearts on having him become anything but a Friar Preacher. Thomas Aquinas, educated by the Benedictine monks at Monte Cassino in his tenderest years, initiated into the liberal arts at the newly founded University of Naples by Peter Martin and Peter the Irishman, had roused the ire of his family by entering the Order of the Dominicans. They pleaded with him, expostulated with his superiors at Rome, enlisted the good offices of Pope Innocent V, imprisoned the youth for nearly a year in the paternal castle of San Giovanni, tried to break his vocation by introducing into his cell one night a gaudy temptress well known to the camp where his brothers, Landolf and Reynald, were looked upon with favor as blood relatives of Barbarossa. Thomas, too, was hard as adamant against the tearful appeals of his two sisters, whom he finally persuaded in his turn to enter monasteries. He evaded the Countess Theodora, his mother, who followed him to Santa Sabina in Rome; argued out the question of his vocation firmly but respectfully before the Pope; submitted to the indignities of a cruel imprisonment while daring to put on a habit which had been smuggled in to him by a friend; drove off with a charred faggot the woman of sin and, finally, escaped on horseback in the dead of night from the two brothers pursuing him to the frontier. John the Teuton, on his way to the General Chapter at Cologne in 1245, out of sheer pity no doubt, for the lad, saw fit to remove him from the molestations of his own family. There is no reason to accept the theory that Thomas was sent to Cologne in order to enjoy the advantages of a schooling under Albert. The oldest chronicles make the discovery of Thomas one of the chief glories of Albert.

In Paris, the General and the silent student did not tarry long. The gay city did not bewitch the mind of the lad who, having just read some of the Fathers of the Church, was turning over in his mind their profoundly touching deductions from the inspired words of Holy Writ. On foot, begging their food along the way, and chanting the Office when not discoursing on heavenly things, the two had come from Paris to Cologne.

Albert must have been interested on beholding the stripling, so calm, so quiet, with big open eyes, auburn hair, and powerful frame. Any lad who had undergone such experiences (which, no doubt, were discreetly made known by the General behind the back of Thomas), would have elicited more than his passing interest. So Thomas Aquinas took his place among the crowd of students around Albert's chair. He was slow to speak. He never asked questions or confessed to having experienced difficulties. Could it be that he did not fully grasp what was being said? So thought his fellow students, and one, more charitable than the rest, volunteered to help him privately over the difficult places. Probably he was touched with pity for the stranger who, because of his silence, had become the butt of all the practical jokers in the school and was generally known as "the dumb Sicilian ox." Thomas courteously accepted the good offices of this self-appointed tutor, until one day when the latter happened upon an unusually difficult passage which he could not explain, the quiet lad unraveled it to his tutor's amazement. He begged as a special favor that nothing be said about the incident. As a reward for this secrecy Thomas, on his part, assumed the work of explaining Albert's lessons.

Now it happened, shortly after, that Albert in his lectures was discussing the difficult book *On the Divine Names* by the pseudo-Dionysius. Quite inevitably he here came upon a most knotty problem, which he proposed to the students. A rivalry ensued among them as to who could answer best. They agreed to write out their solutions and hoped, by a comparison of the answers, to be put upon the road that might eventually lead in the right direction. Was it in mockery that all, save the one sworn to secrecy, besieged Thomas for his answer? Quietly he set to work, and before the rest had marshaled their puny arguments and scant erudition he had finished his own reply. With that he hurried off to other tasks in the choir or convent. A gust of wind carried the written paper into the corridor. Here Albert discovered the memorandum, and not knowing whose the cramped handwriting might be he made diligent search until he learned the identity of the author. He was pleased to learn of the chivalrous conduct of the young student toward his tutor, and determined on his own account to test the caliber of his man.

A public disputation was due on the following day and Albert informed Thomas that he would be called upon to defend a thesis. Without a chance for elaborate preparation Thomas defended his thesis admirably. His lucidity of argumentation was a match for his erudition. But Albert would test, too, the character of the lad to see whether his knowledge had puffed him up with pride: "Brother Thomas," he exclaimed in a tone of apparent reproach, "you seem to answer more like a master than a respondent." But Thomas answered modestly:

"Master, I know not how to treat the question otherwise." To which Albert replied: "Well, then continue according to your method, but remember that I have many objections to make." And forthwith Albert began to ply him with questions, difficult, subtle, and abstruse. Thomas, with wondrous self-possession, disposed of all the objections urged by Albert in right good earnest. Finally the questioner was lost in wonder over the riches of wisdom in one so young. Remembering the nickname by which he had passed among the students, Albert, with a touch of grim, blunt sarcasm, which none could miss, cried out: "You call this man a dumb Sicilian ox; but I declare to you that so loud will be his bellowing in doctrine that it will resound throughout the world."[8] Albert had found a man after his own heart, one who though he did not possess Ulrich's capacity for friendship was, nevertheless, not immune to the exchange of confidences upon which true friendship must be based. Albert's heart passed out to Thomas and embraced him as one who could make his dreams come true. Knowing what it was that the world needed, if it was not to wreck itself upon the rocks of pagan rationalism and the reefs of Christian indifference to the claims of reason; realizing too, that his own work could never be more than the pioneer task of dragging together the most scattered fragments of the new learning, which another must purge of error and inform with the Catholic spirit—the whole-souled man that he was, he now took Thomas to his heart of hearts. He obtained permission to have Thomas's cell next to his own; he invited him to share in the results of his own researches; he put extensive notes and comments at his disposal; he chose him as walking companion, since thus they might discuss the deep problems which, with the new light borrowed from Greece, seemed to call for a fuller answer; and finally, he installed him in his own pulpit when the many outside duties which he was called upon to perform forced him to absent himself from the city for a time or from the classroom for a day or two. An intellectual friendship had been born the like of which had not existed since the days in Athens when Gregory Nazianzen and Gregory of Nyssa companioned each other to and from class, knowing only one other street in the city besides that to the university—the one which led to

---

[8] H. Scheeben, Chronologie, 31; A. M. Walz, "*De Alberti Magni et Scti. Thomae Aquinatis personali ad invicem relatione,*" in *Angelicum (1925), 299- 319.*

the church.

How far Albert was prepared to go in his endeavors to see his pupils put upon tracks that would carry them to high places of responsibility appears from his eagerness to see Thomas Aquinas sent to Paris to lecture at the university in preparation for his bachelor's degree. John the Teuton, as General of the Order, had turned to Albert for some able professor to fill the vacant chair at Paris in the beginning of the scholastic year 1252. From the tone of the General's letter it is plain that he had no inkling of Thomas's fitness. Some even hold that the General was sounding out Albert's willingness to accept the post. In answering this letter of the General, who plainly wished a German for the place, Albert suggested the name of Thomas. The offer was instantly if politely rejected. As the General, after the Chapter of Bologna, May 19, 1252, hastened to the papal Curia on important business, which he was frequently called upon to do, Albert turned to Hugh of St. Cher who happened to be acting as legate in Belgium. John and Hugh met at Constance in August of the same year. Undoubtedly Thomas's fitness was discussed, for he was ordered to Paris without delay. The unselfishness of Albert appeared to good advantage here, for it was at a personal loss and to the disadvantage of the Cologne school that the quiet Sicilian was called upon to assume this task.[9] And as Thomas departed for his new post it was not with trepidation, for somewhere among the few belongings he took with him, were the elaborate notes he had taken down, in his crazy handwriting and crazier shorthand, of Albert's lectures on Aristotle and the Lombard.[10] These were texts upon which he would be expected to dilate. And if Aquinas is at his best in the treatment of moral questions—a fact which seems to have escaped most of his commentators throughout the centuries—it is, no doubt, due in great measure to the fact that these tracts were precisely the ones on which Albert had spent most time and labor at Cologne during his regency.

---

[9] H. Scheeben, ibid.; H. Finke, *Ungedruckte Dominikanerbriefe des 13. Jahrhunderts (Paderborn: 1891), 51;* Analecta Bollandiana (1901), 279.

[10] A. M. Walz, *op. cit.*, 37, 52; P. Mandonnet, *Les Ecrits authentiques de S. Thomas d'Aquin* (Fribourg en Suisse: 1910), 154.

Chapter V

PREACHER OF THE WORD

ALBERT was no bookworm, lacking contacts with the outer world. His predilection for the moral parts of theology, which characterized his teaching at Cologne at this time, would afford sufficient guarantee to hold that he had a sharp eye—perhaps an eye single—on the social questions agitating the minds of the people. Contact with them would serve to enhance the value, practicality, and directness of his teaching. So, like a true Friar, he preached frequently to the people.

That he had a genuine conception of the Dominican vocation and ideal, which would have every one of its members a powerful dispenser of the Word, appears from his commentary on the words of St. Luke (xvi. 21): "But the dogs came and licked his sores." He applied these words unmistakably to the members of his own Order, who even at so early a date were called, by a popular play upon their name *Dominicani*, the *Domini Canes* or "watchdogs of the Lord." In explaining the episode of Lazarus at the gate of Dives he writes: "In our own times this has been verified. For the roving dogs are the Order of Preachers who do not wait at their homes for the poor but go out to them and lick the ulcers of their sins having in their mouths the bark of preaching... For these good dogs have in their teeth the bite of reproof and confusion... Every good preacher is a living dog because he has the grace of a bark in his preaching, of reproof in his tooth and of healing in the counsel of his tongue. But a dead lion is that austere prelate who gives no evidence of the works of a prelate and ruler."[1]

His sermons were direct, solid, and illuminating. As a rule, he took the Sunday Gospel or Epistle—which only a few decades of years before had been selected by the Church from the New Testament as the

[1] *Comment. in Lucam*, Opp. XXIII, 443. This interpretation of the name Dominican has been thoroughly studied by P. Mandonnet, *Note du symbolique médiéval; Domini Canes*, in *Revue de Fribourg* (October, 1912). How this symbolism has played a part in Dominican art and heraldry has been established by C. M. Daley, *The Dominican Shield* (Washington: 1932).

parts with which the people must needs be familiar in order to know and practise their faith—and, after painting in one or two arresting sentences the Scriptural background for a proper understanding of the full body of the pericope, discoursed on his chosen text. Carefully he divided up his sermon, for men might have vast knowledge or erudition, but they knew what they knew and wished to have it treated in an orderly and connected way. Because he used the allegorical sense of interpreting the text he had a large field for new, fresh, and original moral observations, as well as for devotional and practical applications. He used everything within reach for this purpose, not disdaining his large acquaintance with medieval life. Many of his sermons have a distinctly medical—therapeutical and prophylactic—tone, where common diseases, their symptoms and remedies, are detailed in an effort to drive home the fact of the existence, omnipresence, and malignity of soul-sicknesses and the need and uses of spiritual healing. Perhaps this frequent insistence on medical lore made Albert's sermons palatable to people who, without a sufficiency of expert physicians, had a mortal dread of the many plagues and epidemics which so frequently swept over a Europe unacquainted with the utilities of sanitation, diet, and physical rest. His was a practical attempt to get at men's souls through their bodies. Again, he introduced into his discourses personal reminiscences which must have appealed mightily to a people without the modern machinery of news gathering and, on that very account, highly interested, nay curious, about things and men, not least of whom was the preacher whose name was in the mouth of the learned professors of the world. This stooping to the common mental estate of the people was one of the charms of all Albert's preaching. He was at pains to put himself in touch with his hearers. Hence it comes that Albert's sermons are a prime fountain of information concerning his own character and personality. He revealed himself and needed not to be ashamed of the revelation. In this respect he was less historical than Humbert de Romans who, in prefatory notes to the skeleton sermons and sermon models intended for people of every state and condition of life, vouchsafed us extremely valuable sidelights on the customs of the times. Moreover there was little similarity between Albert's sermons and those anecdotes of an historical kind which Vincent of Beauvais, Stephen Salignac, and Stephen Bourbon—all Dominicans of great knowledge, wide travel with keen and open eyes, and a flair for the gossip of the towns and city marts—left behind as a godsend to preachers and as a mine of information to succeeding ages. Albert wove into his sermons the poetry of nature and the music of the forests, becoming at times almost lyrical. He knew his auditory perfectly, but understood not less well all the subtleties of oratory. Just as in St. Augustine there was a frequent use of colloquialisms and popular turns of thought and the playing up of contemporary happenings, so in Albert there was much that cannot be fully understood and duly appreciated without a workable knowledge of medieval men and the times which made these men what they were, with all their virtues and all their faults. To read these sermons in such a way as to get their full savor one must frequently refer to Du Cange's *Glossary of Medieval Latin*—for Albert's Latin was supple enough to make room for expressions we might call slang, but which in those days were but new literary forms, supplementing the Latin pagan tongue. This latter had now come not only under the influence of the Church, which gave a new meaning and content to ancient words, but also under the influence of peoples who were trying to put into coherent speech subtle soul-experiences which the word brokers of the period of Latin decadence were too superficial to deign to take notice of.

By making his sermons so actual and popular Albert offered the people *dicta*, or sayings and slogans, which, repeated often enough and long enough, attained to the dignity of proverbs. Only an infinitesimally small number of these have come down to us, and even these, in any other than their naïve homely form, would seem rather didactic. About their archaic German hangs an air of freshness that appeals. They are hewn keystones of thought. They are concrete as they must needs have been for a people unaccustomed to the subtleties of fine shadings of thought. They are brutally blunt, but never dull. There is no mistaking their meaning and no chance of missing their moral. Among the best of these maxims may be quoted the following:

"An egg given by a living man for God's sake is much more meritorious for him than a house filled with gold given after death."

"Were a man who owned everything that God ever created to give it away at death for God's sweet sake it would not profit him half as much for eternal life as to give an alms for love of the Lord while alive."

"To accept love and suffering from God's hand with perfect

humility, seeing in both the gifts of His Providence, is of more value to the soul than to break a wagonload of birches over one's shoulders daily."

"To pardon those who have harmed us in body, goods, or name is a much more meritorious act than to cross the ocean and cast ourselves into the Holy Sepulchre."

"Just as the priest receives Christ corporally at the altar so man receives Him spiritually in the soul every time he abstains, for love of Him, from some fault, be it only an idle word or a vagrant glance."

"If I were in search of learned ecclesiastics, I would go to Paris, but if I wished to learn the mysteries of God I would go for an answer to the man who is voluntarily the poorest. For we must exchange the lowest for the highest, as Christ made plain in His words to the rich young man: 'If thou wilt be perfect sell all thou hast, give the price of it to the poor, and come follow Me.' "

"A suffering man often imagines that he is of no account in the sight of God, but when he is unable to pray or perform good works his sufferings and desires afford him a deeper insight into the divine than is vouchsafed to a thousand healthy men."

These and hundreds of other oracular and sententious sayings, for whose individual authenticity no man would be bold enough to argue, were current among the people of the Rhineland, who had had a natural liking and aptitude for such sayings since those barbarous days when their forebears in the swamps and forests heard the judicial sentences of the *Vehmgerichte* meted out in just that way by the elders and patriarchs of the tribe. A citizen of Cologne, John Laicus, gathered them together in a volume which he called *Schatzkaestlein* or "Treasure Chest." They were hawked and bandied about so commonly in the ages that followed that they insinuated themselves into the writings of Eckehard, Suso, and Tauler, and the *Gottesfreunde* along the Rhine who cultivated mystical teachings and ascetical living in a corporate way.[2] *The Chronicles of Colmar*, where stigmatizations of nuns are described as a normal condition of affairs for nearly three quarters of a century, are redolent of these maxims. They have not gone without effect on

[2] M. Grabmann, Wesen und Grundlagen der katholischen Mystik (München: 1923), 14-16; and Die Kulturwerke der deutschen Mystik im Mittelalter (Augsburg: 1923), 24, 29, 36 et passim.

Thomas à Kempis and that school of spirituality with which he was identified.

During the seventeenth century it was common in the mountainous districts around Salzburg to place in the church vestibules paintings of Albert enlightened by Christ in the art of conversation. A scroll in popular language, sometimes even in dialect, made known to the people what had been communicated to Albert from on high. The central painting was flanked on both sides with seven small images, each representing the perfection, or counterparts of the virtue of which there is mention in the text of the scroll. This remote imitation of the old Greek triptychs, through the use of the Albertine maxims, had a healthy influence on German art just at a time when it was in danger of abandoning attention to detail for a mad devotion to the broadly pictorial and highly photographic.

Now Albert was not adverse to such a drastically homely utilization of his sermons. He rather encouraged it in every way. Evidently he felt that the people must carry away something from the sermon if it was not to defeat itself, not be love's labors lost, not a flat failure in attaining the purpose of every discourse which is nothing else than the conversion of the individual heart. And he needed not to be a prophet to realize that the popular memory is very short for everything but scandal. Hence, he put himself to the trouble of drawing up summaries of his sermons which he repeated impressively when he was about to finish. These were like nothing so much as litanies of dogmas to be believed and faults to be avoided.[3] Here is one that quite deservedly remained immensely popular in his day and in subsequent ages, in fact, up to the time when flowery, and apostrophic and rhetorical prayers, with no dogmatic content, drove from the private oratories of the people those ancient formulas redolent of the Church's liturgy.

> "Be Thou Blessed, O Humanity of my Savior, which was united to the Divinity in the womb of a Virgin Mother: Be Thou Blessed, O sublime and eternal Divinity, who was pleased to come down to us under the veil of our flesh! Be Thou forever Blessed who, by the

[3] M. Weiss, *Primordia Novae Bibliographiae B. Alberti Magni* (Parisiis: 1905), 243, 251. G. Meersemann (*Introductio in Opera Omnia B. Alberti Magni*, Bruges: 1931), 123, suggests that there are so many prayers purporting to be of Albertine origin that the matter is deserving of widest research and deepest study with an eye to a definitive edition.

power of the Holy Ghost, didst unite Thyself to virginal flesh! I salute you also, O Mary, in whom the fullness of the Divinity dwelt! I salute you in whom the fullness of the Holy Ghost dwelt! May the most pure Humanity of the Son be equally Blessed, which, consecrated by the Father, was born of you! I salute you, O unspotted virginity, now raised above all the choirs of angels. Rejoice, O Queen of Heaven, who didst merit to become the temple of the spotless Humanity of Christ! Rejoice, and be glad, O Virgin of virgins, whose pure flesh united the Divinity with the Sacred Humanity! Rejoice, and be glad, O Spouse of the holy Patriarchs, who was deemed worthy to nourish and suckle at thy breast the Sacred Humanity. I salute thee, ever blessed and fruitful virginity, which didst merit to obtain the fruit of life and the joys of eternal salvation. Amen."[4]

This and other like popular statements of Catholic belief, breathing a typically tender German piety and devotion to the Person and Humanity of Jesus, were learned by the youths in the schools, never subsequently forgotten, and never used without great spiritual profit. The comparatively recent introduction of the Divine Praises after Benediction of the Most Blessed Sacrament is a belated attempt to achieve what Albert effected in his own day. Someone has written that St. Vincent de Paul, by distributing at the church doors of Paris printed statements of the many works he had inaugurated, what they had accomplished, and what could be done with more resources at command, was the real father of modern advertising methods. Might one not say that he was antedated several centuries by Albert, who did not believe that Catholic knowledge was some esoteric teaching for the favored few, some exotic growth that could not take root in the popular heart? Rudolf of Nijmegen gives us a clue to the methods Albert adopted to reach the people. He writes: "What shows us how much Albert strove to impart, even to the people, the result of his learned researches, and to change the problems which he solved into virtues calculated to engender piety in souls, are the four books of the *Sentences*, which he transformed into so many formulas of prayer."

"He wrote also a short paraphrase of the Gospels and then reduced

[4] Rodolphus de Novimagio, *Legenda*, 19.

them to prayers, in order that the mind and heart might at once be enlightened and inflamed with God's praise. He was not content with the usual invocations in the Litanies; but, after having enlarged them, he composed in honor of each of the saints a prayer of a few words, but full of meaning."[5]

The prayers constructed out of the Lombard's *Sentences* were discovered and edited by Nicholas Thoemes at Berlin, in 1893. There still remain unedited several prayers to the Eucharistic Christ, the Holy Spirit, and the Blessed Virgin. We can still look forward to the publication of prayers composed in honor of each of the saints mentioned and invoked in the Litany of the Saints.

If these and many other formulas and prayers have been lost to the ages or left unedited, such is not the case with the fervent outpouring of his soul after his Sunday and festival sermons. These prayers breathed the air of the sanctuary and were filled with an authentic Scriptural perfume. They came hot from the heart, without any literary artifice, without any straining after pious effects. If a man thinks twice before weeping in public, the same holds good of praying in public. Hence, these prayers were manly, virile, solid–precisely the same characteristics that are to be found in all Albert's written works. They were a native product of an age of faith, with no awkward posing or forced tears. The Christian piety of that age has nothing finer to offer as a sample of what it could do at its best. There was none of the frenzy and rhapsody of those unorthodox prayers composed by good men of a later age whose hearts (perhaps, glib tongues too) ran away with their heads. Later on a theologian like Contenson, when finishing the individual chapters of his golden but criminally neglected and forgotten *Theologia Mentis et Cordis,* would do exactly what Albert taught. These Albertine prayers for Sundays were frequently reprinted during the centuries, were even translated into Flemish by the poet Louis de Velthem before the end of the twelfth century,[6] and became an efficient means of fixing in the minds of the people the content and lessons of the Sunday Gospels. Albert had learned to practical advantage a lesson from St. John Chrysostom who had been in the

---

5 *Ibid.*

6 G. Meersemann, "*Albert de Groote in de Nederlanden,*" in *Thomistich Tijdschrift (1931), 170 sq.*

habit of boiling down his sermons into prayers which his admiring hearers committed to memory.

By such diversified means Albert soon began to exert a powerful influence in Cologne and the country round about. If, as St. Augustine tells us, the world woke up one morning to find itself Arian because it had been singing and whistling the jingles into which Arius had injected his heretical teaching, then something in the opposite direction was attempted by a resourceful professor who knew his theology well enough to be able to put it into the simplest, most picturesque, and appealing form—a feat as rare as it is difficult and an achievement which makes Albert one of the greatest home missionaries of a frankly missionary Order. His methods will serve in his own institute as a model for a host of apostles at home and abroad, even such as have the delicate task of imbuing royal minds with truths that only too often can prove inconvenient to men who, quite unconsciously, come to think themselves above the law because their will is obeyed unquestioningly by a cowed race. Friar Lawrence, who wrote a *Somme* for the French Dauphin a few decades of years later, is intellectually a legitimate descendant of Albert.[7]

Naturally such thorough grounding in and frank acceptance of the truths of the faith brought numberless penitents to the feet of Albert. The early chronicles are one in insisting on this point—Albert had the understanding mind and the commiserating heart. Is it any wonder, then, that he was besieged by penitents and prodigals in a day when men sinned lustily, no doubt, but did not rebel at penances which were not too ridiculously incommensurate with their offenses? None of his contemporaries complained when Albert imposed a severe penance of seven years duration. Rudolf communicates this information for the purpose of driving it home that Albert had such a reputation for sweet reasonableness as to attract a sinner for whom such a penance did not seem disproportionate and incongruous. What, then, must he have been with those pious souls who had not gone off into a far country to squander their inheritance of grace? Need we wonder that he was a favorite confessor with nuns athirst for the waters of perfection? Need we wonder that in the most unlooked-for places he goes minutely into

[7] P. Mandonnet, "*Laurent d'Orléans, auteur de la Somme-Roi*," in *Revue des Langues Romanes (1913), 20-23.*

subjects which from the way he speaks are frankly distasteful to him, as when, in his *Commentary on the Lombard,* speaking of the faults against purity, he confesses: “it is true, we ought never to raise, and much less discuss these immoral questions, which we can scarce mention without shame. But the monstrous sins which are nowadays brought to the holy tribunal unhappily too often oblige us to speak of them. They who seek to excuse their faults by saying that such acts are conformable to nature should be taught that they are, on the contrary, opposed to it.”[8] Perhaps it was the gnawing of the worm of conscience that brought King William to Albert at Cologne. Else why the utter mystery and deep silence about the purpose of his coming? Was this the reason, too, why so many patricians of the Empire sooner or later found their way to Albert’s cell? The same mystery shrouds their secret parleys with the professor who knew the claims of justice so well that he could be depended upon to give the correct decision in delicate cases of conscience and who was ensouled with such a sympathy that he could be depended upon not to quench the smoking flax.

---

[8] Comment. in Sent. Dist., XXXI.

Furcht·got·wan·die·stund·seins·urteils·ist·zukunftig

CHAPTER VI

PROVINCIAL AND REFORMER

AT the General Chapter of the Order, in the spring of 1254, the German provincial, Herman of Havelberg, was deposed. Now, late that same year Albert, who was acting as vicar provincial during the interim, called a provincial Chapter to meet at Worms. The brethren showed their confidence in him by electing him provincial. For the next few years he would have authority over more than one thousand brethren scattered in forty convents, and many small establishments, from the Hungarian frontier to the mouth of the Rhine. At the time this vast stretch of land comprised Austria, Bavaria, Suabia, Alsace, the Rhenish Countries to Feldern and Utrecht, Holland, Sealand, Friesland, Brabant, Flanders, Westphalia, Hesse, Saxony, Thuringia, Meissen, Schleswig-Holstein, the Marshes, and the free city of Lubeck. For a man of sixty the thought that he was bound in conscience to make a personal visitation of these lands regularly must have been little short of terrifying.

Like the practical man he was, Albert would excel in giving good example to the brethren. The Friars, in the big and large, would be no better than their leader. His observance of the vow of obedience, by reason of his office, was restricted. Hence, he would compensate for this by a more vigorous observance of the vow of poverty. On foot, generally in company with his intimate friend, Ulrich of Strasburg, he traversed the vast stretch of land committed to his care, over ribbonlike paths which could not be dignified with the name of roads, through mountain passes infested by wild beasts and, in some regions, by men just a few removes from savagery. He wore shoes of a rough make, thus subtly rebuking the Spirituals who sought to make a favorable impression upon the people by exaggerating the sanctities of going barefoot. He begged his food at the nearest door when hunger urged, and where no religious house was to be found slept outdoors. Like St. Paul he did not wish to be a debtor to anyone, so in his refined delicacy he left behind in convents the books he had composed along the way during his brief periods of rest. Thus, also, he sought to stir up in the brethren a hunger for learning. Peter of Prussia says well: "He was not an egotist in regard to his knowledge, and he acted thus in order to show that he renounced all claims to property, and that he did not even consider the books which issued from his own prolific pen as belonging to himself."[1] He exacted nothing he himself did not practise. Hence, there could be no murmuring nor resentment among the brethren on the receipt of a letter of such tenor:

> "Brother Albert, Provincial, and the servant of all, to our beloved Brethren, the Priors and Convents of the German Province: health and brotherly charity in Christ. Fearing lest the evil of proprietorship, which is contrary to our blessed condition of the poor ones of Christ, should be introduced among you, we forbid every Religious to possess money or other objects for his own personal use, or for that of others. The Superior himself should know how this money or other objects are employed. Should anyone contravene this prohibition, that is, should any Religious, whosoever he be, dispose of money, or retain any object, unknown to his Superior, we shall hold him to be a proprietor, and punishable according to the utmost rigor of our laws, as a violator of the Constitutions of our Order."

And the brethren soon came to learn that he meant every word he said. For at the very Chapter in which he was elected to office he gave orders that the corpse of the lay brother at Pettau, in the diocese of Salzburg, on which money had been found, should be disinterred and cast into the common sewer.[2] This drastic measure gave special impressiveness to the regulations passed at the same assembly of the brethren: "Whosoever exercises the ministry of preaching in country districts should know that he is absolutely forbidden the use of vehicles in his journeys. He cannot, without a lawful reason, enter anyone's carriage. By a lawful reason, we mean the case when, traveling in uninhabited districts, he is unable to meet with an inn or the means of

[1] Petrus de Prussia, *Vitae*, Chap. XXVII.

[2] H. Scheeben, *Chronologie*, 160 und 27.

subsistence; when it is needful to visit the sick, and when there would be danger in delay; when it is necessary to convey a Brother to a Convent who has fallen ill on the way; when a Prince sends for us on important business, and in order to arrive the sooner. Let all who act contrariwise receive the discipline in presence of the whole community, and fast on bread and water in the middle of the refectory. These punishments cannot be remitted by dispensation."

The following year, at the Capitular Chapter at Augsburg, the same decree was repeated with more emphasis. "We impose upon the Prior of Worms, for having used a carriage and clothed two lay brothers without permission, seven day's penance on bread and water, five Psalters, and five disciplines; on the Prior of Minden, five day's penance on bread and water, five Masses, three Psalters, and three disciplines, for having come to Chapter on horseback; on the Brethren of Treves, for taking women into the Choir of their Church, the Convent, garden, and workrooms, three days on bread and water, three Psalters, and three disciplines. Likewise the Religious who this year have come to the Chapter in carriages or on horseback, or who, on other occasions have made use of the same, must be punished for this grave and scandalous violation of rule."[3]

In our tepid days such rigor seems almost repulsive. But it was general in the legislative enactments of the time and faithfully observed. Vocation to the Dominicans was not meant to be a carnival existence. Yet vocations increased so rapidly that Albert opened new convents at Strasburg in 1254, Seehausen in 1255, Rostock in 1256, and Mainz in 1256, while enlarging at least a dozen others, especially at Cologne and Utrecht. In all these convents he established regular observance and at the meetings of the superiors held at Augsburg, Erfurt, and Ratisbon, made diligent inquiries as to the manner in which the common life was observed. To prosper the practise of community life, Albert wrote the following letter which speaks eloquently of his solicitude: "The memory of the painful burden imposed on my feebleness by holy obedience, and the daily solicitude which it causes me, press me to impart to you, who are absent, the counsel given to the Brethren present at the Provincial Chapter. In order, then, that the government of the Religious committed to my care, a government for

[3] Petrus de Prussia, *op. cit.*, Rodolphus de Novimagio: *Legenda* 27.

which I am no longer alone sufficient, may be effectually shared by the Priors of the respective Convents, I hereby put in force as a salutary measure what the General Chapter long since ordained, namely: that each Religious shall lay open his conscience once a year to his Prior, and declare to him every fault of which he finds himself guilty, so that the state of his soul may be perfectly known."[4]

This letter is dated early in the year 1256. It is possible that Albert, who was on his way to the General Chapter at Paris in June, wished to relieve his mind of any fears about irregularities creeping in during his absence. And, perhaps, he had some premonition that he would be detained there, as nearly always happened when seen by his superiors at close range. For at many a Chapter the supreme head of the Order had commissioned him to do work which had reference to the common good of all the provinces. At all events, he was not far afield on this occasion, for he was sent from Paris to Anagni by Humbert de Romans, the General, to argue out before the Sovereign Pontiff the cause of the Friars whose presence in the teaching world of Paris was resented by a coterie of disgruntled university professors.

But Albert was too great a man to allow himself to be entirely absorbed by these duties and by his writings and preachings from which he never ceased until the closing years of his life. Within a few months of his election Albert, on February 17, 1255, was carrying on negotiations with the Archbishop of Cologne concerning some bequest, probably intended and used for the convent of the city, which was growing more popular every day as a seat of learning.

Almost at the same time he began to display a new aspect of his rich and resourceful nature. St. Dominic, realizing as every observant man must do, the self-sacrificing spirit of women, which could be harnessed up for the good of religion, had consecrated many an hour to the nuns wherever he went. He was so willing to make the sacrifice of dispensing with the services of the best brethren (even his own brother, Blessed Mannes, whom he sent to Madrid for this purpose) for the spiritual development of communities of nuns, especially those who professed his own rule, that this spirit of cooperation and helpfulness became traditional in the Order and characteristic of every man who ever accomplished anything worth while. This has become

---

[4] H. Scheeben, *op. cit.*, 161.

a taunt in the mouth of historians like Hauck.

Now Albert was simply following a tradition in his dealings with nuns. This course of action deserves to be accentuated since it brings out facts of Albert's character and piety which his academic life did not give him an opportunity of displaying. We see the man of courtesy and chivalry who was willing to put himself to the greatest pains to confer small favors, do little deeds of kindness and consideration, take upon himself onerous tasks to make the yoke of religion a bit lighter for others. He who on occasion could be as hard as stone when a principle of truth was involved, who could hurl epithets with fatal facility and still more fatal accuracy, was the very soul of tenderness with nuns. No trace of softness, sentimentality, or mawkishness humanized his dealings which, from beginning to end, were intended and directed to the spiritual progress of these women of the consecrated life. If grace presupposes nature, then a man like Albert, of gentle birth and noble instincts, refined by prayer and self-discipline, can well be looked upon as an ideal director of the spouses of Christ.

Rudolf of Nijmegen paints a very engaging picture of this phase of Albert's life and activity. "In the diocese of Cologne there is the city of Soest which was once very rich. Here a Religious of the Order of Friars Preachers, named Eberhard, often preached the Word of God, and many of the nobility of the neighborhood, distinguished alike for their rank and wealth, resolved with his advice, to consecrate their daughters to the service of God." A contemporary, Henry of Hosthoven, tells us that the first idea of erecting a Dominican convent at the place where Paradise afterwards sprang up, was due to the fourth General of the Order, John of Wildhausen, who tarried at Soest in 1252. He ordered Henry, together with Eberhard Clodt, to proceed with the purchase of suitable land. Difficulties of all sorts, which sprang up, could not deter them from preaching. And, as so often happened in those days of faith and generosity, sermons were followed by ample donations. And at once the small gentry came bringing gifts and, better still, their daughters: Arnold von Wedenbrugge with his wife and daughters; Gerard von Lo with his two daughters; Adelaid von Rothen with her daughters; Henry von Ruden with his wife and daughter; Christina von Dortmund with her daughters, houses, and property. Other lords and burghers of the neighborhood of whose names there are no records converged toward Soest. Now Rudolf continues:

> "The women and young maidens inhabited a common dwelling, and commenced to climb the mountain of perfection, without, however, binding themselves to any specific rule or adopting any particular habit. The reputation of these noble virgins soon spread abroad like the aroma of precious nectar, and the number of those who were desirous to conform their lives to their example daily increased. The necessity of giving form and stability to this holy enterprise was now felt, and the Chevalier Arnold, minister of the Bishop of Osnabrück, sought out the illustrious servant of God, Albert, in order that he might found, by his authority and wisdom, a Convent of women, according to the Rule and with the habit of St. Dominic. Albert consented: and when he learned how this pious community was prepared to run after the sweets of the Spouse, he praised God with all the powers of his soul. He instructed them in all that related to the Rule of the Order and the enclosure to which they would be obliged to submit; then, when he saw these souls established in the love of God, he fixed the day on which he would separate these daughters from the world, these precious stones, these choice flowers, in order to lead them into the place where they would be able, like wise virgins with their lamps burning, to serve Christ, the Spouse of virgins. On a Friday, after he had offered the holy Sacrifice before them, and in presence of many noble knights, he conducted them in procession, accompanied by the clergy and people, to a spot outside the city walls, and which was called at the period Alvoldinghausen. The virgins walked barefoot and were clothed in poor garments, for they had devoted their persons and possessions to the sanctuary wherein they purposed always to dwell. Before the altar of an ancient Oratory dedicated to the holy Virgin, they made in Albert's hands a vow to embrace, they and their successors, the Order of St. Dominic."

Henry of Hosthoven still adds these further details regarding Albert which bring us closely into touch with him: "In a fervent address, he pointed out to them how it behooved them henceforth to live according to the Rule of St. Augustine and the Constitutions of the Friar Preachers, to love the community for the love of God, to despise self, to obey humbly, patiently, without murmuring, without hesitation, and joyfully; how they ought to comport themselves, regulate their occupations, cordially love one another, and thus render themselves worthy of the benefits which the Order accorded them. He explained to them the nature of the monastic vows, and promised them the rewards of heaven if they faithfully persevered therein. Then the venerable Father closed on them the doors which would forever separate them from the world and guarantee the observance of the Rule. The Sisterhood chanted during the ceremony: 'I have despised the kingdom of the world and all earthly attire for the fervent love of my Lord Jesus.' All being now finished Albert bestowed on them his benediction. He also allowed, with the sanction of the Apostolic Legate, Cardinal Hugo, the two daughters of the Chevalier Arnold, Gertrude and Oda, to pass from the Benedictine Order into the newly founded Convent. Arnold himself quitted the world, received the habit of St. Dominic, and undertook the temporal administration of the new Convent, while his wife Cunigond was elected its first Superior. Thus were they able to choose the sublime life of evangelical perfection. From that moment Arnold desired that the place should be called Paradise, either on account of its charming situation, or for a spiritual reason. As our first parents, by their disobedience, lost the happiness of paradise, these spouses of Christ must strive to recover its joys by obedience."[5] In that last sentence Rudolf hinted at the dominant note of Albert's direction and instruction of nuns. Obedience must characterize their entire lives, for only thus could they entertain any hope of coming off victoriously in the new manner of life they had chosen.

Henry goes on to give us the practical, common-sense directions Albert left behind him for the guidance of the nuns. Mindful of the havoc he had seen in the women's convents in Italy, and perhaps in France, he warned them against admitting too many novices or unsuitable recruits, and dissuaded them from entering upon too grandiose building projects. Only when a sufficiency of alms permitted should they erect other buildings, but these should always be so

---

[5] Rodolphus de Novimagio, Chap. XXVII; J. Seibertz, "*Geschichte der Stiftung des Klosters Paradies bei Soest,*" in *Zeitschrift für Vaterlandische Geschichte und Altertumskunde (1856), 267-328.*

arranged as to insure regular discipline and monastic observance. Later on, as Bishop of Ratisbon, Albert will return to Paradise to consecrate the church and altar that had been erected through the generosity of the faithful and to show by his practical interest his undying solicitude for the nuns whose number, under the blessing of this new spiritual patriarch, increased like the children of Abraham.

But scenes of another kind and experiences bitter enough to test the soul of a hero were awaiting the man to whom the peace and recollection of the convent at Soest must have seemed as a breath of heaven. After having acted as witness and executor for the Archbishop of Cologne in the matter of a bequest in January, 1256, we find Albert, in the capacity of a papal legate, hurrying to Poland, Prussia, and Livland in obedience to an order of Pope Alexander IV.

These lands had been partially evangelized by St. Hyacinth and his brother, Blessed Ceslaus, who on their way to the Holy Land, had tarried in Rome long enough to meet St. Dominic and receive the habit from his hands. Fired with apostolic zeal they abandoned their pilgrimage to the Holy Sepulcher, using their energies instead to penetrate to the most inaccessible regions of Eastern Europe with the gospel of salvation. Unfortunately, much of the good effected by them was neutralized by the scarcity of missionaries. This missionary handicap was in the process of solution at the time in the foundation of a society of foreign missionaries among the Dominicans. The men in question, wearing as a distinctive mark a red girdle, and governed by a few additional rules suitable to their specific work of evangelization, were called "The Wandering Brethren of Christ amongst the Pagans." The two convents, established on the frontier where these missionaries could learn the barbarous tongues and customs of the people among whom they were to labor, could boast of only a few volunteer Friars from the German province. The second reason for the partial miscarriage of much of St. Hyacinth's work was due to the almost chronic invasion of the Mongolian tribes who spread death and destruction everywhere. The saint himself on more than one occasion had had to flee before their fury.[6]

These two reasons, no doubt, lay at the very bottom of the Pope's letter in which Albert was exhorted to stir up a missionary zeal and

---

[6] *B. Altaner,* Die Dominikanermission des 13. Jahrhunderts (Habelschwerdt: 1924), 160.

enthusiasm among the brethren, especially for the sore-tried mission stations in Prussia and Livland. Did Albert sense a gentle rebuke in his selection as papal legate to the East and in the papal exhortation for renewed enthusiasm for the missionary cause? Did he accuse himself of criminal negligence for not having emulated the zeal of St. Dominic, whose dream throughout life had been cruel martyrdom at the hands of the Cuman Tartars? Whether it was the rebuke of a tender conscience, or the desire to supply the brethren with an example of heroic readiness to go to the field afar, or an effort to see for himself the deplorable condition of affairs, Albert with a band of priests and religious hastened eastward with his plenary legative powers. He soon saw for himself how much good had been undone, how religion was languishing for lack of preachers, and how the people, surrounded on every side with the crassest savagery, were fast falling back into the most unspeakable habits. Thus, he relates,[7] how he saw among the Slavonians that the tribe of the Cumans put ruthlessly to death deformed children and old people, and boasted gleefully about their deeds when showing strangers the graves in which the poor victims had been buried. The cripples were done away with because they would never be able to bear arms. These savages determined the number of their offspring lest they be unable to rear them. The decrepit were killed because they could not work and their sustenance would be a burden. With fine scorn at such inhumanity, Albert remarks that these people dared to call themselves Christians. As is his wont, he moralizes a bit to this effect : One could understand, excuse or condone such horrors among people ignorant of the Gospel and the dignity and rights of man, but there could be no imaginable explanation for such customs among Christians who know that men are living images of God and through the Blood of Christ members of His mystical Body—hence worthy of respect and reverence; hence freemen, each and all, possessing rights which no man can take away; hence, also, too highly placed to be bartered away like slaves or butchered like cattle.

Seldom in his written works did Albert rise to such heights of savage and righteous indignation. He reveals himself as the eloquent pleader for the rights of man and for those hapless ones whose coming and tarrying in this world was permitted and effected by a loving

---

[7] Opp. II, 329; Opp. VIII, 740.

Providence, not only for their own spiritual refinement but also for their sublime mission of calling out the best, noblest, and most magnanimous in the hearts of more fortunately placed men. It is difficult to find in Albert's work a nobler passage than this impassioned cry of an angry but strong and robust man in behalf of those who are suffering from the spurns and whips of fortune. It is easy to conjure up before one's mind with what force he must have preached to these hardened peoples; how he must have scourged them with his scorn; how he must have tried with the magnet of his voice to draw from their flinty hearts one spark of plain, downright humanity. No records of his success in the frontier lands have been preserved except the general statement of Rudolf of Nijmegen[8] that he had the consolation of having restored many souls to the Church. If after this date the company of Dominican campaigners for Christ among the Mongols was increased by many German volunteers, the reason is not far to seek.

On his return to Cologne Albert, whose mind must still have been harrowed by memories of the horrible sights in the frontier countries, saw that the time had come for him to bring to a happy conclusion a quarrel between the city merchants and Archbishop Conrad of Hochstaden. For seven years he had put forth his best thought and effort to arrange adroitly some understanding and settlement between the contending parties in the bloody feud. Like most intestine riots, this quarrel began with the greed of the city merchants who, in order to store up more hoard by pyramiding commerce and bargaining, sought to withdraw themselves from the sovereignty exercised over them by the prince archbishop, universally recognized as the second most powerful man in all the Empire.[9]

But Conrad was not the man to let go by unchallenged this encroachment upon his prerogatives. He arose mighty in his wrath and anger. First, he imposed a heavy toll on all imports and exports, opening a customhouse at Neuss, across the Rhine from Cologne. He next set aside completely the merchants' disavowal of his own right to coin money at pleasure and not, as had been agreed upon decades

---

[8] Rodolphus de Novimagio, *Legenda*, 30-31.

[9] H. Cardauns, *Konrad von Hochstaden, Erzbischof von Köln* (Köln: 1880), 194 sq.; E. Michael, *Geschichte des Deutschen Volkes* (Freiburg: 1903), III, 89.

before, on three occasions only, namely: on taking possession of his see, on receiving the pallium, and on welcoming the envoys of the Holy See. Being thus gravely hurt in their pockets, the citizens and the burgomaster remonstrated with Conrad and ended by threatening him with dire consequences. Nothing intimidated, the archbishop left for Andernach where, gathering a goodly number of armed boats, he declared open war upon the citizens. During Lent, 1251, he sailed down the Rhine, and took up his position at Neuss. Enraged that the cowed citizens made no show of fight but quietly settled down to a siege, he followed the suggestion of an engineer in his fleet by sending a boat, loaded down with explosives and combustibles, across the Rhine in order to blow up, or else set on fire, the merchant fleet on the opposite shore. When his own craft was burned without causing any damage to the merchant marine, Conrad was ready to accept the advice of Herman von Rittenhoffen to lift the siege and open friendly parleys with the agents of the city merchants.

The decision on the points in dispute was left in the hands of Hugh of St. Cher, who as papal legate in Belgium, was in frequent communication with Albert, the second umpire in the case. Several documents having reference to this dispute show how slowly an amicable arrangement was arrived at. An entire year was required to establish the reciprocal rights of the litigants. Conrad was permitted to coin money twice only and required to use a clear, sharp stamp so as to make counterfeiting practically impossible. The toll at Neuss and other points along the Rhine was abrogated. He was also to promise to defend the city and its inhabitants—Jews and Christians. On their part, the citizens were to swear under oath never to introduce in any way whatever contraband goods, thus evading the municipal tolls. Besides, they must defend the rights of the archbishop, their liege lord, and recognize his jurisdiction. Albert had shown consummate diplomatic skill and statesmanship in drawing up this platform. Perhaps, in his buoyant way, he dreamed that the matter had been definitely adjusted. Having no slippery, scheming nature himself, Albert probably credited his fellows with the same uprightness of character and honesty of heart. When just about this time he was called to Italy, he departed with no misgivings about the civic peace of Cologne.

Did the struggle burst forth just because the man who was everywhere hailed as an angel of peace had left Cologne for the purpose of bringing about an understanding on a more momentous question? Conrad, who considered that he had been exorbitantly penalized, kept up a campaign of petty nagging and petty fogging against the merchants. About the year 1256 he thought himself so gravely injured in his honor and authority that he felt justified in gathering his men at arms. Mounted on a powerful war horse the archbishop rode at the head of his troops. He looked a warrior every inch and displayed the courage of a conqueror. The citizens marched out, sullen, stubborn, and determined under the command of Thierry of Falkenberg. Near the village of Freehen the armies came to blows. The eagles all but settled upon Conrad's standard. But just as he was about to leave the field, assured of victory, Thierry brought up suddenly a few detachments of fresh reserves, who, fearing defeat, fought like demons. Dismay seized upon Conrad's men. They first yielded. Then they fled in confusion. Conrad, like the doughty fighter he was, saw his men fade from the ranks. His cries could not be heard or else were not obeyed. He almost performed miracles of courage and valor. But, finally, with his war steed shot beneath him, Conrad leaped upon a fast charger to seek safety in flight and find disgrace in defeat.

Albert at Anagni, as documents show, knew at least in a confused way what had befallen. Peace seemed very far removed as both disputants held out unrelentingly for their rights. Negotiations were still dragging along when Albert returned from Italy. On Maundy Thursday, 1257, both parties agreed to refer the decision to a board of arbitration composed of Gosswin, dean of the cathedral, the provost of St. Severin and the Holy Apostles, Philip, warden of the cathedral, and Albert. Again he had a chance to go over the entire ground of the dispute with its numerous complaints, wrongs, and pretensions. With a spirit of impartiality and a sense of justice Albert replaced the rights and jurisdiction of the archbishop and the rights and duties of the citizenry in their proper spheres. But the peace did not last long; and later Albert will be called upon again to take up this dispute with which, by this time, he must have been most heartily disgusted.

As if all these duties were not sufficient to engage the time and energies of a single man, we find Albert during this period, probably while making a visitation in the Duchy of Brandenburg, consulting with the Abbot of Lehnin about the granting of a dispensation of blood relationship in favor of John I, Margrave of Brandenburg, and Jutta, the daughter of the Count of Saxony. The matter had been referred to the Pope for adjudication and Alexander IV delegated these two men to act in his name.

CHAPTER VII

DEFENDER OF THE FRIARS

WITH kaleidoscopic swiftness the scene changes again but not the central actor. That something fatal was impending in Christendom seems to have been sensed everywhere by the more devout followers of the Lord Jesus. Probably, at no other turning point in the history of the Church were there in circulation so many frightening private revelations portending gloom and evil. While we are perfectly free to reject the supernatural origin and compelling force of these visions, we cannot explain away the historical fact of their existence and influence upon the masses. Thomas of Cantimpre, who was a busy and restless collector of popular sagas, whether visions or town gossip, relates the following story which was not contradicted by any contemporary who easily might have ascertained the facts for himself, or the truth of the report.

> "The Provost of a Monastery of Augustinians in Bavaria, Gavilus by name, a man of most holy life, went to Rome two years before the great tribulation fell upon the Friars, in order to transact his affairs. Being one day at prayer in the Basilica of the Prince of the Apostles, he beheld in ecstasy the church suddenly filled with a large multitude of serpents, whose frightful hissing alarmed not only those who were present, but even the whole city of Rome. Seized with fright, the Provost soon beheld a man clothed in the habit of the Friar Preachers enter the temple. While with astonished looks he viewed the unknown, it was divinely revealed to him that this stranger's name was Albert. Then the reptiles fell impetuously upon the Mendicant Friar, covered him with stings and clung to his feet, hands, arms, breast, and his whole body. But the pious Friar with manly courage soon shook himself free from their mortal grasp, and ran to the ambo, where he began to read the Gospel according to St. John. When he came to this passage, 'And the Word was made flesh,' the hissing of the reptiles suddenly ceased, they were chased

from the church, and peace was restored. The holy man understood not this vision, and he returned into his own country. But one day while he related to his sister, a holy recluse of Germany, what he had witnessed at Rome, the latter, being filled with holy joy, replied: 'Marvelous thing! this Albert whom you beheld in your ecstasy has arrived, I am told, at the Count of Ottenheim's to treat with him respecting this country.' The Provost rejoiced exceedingly at this news, and said: 'I am desirous to see and examine if it be really he, for I hope to recognize again the countenance which he had during the vision.' He then ran in haste to the Castle of Ottenheim, where he identified Albert by certain marks, his attitude, countenance, the color of his hair, and his small chin. He related to him his vision, but neither could comprehend its meaning. What is certain is that in the famous dispute which took place later on between the Mendicant Orders and the University of Paris, the whole occurred exactly as the Provost had seen it in his vision."[1]

That trouble was brewing in the university was plain to Albert during his years of teaching at Paris. Difficulties had arisen at the university with the first appearance of the Friars. Did men dislike them because their manner of life was a rebuke to the loose morals of students and professors? Did men envy them their popularity with the people? Did the professors resent their forceful entrance into the teaching corps which the seculars wished to keep a closed corporation? Did they wax angry at the Friars' influence over the student body and at their many conquests of the best heads among the young? Was it a reflection upon the teaching methods of the professors to find streams of students going to the Mendicants' schools? Did their espousal of Aristotle, and Albert's purging of him, constitute the bone of contention? Did the frank opposition of the Friars to the materialism of the day, in their teaching and manner of living and their spectacular rejection of Oriental pantheism, revived Monopsychism and Averroistic fatalism—all of which had been taught in guarded terms and watered-down forms by Paris professors—make the Friars odious because feared by a large contingent of the doctors? The truth of the

[1] Thomas Cantimpranus, *Bonum Universale*, II, Chap. 10, n. 21-26.

matter is that all these things conspired to produce an undeniable antipathy to the Friars, dating back to 1218 and gaining force and venom with each success these interlopers reported. For that the Friars were considered such is plain from the storm aroused when they obtained their first, and three years later, their second chair in the Paris University.[2]

Albert had been a witness to this growing opposition. Perhaps he had heard with his own ears the vitriolic tirades of the professors, or more likely still, the blistering rimes of Ruteboeuf, the court jester of Louis IX, whom the doctors had engaged (perhaps at a handsome fee) to vilify the Friars. It was common talk that they had won their first victory over the professors when the Pope wrote fearlessly to the holy king that, even at the instigation of the university, he should not proceed beyond his prerogatives by mixing in university affairs which were reserved to the Holy See. Albert may have seen on frequented street corners the placards, purporting to come from the devil but actually posted by the professors, in which the Friars were traduced and pilloried. Matters of this kind appealed little to Albert who was essentially peaceable by nature. Perhaps he thought the antipathy would die down. Had it been his aim in making his lectures as learned and attractive as possible to undermine the opposition quietly?

But in 1255 a treatise appeared in Latin, and quickly in a French translation for popular consumption, bearing the screaming title *The Perils of These Latter Times.* It came from the fertile and deft pen of William of St. Amour, a professor who enjoyed a certain standing for his researches in Aristotelian lore, an able and eloquent teacher, an artistic peddler of backstairs gossip, especially against the Mendicants, a teacher who had been hauled twice before the archbishop for suspected doctrine and once before the university senate for questionable conduct, a magician of words which helped him to save his academic standing and good name, violent, heartless, unscrupulous, generally called the most artful liar of his time, adept at spreading half truths, broadcaster of dark innuendos, trained in the art of posing as a persecuted man, a martyr—in a word, a brilliant shallow juggler, who

---

[2] J. Bierbaum, Bettelorden und Weltgeistlichkeit an der Universität Paris (Munster: 1901), passim; F. X. Seppelt, *Der Kampf der Bettelorden an der Universität Paris um die Mitte des 13. Jahrhunderts (Breslau: 1908), 110 sq.*

played to the galleries and stopped at nothing to elicit a round of applause or a roar of hisses from his volatile audience. He was the voluble spokesman of the disaffected group of professors, and in the university, as in the army, the chronic grouch is always sure of an audience. This fiery Burgundian carried off the day with his screed. His charges were hotly discussed in every wine shop of Paris and in every classroom of the university. He attacked the Friars, especially the Dominicans, who from the first had been uncompromising in their demands for academic recognition. Every disgruntled student who had been plucked in examination or worsted in public discussion at the Friars' schools instantly became an advance agent for William's views. The strangers with revolutionary leanings joined up with William, for he attacked the king, princes, nobles, and bishops for the high favor they showed the Friars. He excoriated the populace for its craven spirit in listening to the newfangled monks. Paris was in a state of high turmoil. There was no denying it. We know from contemporary writers that the Friars were obliged to stay indoors for days at a time. Louis IX, in 1255, just returned from one of his spectacular if high-souled and disastrous crusades, wished to submit the quarrel to the judgment of the several bishops of the Sens and Rheims provinces together with representatives of the university and the incriminated Orders. But the Dominicans demanded that the issue be submitted to Rome.

The Sovereign Pontiff realized that this dispute was no longer a mere academic quarrel in the schools but constituted a snare to the faithful through the false teachings of the *Perils.*[3] And the Dominicans were too much involved in the dispute to remain silent, especially as Hugh of St. Cher, Cardinal of Santa Sabina, enjoyed the confidence of the Pope, and the Dominican General, Humbert de Romans, was always free to come and go at the papal court. Finally, the protestations of the two prevailed and Alexander appointed a Commission of four cardinals to scrutinize the book. Humbert on his own initiative called Albert from Cologne to report to the convent at Anagni, where he himself had taken up quarters to be near the seat of operations.

Contrary to the assertions of some of the older chroniclers,

---

[3] *S. Bonaventura, Opp. (Quaracchi), V, 7; X, 10, 45; A. M. Walz, Delineatio Vitae S. Thomae Aquinatis (Roma: 1927), 56; A. Mortier, Histoire des Maîtres Généraux de l'Ordre des Frères Précheurs (Paris: 1903), I, 471, is entirely untenable.*

historians today prefer to hold that Albert was well acquainted with the merits of the dispute when he set out from the Provincial Chapter at Erfurt, in the summer of 1256, for Anagni, where he arrived before the end of September.[4] At the General Chapter in Paris, in June of that same year, at which Albert was present, the persecution of the Friars was discussed in detail by Blessed Humbert. Perhaps even there the General commissioned the most famous teacher of the Order to take up the gauntlet in defense of the Friars. It is almost impossible to accept the statement of Henry of Hereford[5] that Albert had only two days during which to study up the case and marshal his arguments. Nor do historians accept the assertion of the same chronicler, much in accord as it would otherwise be with the temper of Albert, that, not having seen a copy of the *Perils* he had it hastily copied out by scribes, and having had it delivered to him, piecemeal, chapter by chapter, he assimilated its contents. What evidently Henry of Hereford had in mind was the established fact that the copyists prepared the work hastily for the cardinals of the Commission, who had not seen it, with the possible exception of Hugh of St. Cher to whom, as a Dominican, it must have been of supreme and personal interest and concern.[6] It is clear from the documents that there were no meetings of the cardinals before the arrival of Albert. It is, therefore, just to assume that before the first formal meeting, Albert made it his business to approach the eminent judges with whose decision the fate of the book rested—Eudes de Chatteauroux, cardinal-bishop of Tusculum, John Franciago, cardinal-priest of San Lorenzo, Hugh of St. Cher, cardinal-priest of Santa Sabina, and John of Ursini, cardinal-deacon of San Niccolo. Albert was anxious to have matters expedited, as a deputation of university professors was on its way, under the leadership of William of St. Amour. One could never tell or guess what ruses would be resorted to in an emergency by such crafty men as Odo of Douais, Christian, canon of Beauvais, Nicholas of Bar sur Aube, John Belin, and the Englishman, John of Gecteville, rector of the university.

On the appointed day the Pope, surrounded by his court and the four eminent judges, listened to Albert as he dissected the vicious book,

---

4 *H. Scheeben, Chronologie,* 44-46.

5 Henricus de Horvardo, *Chronicon*, 197.

6 H. Scheeben, *op. cit.*, 46.

refuting the false charges step by step. He left no loopholes. He slurred over no difficulties.

With imperturbable calmness he showed that the Religious Orders of the Church simply reduced to a systematic mode of life the three evangelical counsels enunciated so clearly by our Lord in the Gospels. Religious have a right to preach and teach and hear confessions. They are not bound to depend for their livelihood upon the labor of their hands. The vow of poverty, especially as understood and professed by the Mendicant Orders, does not mean a forced mendicity but rather a subsistence on voluntary alms. And those who perform intellectual work, whether preaching or teaching, have a right to look for the alms of the faithful. These and many other things Albert discussed with relentless logic, a large array of arguments and a directness which cut the ground from under the charges of the Paris professors.

When Albert had finished the cardinal judges delivered their verdict. The book because of its error, bad will, and malice should be formally condemned. This was done by Alexander IV on October 18, 1256, in his bull *Quasi Lignum Vitae*, in which the entire book was condemned as iniquitous, criminal, and execrable. He commanded all who possessed the same to burn it within eight days under the pain of excommunication, and he forbade anyone, whoever he may be, to read it, approve it, circulate it in anyway or sustain it under any guise. This condemnation was pronounced publicly in the cathedral of Anagni on October 23, 1256, and the book was burned in the presence of the Pope. It was, shortly after, consigned to the flames publicly in Paris before the entire university and the king, St. Louis IX.

The Paris deputation arrived after the work had been given to the flames. Their remonstrances fell on deaf ears. They were constrained to subscribe to the ordinances of the papal bull. Odo of Douais and Christian of Beauvais promised on oath, and before Hugh of St. Cher and John Ursini and other witnesses, to obey it. They also swore to receive the Friars among the teaching faculty of the university; to resist all attempts at breaking up the schools of the Mendicants; never to consent to the removal of the Friars' schools to any other place. Furthermore, they swore to teach and preach that the mendicant state, embraced for love of Christ, is a state of perfection; that its members need not subsist on manual labor; that they lawfully could teach, live on alms; that the Orders of St. Francis and St. Dominic were good, approved by the Church as also by God, who showed this forth by miracles wrought after the death of the holy founders.

William of St. Amour was not so tractable. He was forbidden under excommunication to return to France, to resume teaching or writing, or to enjoy the fruits of his several benefices. Sullenly he retired to his estates in Burgundy, disgraced but not submissive. In 1263 he was permitted to return to Paris where secretly he began to stir up anew discord concerning the Friars.

Albert's was a complete victory and he has deserved the gratitude of all religious orders. Something of this gratitude breathes forth in these words of Rudolf of Nijmegen:[7] "It is thus that Albert became the instrument in the hands of Providence, or rather of the glorious Virgin Mary, towards whom the Friar Preachers had ever the most tender devotion, to deliver the new Orders from persecution, and to put their redoubtable enemies to flight."

On the earnest solicitation of the Pope and cardinals, who must have been ravished by the knowledge and eloquence of the renowned man, Albert was permitted to remain at Anagni to conduct the Curial University. For in those days the Popes set up a school wherever they happened to be holding court. It was no unusual sight to see ecclesiastics of the highest places humbly take their seats among the clerics and students from the environs. It is a mistake to hold that Albert was appointed on this occasion to the post of Master of the Sacred Palace, or official theologian of the Pope. He acted in the capacity of a professor, following the Curia, no doubt, when it moved from Anagni to Rome in December, 1256, till May, 1257, and then from Rome to Viterbo until October.

During these months he explained and analyzed the entire Gospel of St. John with so much learning and unction that his august auditors declared that they had never heard anything like it from the lips of man. He laid his prodigious learning under contribution and availed himself largely of his knowledge of birds and their habits, especially the eagles, to make clear the full meaning and import of the Words of Holy Writ. For in the symbolism of the Church, St. John is compared to an eagle because of the sublime heights to which he rises. Here was an opportunity for Albert. In his allegorical and mystical interpretation

---

[7] Rodolphus de Novimagio, *Legenda*, 34.

of St. John was he thinking of his youth on the banks of the Danube and did he make his august hearers hark back to that golden period of their own lives? For among a vast amount of other actual observation, he said of the eagle, and later applied his words symbolically to St. John: "Its flight is bold; it is a bird of prey but loves to share its spoil; it perches and flies alone and not in flocks like other birds; it builds its nest alone in the crevices of the rocks, or in other inaccessible places, in short, it very often puts an amethyst among its eggs to deter serpents from approaching."[8]

In an incredibly short space of time Albert had gone through the Gospel, and on the request of the pontifical court essayed to discourse on all the canonical books. Since we have no traces of this commentary, it is just possible that he did not work over and enlarge his notes, as he did in the case of the Gospel of St. John. Perhaps, too, the lectures were lost in the process of moving so frequently from one place to another.

But he was requested also to pour forth the riches of his knowledge on Aristotle, whose teaching had been defaced by the tendentious interpretations of Averroes. These oblique interpretations were rapidly finding their way into the Christian schools of France and Italy, and thus aroused the well-grounded fears of the Pontiff. Whatever the reason, pretext, or occasion may have been, Albert carried on a public disputation on the doctrine of Averroes that all bodies together possess but one intellectual soul. Since this error on the unity of the intellect "is most dangerous and counts many partisans, and since its defenders maintain that philosophy imposes it, though it is contrary to the faith, it is necessary to combat it with philosophy." And in right good earnest he demolished the cocksure teachers who, relying solely on philosophy, seemed even then to assume a supercilious air and condescending attitude toward the Christian. And later on, referring to these lectures,[9] Albert adds: "All these doctrines were once maintained by me before the Pontifical court when I resided there by order of my Lord, Pope Alexander." And at this same time he answered many difficulties urged by the Averroists. The former series of replies at Anagni he later published as a separate book and subsequently

[8] Opp. XXXIII.

[9] Opp. LXXV, *De Anima*; F. Pelster, *Kritische Studien*, 140.

incorporated them in his theological *Summa.* The latter, long known only by name, were discovered in our own day and published by Mandonnet.[10]

It is to be assumed that Albert reached Cologne in time for the opening of scholastic work in September. The first documentary evidence of Albert's presence in Cologne is dated March 20, 1258, when he signed a deed as "lector of the Preaching Brothers of Cologne." He affixed the same signature to every document during this period. Hence, it is plain that he was engaged in teaching class each day. The only indication we have concerning the subject matter of his lectures are the notes, or *reportata,* of Conrad of Austria on the *Quaestiones Disputatae de Animalibus.* This work has been discovered only recently and still remains unedited.[11]

But it is evident that, aside from his own personal work in the classroom, Albert was intrusted with the entire academic life of the *Studium* at Cologne. Hence, it was his business to keep a sharp eye on the professors and their work so as to ascertain whether they were putting forth their best efforts to maintain the high pedagogical ideals about which the Order was so much concerned. All academic questions were, in the last instance and analysis, referred to him for decision. Any new direction, either in the matters to be treated of or in the method of handling them, must come from his enthusiasm and suggestiveness. He was responsible to the Order for the way its regulations were carried out at Cologne, which set the standard for all the lesser, more insignificant Dominican schools in German-speaking countries.

Furthermore he was expected to ascertain from personal observation at the weekly and monthly academic disputations and from examination of individual students what were their respective talents, interests, and aptitudes; how the youngest brethren could best be helped in their work; what handicaps must be removed from their path; what personal difficulties between professors and pupils must be ironed out with dexterity and understanding. Here was a vast field for the display of interest in those who with their high ideals dreamed high, sometimes impracticable dreams. The large number of students

---

[10] P. Mandonnet, *Siger de Brabant et l'Averroisme Latin* (Louvain: 1911), II, 29-52.

[11] F. Pelster, Zeitschrift für Katholische Theologie (1922), 332 sq.

who swore on Albert's words to the end of their lives and propagated not only his ideals and methods, but also his reputation, is the best proof of that personal attention and inspiration which he knew so well how to show toward those promising youths who were not afraid of hard work. There was Ulrich of Strasburg who later on, after careful observation of men in many places, wrote that Albert was the intellectual wonder of his age;[12] there were Dietrich and John of Freiburg who turned on Albert's suggestion to the moral theology of the Church as the field of their special investigation; there was Ripelin of Strasburg whose *Compendium* of theology was such a faithful echo of Albert's teaching that it passed as one of his authentic works almost up to our own times; there was John Glogan who transplanted Albert's ideals to Cracow, where they produced a long line of Polish theologians and philosophers at a time and in a place when there were scarcely any writers in the land. There were at least a dozen other Dominicans whose eminence in sacred science bear witness to Albert's interest in their first faltering steps and his encouragement in their progress. Albert did extend himself through decades of years in the disciples whom he formed and ensouled with his own superb spirit.[13]

But the Order profited in a larger way from Albert's pedagogical experience. It was laid under contribution directly by Humbert de Romans who has ever been looked upon as the perfect incarnation of a superior according to the ideals of St. Dominic himself. He appeared at a time when the Order was at the very highest notch of its power and efficiency. After having given an impetus to the observance of the rule in all its vigor he turned his attention to the apostolate, especially the foreign missions. He put it down as basic that study and observance have ever belonged together essentially in the Dominican scheme. Any lowering of pedagogical ideals reacted unfavorably upon monastic observance. Study was a necessary condition of spiritual health and apostolic robustness in the Order. Hence, Humbert in seeking to promote observance of the rule was necessarily forced to

---

[12] M. de Bouard, "*Une Encyclique Médiévale,* " in *Revue Thomiste* (1932), 118-143; M. Grabmann, *Mittelalterliches Geistesleben* (München: 1926), 175 sq.

[13] M. Grabmann, L'lnflusso di Alberto Magno sulla Vita Intellettuale del Medio Evo (Roma: *1931), 37,* 85.

insist upon prosecution of learning among the brethren.[14] From the very beginning of his generalate he left no doubt in anyone's mind as to his position on the question of the Order's educational program.

Under no other General were more stringent rules, more minute enactments regarding study, passed. This enthusiasm was, no doubt, the normal and healthy reaction of the changes introduced upon the intellectual and pedagogical horizon by the colossal and daring championship of the new Aristotelian ways by Albert and Thomas. There was a cautious opposition by the timid and hide-bound. But with such as these Humbert had little patience. Undeterred by fear of what this carping contingent of professors, left over from another generation, might say or seek to foment among the intellectually lazy, who found it easier to swear in the words of the old pedagogues instead of extracting the good from the methods of new teachers, Humbert summoned the most progressive professors in the Order to the Chapter at Valenciennes in June, 1259.[15] There was Buonuomo, the fourth Dominican to take his master's cap at Paris where he taught with conspicuous success; Florence Hesdin, who needed not blush to teach side by side with Thomas Aquinas; Peter of Tarentaise, writer of no mean repute, a man who pacified Lyons at a critical time and passed thence to the papal throne as Innocent V; Thomas, who wrote down his pedagogical ideals in *De Magistro*, which quite unwittingly is a panegyric of himself in his educational apostolate and, finally, Albert of Cologne, patriarch of them all in years. These five masters had had enough experience in teaching to warrant the hope that instead of beating the air, they would get down to the roots of the difficulties confronting the educators of the Order. They were not radicals who would cast out the wisdom of the past in their enthusiasm for the new learning. But, by the same token, they were progressive enough to wish to profit from the lessons which the present had taught them. This ideal Commission, charged with the high spirit of Humbert, set to work in good earnest. By a careful exchange of opinions and by a comparison of the results obtained by following determined trends in

---

[14] Humbertus de Romanis, *De Vita Regulari* (ed. Berthier. Roma: 1880), I, 146; H. Denifle, "*Quellen zur Gelehrtengeschichte des Predigerordens,*" in *Archiv für Litteratur und Kirchengeschichte des Mittelalters (1883), II, 177.*

[15] A. Mortier, *op. cit.*, I, 518-534; A. M. Walz, *Delineatio*, 57; E. Michael, *Geschichte des deutschen Volkes* (Freiburg: 1903), III, 90.

academic affairs, it elaborated a system which, when submitted to the Chapter and presiding General, met with instant approval and permanent success.

The entire question of effecting a reform was approached from two angles. In the first place, the Commission insisted upon the freedom of teaching. The professors were to be given every opportunity of devoting themselves to their assigned tasks without interference of any kind on the part of local superiors. In those ardent days, when apostolic priests were needed, it is easy to understand why professors were frequently taken from their classrooms for active work in the ministry. With so few preachers to fall back upon to present solid sermons to the people, who always want substantial meat, and so few orators to invest the spoken word with a dignity and authority that would appeal to the cultured, it is easy to understand that the professors were often compelled to abandon their classes for a time. If there was to be such a thing as a steady stream of able preachers, it could only be on condition that the preliminary preparations were not interfered with for any immediate reasons. The professors must be given a chance to do their work without hindrance. Constant surveillance on the part of the Provincial, conscientious investigation on the part of the annual visitator, would reveal whether meager results from the teaching system were to be laid at the door of the professors or students.

This close and constant scrutiny of the functioning of the educational machine was the second plank of the reform suggested and outlined by the Commission. If professors must be able, capable men, then the same standards must be applied to the students. Dominican schools were to be a training field for the strong, if inexperienced, but not a hospital ward for the intellectually crippled or feeble. Hence, superiors need have no scruples about dismissing the deficient. Hence, too, they were to punish the talented who refused to traffic with their gifts. Hence, also, they were prohibited from assigning tasks to students which would interfere with serious application to study. Hence, again, they were to select students for the higher studies for which they had a natural aptitude and in which they promised to excel—if necessary, separate schools for the study of special branches were to be established in each province, or in default of this, students were to be sent to other provinces where such specialized schools existed. The prior was to attend classes every day, not only to observe what was going on, but also to give good example, and, incidentally, to save himself from intellectual deterioration. The brethren in the house, not otherwise engaged, were held to the same law of attendance at classes. Weekly intellectual debates, or tournaments, must be held in every branch of study taught in the house, and attendance was compulsory on all. Monthly public disputations, to which externs were free to come, must be conscientiously not mechanically conducted. Preachers and confessors must attend these academic exercises, and daily examinations on subjects taught were exacted of them. No weakness or favoritism should be allowed to impair the effectiveness of these regulations.[16]

As can be seen at a glance, these suggestions struck at the very root of the abuses of the time. While the educational freedom of the professor was guaranteed, arbitrariness of method and slovenliness in preparation for classwork were rendered impossible. Teaching was to be a professor's sole business. Just on that account superiors were enjoined to see to it that the teaching was of a high grade of excellence. Those who did not teach or were not actively engaged in the works of the ministry must study. Any other occupation was intolerable and insupportable in a Dominican house. Those who could not make or refused to make study ancillary to piety and apostolic work were intruders and interlopers in the Dominican scheme, and for the sake of the common good, for the purpose of avoiding internal corruption and public scandal, should be dispensed with forthwith, without fear or scruple. To promote study and preaching, the sacred offices of the choir were to be conducted with a certain holy alacrity and expedition. The time thus salvaged must be used for the salvation of souls, which saving work could not be accomplished without consistent and persistent application and consecration to study. The old Benedictine maxim had been to the effect that "to labor is to pray." Humbert enunciated the genuine Dominican maxim that "to study is to pray," and the Commission he convoked at Valenciennes was inspired with his authoritative teaching on this point.

If the next centuries beheld the Dominican tree burst forth in a multiple blossom of learned men, it was because the curriculum outlined by the Commission and the spirit labeled "Dominican," which

---

[16] A. Mortier, *op. cit.*, 544-568; Echard et Quetif, *Scriptores*, I, 140.

must animate it, were never disregarded in any large way or abrogated in essentials. And this does not mean that the brethren were expected to look upon the academic program like a fetish, that they were not to keep a sharp eye on the progress of pedagogics so as to incorporate the newest and best in their academic charter. Albert and Thomas subsequently came back on at least two occasions to this work, incorporating suggestions that had come to them as a consequence of their living contact with learned men and institutions. But the broad, elastic, and adaptable platform of freedom for real teaching and universal obligation of hard study was never abandoned or essentially substituted for another. As long as the Dominican Order can nurture at its bosom scholars in any field of knowledge—for all knowledge can lead to God—as long as it can generate a race of preachers who, by solid dispensation of the Word, can fortify men for the road that leads to God, it will not hesitate or apologize for the frankly intellectual bias given it by Albert and his four associates on the Commission of Valenciennes.

CHAPTER VIII
A BISHOP OF SOULS

IT WOULD seem that at the Chapter of Strasburg, in the autumn of 1259, which Albert attended in the capacity of a definitor, the first vague rumors about his appointment to the bishopric of Ratisbon were heard.

As soon as Humbert de Romans learned of the proposal, he wrote Albert this long and impassioned letter: "We, Brother Humbert, an unprofitable servant in the Order of St. Dominic, desire eternal salvation in paradise, and on earth the renown of innumerable merits and of good example: To our beloved son in Christ, Albert, Lector at Cologne. We have received news from Rome which would deeply concern us did we not place the fullest reliance in you. We learn that the Court of Rome destines you to a diocese. We must credit the report, since it comes from the Pontifical Court, yet no one, of all those who know you, believes that it will be possible to gain your consent thereto. Who would imagine that you, having now reached the term of your glorious career, would be capable of imprinting a stain on your own glory, and on that of an Order to whose progress you have so largely contributed? Who, then, we ask you, beloved and dear Brother—we do not speak of our own, but of all the poor Orders—would henceforth be able to resist the temptation to accept these appointments if you receive them? Oh! we implore you not to suffer yourself to be moved by the counsels and importunities of their Lordships of the Court of Rome, where they do not view these matters in so serious a light. Let not the slight imperfections of an Order, which cherishes and honors all its members, and glories especially in possessing you in our Lord, discourage you. Should these moral hardships, moreover, become still greater, ought not they to be borne by a man of your merit, with the shoulders of a giant? Suffer not yourself to be overcome by the Pope's command, which, in such cases, is more in words than in intention. Violence is offered to no one who seriously resists. This holy and passing disobedience will augment your glory rather than diminish it. Consider the lot of many of those who are raised to this eminent position. What is their reputation? What good have they performed? How have they ended? Reflect attentively on the troubles and hardships which they encounter in the government of the churches in Germany, and how difficult it is not to offend God or man therein. How will you be able to bear the embarrassments of temporal concerns and the danger of committing sin, after having cherished the Holy Scriptures and purity of conscience so much? If it be the good of souls that tempts you, remember that you will annihilate, by a change of state, the innumerable fruits which you have borne, not only in Germany, but in almost every part of the world, by your reputation, your example, and writings; while those which you will produce in the Episcopate are very uncertain. Observe, moreover, beloved Brother, how the Order has been delivered from great tribulation, how it is now reestablished in peace; what then will befall it if you plunge it again into deep sorrow? We would rather learn that our beloved Brother is in the grave than seated on an episcopal throne. We implore you, then, on bended knee, and in the name of the humility of the most holy Virgin and of her Divine Son not to abandon your state of abasement. All that the enemy of salvation has perhaps planned in darkness for the ruin of many will then be changed into a twofold glory both for yourself and for our holy Order. Forward to us a reply which will console and rejoice us and our Brethren. Pray for us! The grace of our Lord Jesus Christ be with you! Amen."[1]

In all probability this letter was written in January, 1260. It could not have reached Albert in Cologne from Belgium, where Humbert was tarrying at the time, much sooner than the early days of February. We may be permitted to assume that by this date Albert was in possession of the papal bull appointing him to the see of Ratisbon.

What was the reaction of Albert to this impassioned letter which deserves to hold a unique place in ecclesiastical literature? We may take it for granted that he read the letter attentively and pondered long upon its contents. But as far as the documents go he made no reply. Nor do we know that he communicated in any way with the Pope with an eye to the recall of the appointment. If, finally, he determined to present himself for consecration, it must have been for reasons which in his eyes far outweighed the arguments of Humbert. What these

---

[1] H. Scheeben, *Chronologie*, 154-156.

reasons were Albert never revealed to anyone. Nor can we find anywhere in his voluminous writings the slightest hint as to the motives which impelled him to disregard the wishes of a man whom he respected and loved. Albert settled the matter between his conscience and God. Whatever historians, who presume to wear the stole of clairvoyants, may say about the reasons which induced him to accept the episcopacy can never purport to be more than clever guesses.

In the absence of any convincing reason for not heeding the earnest entreaties of Humbert, the papal references to Albert's knowledge and judgment seem almost prophetic of what would follow upon his consecration not only for the Church of Ratisbon but also for the Church Universal. Under date of January 9, 1260, the following brief was drawn up.

"Alexander, Bishop, Servant of the servants of God, to Brother Albert, Lector at Cologne. The duties of the office which has been committed to Us, oblige Us to occupy Ourselves with the churches, and to labor, for their increase. But it is incumbent on Us, before all to provide with great care for those in widowhood, in order that they may not remain too-long destitute of pastors capable of discharging the ecclesiastical functions and of increasing their temporal interests. But as the Church of Ratisbon is now deprived of this consolation by the retirement of Our Venerable Brother, its former Bishop, We are interested, as is fitting, with paternal affection in all that concerns it. Knowing then your numerous merits, and having agreed with Our Brethren the Cardinals, We have resolved to place you over this Church. For, as you have ardently drunk of the pure source of the Divine law, and of the salutary waters of science, in such sort that your heart is replete with the fullness thereof, and your judgment is sound in all that relates to God, We firmly hope that this Church, which is overturned in spiritual matters as well as temporal, will be healed by you, and that your unceasing efforts will repair all its injuries. We therefore command you to obey Our will, or rather that of Divine Providence, to submit to Our choice, to repair to this Diocese and assume its government according to the prudence which the Lord has imparted to you. May you, with God's grace, make constant progress in its reformation! Given at Anagni, this ninth day of January, in the sixth year of Our Pontificate."[2]

Some time between March 1, when he had not as yet been consecrated, and March 29 when he entered Ratisbon, the triple imposition of hands was performed at Cologne. It may have been Laetare Sunday, March 14. Gottfried, coadjutor to the archbishop, was almost certain to have been one of the consecrators. It is not known who carried out the ceremonies of lay investiture, for as a bishop Albert became a secular prince and needed to be invested publicly by the Emperor or his delegate. King Richard, who at the time was in England, is said by an old chronicler to have commissioned Conrad of Hochstaden, Archbishop of Cologne, to confer the regalia in his stead.

Perhaps as Albert, with a few fellow religious, pushed from Cologne to Ratisbon, conscious of his pastoral obligations to the flock that had been sorely visited and partially dispersed by the negligence of its former shepherd, he thought of the words he had spoken in the very presence of the man who had sent him to Ratisbon. For in commenting on St. John's words, "Simon, son of John, lovest thou Me," he had given in advance the ideal of a pastor which he would seek to realize in the immediate future. Albert says:[3]

"It is the test of those to whom the pastoral office is confided. They are not examined with regard to knowledge, for they ought to receive this from the Holy Ghost, but with respect to love, for it is love which is the measure of life, merit, and reward; as it is the cause of fidelity toward the flock. But why is the question put three times? It is because the love of our neighbor exacts three things: first, the ardor of charity, which enables us to love with strength and zeal. Hence it is said, 'The lamps thereof (love) are fire and flames.' Secondly, discernment in love, which causes us to love what ought to be loved, and to know the reason and the means of loving. This is the meaning of the word love (*dilectio*, from *dis* and *legere*). It is also said, 'I am the mother of fair love, and of fear, and of knowledge, and of holy hope.' Thirdly, the order in charity, so as to know in what degree each sheep of the flock ought to be loved. 'He set in order charity in me.' Divine love possesses also three characteristics, since it is written, 'Thou shalt love the Lord thy God with thy whole heart, with thy whole mind, and with thy whole

---

[2] Potthast 17737; Echard et Quetif, ***Scriptores Ord. Praed.***, I, 168.

[3] Opp. XXIII *Com. in Joan.*

soul': With the whole heart, so that nothing may turn us from the Sovereign Good; with entire submission of mind, in order that we may never be deceived; with our whole soul, so as to be screened from every distraction. When the sacred writer adds: with all the strength of the soul, it means the same thing, because the powers of the soul must be used in order to love perfectly."

In order to avoid a noisy reception at the hands of the people, Albert stole into Ratisbon after sunset the night before his formal installation in the diocese. He went immediately to the Convent of St. Blaise where twenty years before he had spent many happy days, despite poor surroundings, as a professor. Early the next day he was led in procession to the Cathedral for his enthronization. The people were glad to welcome their pastor, as a Latin poem still extant bears witness with more good will than literary distinction. The priests came up one by one to pledge their obedience to the new bishop. It was Tuesday of Holy Week, March 30, 1260.[4]

As he looked over the priests who approached him could Albert see upon their faces any telltale stories of the manner of lives they lived? How far many of them had fallen from their first fervor he would soon learn for himself and deplore in his *Commentary on St. Luke*, which he would compose during this period as a kind of diversion from the repugnant sight before his eyes.[5] But he came in contact with the seamy side of his priests through a letter from Pope Alexander IV to the metropolitan district to which Ratisbon belonged. Writing to the Archbishop of Strasburg on February 15, 1260, the Pope bewailed the loose morality of the clergy. "It is through these men," he says, "that the Name of God is blasphemed on earth; it is through them that the Sacraments of the true Faith suffer, for the vessels of the Lord are profaned by their sacrilegious hands; it is through them that religion loses the respect of the faithful; it is through them, in short, that the property of the Church is wasted in the most guilty dissipation. They are the cause of the Word of God not being heeded, because they preach it with impure lips; hence the reason why heretics make us the subject of their bitter mockeries. If the powerful ones of the earth are

[4] Oeffle, *Rerum Boicarum Scriptores* (Augustae Vind.: 1763), I, 680.

[5] Opp. XXIII, Com. in Lucam; U. A. Endres, "*Albertus Magnus und die bischöfliche Burg Donaustauf in* Historisch-Politische Blätter (1912), 829-836.

filled with indignation, if the wicked persecute us, if the profane boldly lay hands on the heritage of Christ, if the whole body of our holy mother the Catholic Church is become the subject of scandal and universal shame, it is because of this corrupted flesh which the knife fails to cut off." He continues thus to call upon the bishops to repress abuses by the severest measures, and to introduce a reformation among the clergy, threatening them with the lot of Heli if they obey him not. "Act in such a way," the Pope concludes, "that, when the great Prince of pastors shall come and shall claim from each one of you the fruit of His ministry, you may stand without fear before His face, and be able to render Him an account of your administrations."

Later on Albert will be able from his own observation and experience to say what he would have preferred to cover over with the charitable mantle of silence. Commenting upon the passage where there is mention of the stars appearing in the heavens, he says: "The stars are the Religious, who, like the stars, should remain fixed in the firmament; they should also persevere in a celestial life, for our life is in heaven. And in the Book of Judges it is said, 'The stars remaining in their order and courses, fought against Sisara.' These stars have three parts to fulfill, which are the observance of the vows of obedience, chastity, and poverty. The vow of obedience they in some sort still observe, as also that of chastity; but the renunciation of the perishable goods of this world is clearly lost, for nearly all are drawn to the love of possession, and even more than the people of the world; therefore it is said in St. Matthew that they shall fall from heaven."

As to the history of Lazarus, "who desired to be filled with the crumbs that fell from the rich man's table" (Luke xvi. 21), Albert says: "They who are set over the churches ought to be rich in science and divine speech, in order to draw sinners and the poor to repentance; and they should bestow on them at least six crumbs" (which he goes on to explain). But at the end he exclaims in accents of deep sorrow, "Woe to us! for there is no one at the present day to give to the poor; the Pastors of the Church are consecrated, according to the expression of the Prophet, with the best oil, without heeding the sufferings of Joseph, that is, of the poor. They delight in repeating these words of the sinner: 'I have at length found repose; I desire to enjoy my goods alone!' " We find still more severe reproaches on the subject in the passage where the Sadducees inform our Lord of a woman who had married seven brothers, one after the other, without having borne children to them. "Many of the churches nowadays," observes Albert, "resemble this woman, which have received spouses, one after another—not seven, but a hundred prelates without deriving any benefit from them." What could one man do in the face of such general relaxation of virtue in those whose business it is and must ever be, to manifest it in a striking way for the edification of the people? Albert was too practical-minded to lose himself in grandiose dreams of exterior ecclesiastical pageantry, when what was needed was a show of Christian virtue in priests. Rudolf of Nijmegen makes it plain that he was concerned about giving good example in his own person: "What the venerable bishop had first at heart, was his ecclesiastical calling. He was justly concerned, like the Chief Pastor of all the faithful, about the sheep as well as the lambs, and, for this reason, he devoted himself above all to the guidance of souls. But he labored with such prudence, that, like that creature which has eyes in every part of its body, he avoided every fault, and ever appeared blameless in the sight of his flock!"[6] And to effect a change among his clergy he struck directly at greed, the root of most ecclesiastical disorders. He was by profession a poor man, though his vow of poverty had been suspended by a papal dispensation at the time of his consecration. But he would safeguard his love for poverty by accepting the hardships of poverty. The grim castle, adjoining the old stone cathedral which dated back centuries, no longer resounded to the laughter of priests and princes foregathering there for carousal and wassail. All superfluous furniture was given to the poor. Horses in great numbers were not stabled in the ample barns to provide an escort for the new bishop when going abroad.

Albert was told by his attendants that his predecessors in going to the Diets had a retinue of thirty mounted escorts. Albert traveled alone or with one companion with whom he kept up a quiet conversation on holy subjects, enlivened, no doubt, by observations on the beauties of nature they saw along the way. Even as a bishop he was ever on the alert to discover shreds of new knowledge about natural phenomena.

He walked by preference and retained the coarse shoes in use among the Friars. Here, then, was a choice morsel for the busybodies around Ratisbon. The new bishop, they said, will most certainly prove

---

[6] Rodolphus de Novimagio, *Legenda* 46.

himself a difficult master because he is pitiless with himself and hence cannot but help being exacting with the people. And as proof they pointed at his footgear, which was so different from the highly polished shoes decorated with silver, sometimes jeweled buckles, which his predecessors had affected. And some glib rascal coined a nickname for the bishop which was soon in every coarse mouth. As he rattled along over the stone-set or cobbled roads, they sniggered as they called him "Boots, the Bishop."

Next Albert turned to the reformation of the clergy, beginning with the religious communities of men and women in his diocese. He visited in person the Benedictine Abbey of Metten, near Deggendorf, where he left behind, after his rigorous visitation, written rules and recommendations for the good conduct of the community. He abetted Peppo, the new Abbot of Upper Altaich, in his reforms. He sent Hermann, Abbot of Lower Altaich, to Metten to see that his suggestions were carried out. Relentless in his persecution of monastic abuses, Albert was never tyrannical. Whenever he observed good will among the monks and readiness to observe his regulations, his expansive heart prompted him to make large offerings to the monastery, so that the religious services might be carried out becomingly. On the very day of his enthronization, he made a large donation to Lower Altaich, the chief monastic establishment in the diocese, and later on, when he had learned for himself how assiduously religious observance was maintained there, he repeated his gifts and privileges. He was zealous to safeguard the revenues of the monasteries, only too often looked upon with greedy eyes by princes and people.

There was, therefore, nothing niggardly in Albert's spirit. One of his first cares was to provide a decent competence for the clergy from whom he demanded a tireless devotion to the works of the ministry, especially preaching. He never tired of maintaining that only those priests had the right to eat who spared not themselves in their ministrations to their flocks. To the Cathedral Canons of Ratisbon he handed over a church at Cham on condition that they keep up the services in a befitting way and desist not from breaking to the people the bread of truth.

Albert missed no opportunity to preach the word of God, since "faith cometh by hearing" and good works without faith are of no account. He inveighed against the worldly-mindedness of the times. Thus, for instance, in the third sermon for the third Sunday of Advent he flayed the women who paint themselves, dye their hair, and twist golden chains or jewels into their tresses. He is filled with the spirit of St. Clement of Alexandria, when condemning in men and women the use of perfumes, silken garments, the exaggerated display of jewelry. He excoriates those who expose indecent or suggestive pictures in their homes. He condemns too much music on harps, kettle drums, flutes, and trumpets; advises against too much theater going; pokes fun at the sentimental songs of the *meistersingers*. These people are victims of a spiritual leprosy. His medical remarks on leprosy, a disease just introduced into Europe by the crusaders returning from the East, must have made the hearing of a sermon by him a most gruelling experience. In his preaching to the people Albert used German and, if later on, he took with him as a fellow preacher the Minorite, Berthold of Ratisbon, whose eloquence attracted crowds numbering on occasion from forty thousand to one hundred thousand, we may be sure that he was not ashamed of his own power of announcing the word of God. In two German sermons of his, which have recently been discovered, there are distinct whispers of an age that will soon boast of Wolfram of Echenback, Walter of Vogelweide, Conrad of Würzburg, Suso, and Tauler.[7]

Knowing the practical mind of his people, Albert did not blush to make the most explicit and concrete suggestions about translating his sermons into everyday practice. He preached almsgiving incessantly. No charitable work was carried on in the diocese which he did not commend in his own forceful way to the people. The duty of visiting the sick, befriending the poor, sympathizing with the fallen were the favorite themes of his discourses. He went about pleading for the members of Christ's mystical Body broken by sickness, disease, or poverty. To encourage the faithful to contribute to the Hospice of St. Catherine, near the famous bridge of Ratisbon, he made generous donations of his own and ordered his clergy to commend the enterprise to the people. To the generous he granted an indulgence of forty days and dispensation from fasting for one year. He gave to his priests broad

---

7 G. Meersemann, Introductio, 122; P. Strauch, "*Kölner Klosterpredigten des 13. Jahrhunderts*," *in* Festschrift Christoph Walter (Norden und Leipzig: 1911), 21, 48.

powers of absolving great sinners who had violated their vows, mistreated their parents, or failed to make a promised pilgrimage, on condition that they offer an alms to the Hospice in proportion to their deeds.

Pilgrimages to famous shrines were in great vogue in the Middle Ages as a salutary form of piety and penance. Now there was such a shrine in the diocese, at the Benedictine monastery at Prüfening, whither large bodies of the faithful travelled annually on foot on the Feast of St. George, Rogation Day, and May 12, the Feast of the Dedication of the glorious basilica. Frequently this last day fell on a week day and only at the sacrifice of much income through loss of labor, could the people participate in the pilgrimage. Albert transferred the feast to the first Sunday after the Ascension, when work would be slack, the roads and weather good, and the desire to be abroad after the stress of sowing time, great and all-compelling. To encourage the people to attend services he introduced the feast of St. Dominic into his diocese, thus showing his spirit of compliance with the wishes of the Order which in several successive Chapters of the time had urged this upon the brethren.

In his private relations with the people Albert realized in the concrete the high ideals of a churchman which he held up consistently before them. He did not make the fatal mistake of aspiring after mass conversions. The priest is a fisher of men taken individually. Hence, the doors of the episcopal palace were always open. Anyone might come, not for idle conversation, for Albert was too busy for such a luxury. But the needy, the suffering, the down-trodden, the man in doubt, in sin, in temptation—these were the objects of his love and solicitude, and for their sakes he would sacrifice whatever he had in hand. With his inbred good nature, his knowledge of psychology, and his multiform experience, he was the ideal counselor in the parlor and the model confessor in the tribunal of penance.

Much as he must have disliked the business of lifting the financial debt weighing upon the diocese as a consequence of his predecessor's extravagance and slipshod business methods, Albert set about in good earnest to do his best to dispose of an encumbrance of four hundred and eighty-six pounds of gold. By a régime of strict economy in the episcopal palace; by the gifts of the faithful, especially the present of a vineyard by Rudiger of Bachem; by the careful administration of diocesan revenues in the shape of tithes, quit rents, and income from real estate, the new bishop, following the advice of experts in financial matters, succeeded within the short space of a year in breathing freely and ridding himself of the importunities of Jewish bankers from whom the former bishop had made heavy loans at great interest.

Toward the end of September, 1260, he attended the provincial synod of the bishops of the Salzburg metropolitan province, held at Landau on the Isar. Besides Ulrich of Salzburg, there were present Conrad of Freising, Henry of Chiemsee, and Otto of Lavant, all of whom welcomed Albert with open arms. Together they agreed that any ecclesiastical sentences or censures decreed by any one of them would be respected and enforced by all the rest. This was evidently intended to strike at those parties who, having incurred censures in one diocese, sought to free themselves by hurrying to another. Such a state of spiritual vagabondage introduced disorders and defeated the very purpose for which the laws had been made. Another decision arrived at was directed against those who, emulating the rapacity of the lords and soldiers, sought by shady methods to defraud the Church, unjustly retaining Church dues or collecting and appropriating Church tithes without authorization. The bishops ordained that a declaration should be published from every pulpit that all those who were guilty of such devious dealings, unless they made reparation within a month, should be deprived with their families and servants of Holy Communion and should be refused Christian burial.

In enforcing the first regulation Albert did not add anything to his popularity with that part of the flock which, in failing miserably to live up to the Christian ideal and on that very account incurring the medicinal punishments of the canon law, was the loudest in its denunciations of ecclesiastical guidance and leadership. Murmurs soon became articulate and were taken up and broadcast by all those to whom the intense practise of religion was becoming irksome.

The enforcement of the second synodal regulation, on the other hand, brought Albert a large inheritance of hatred from the nobles who at that time were indulging in a veritable orgy of rapacity and robbery of Church goods. The almost chronic state of war in the Germany, which fell heir to the quarrels of the Hohenstaufen among themselves and everyone else; the poverty consequent upon the crusades, which in many cases engendered such a false conscience that those who were left behind, or suffered as a consequence of the great campaign, deemed themselves justified in compensating themselves for their losses, real or imaginary, by alienating the goods of the Church; the crooked business dealings of the former bishop that had impoverished many a merchantman, which he was desirous of making good at the expense of the diocese—these and a score of other reasons and causes made the preaching and exacting of strict justice and equity a hazardous program and a dangerous platform of action. Albert, though a temporal prince according to the existing laws of the Empire, had no taste for worldly business. And the nobles sensed it at once from his manner of living, his fraternizing with the poor, his consistent abstention from all secular celebrations and festivities. Thus arose the antipathy of the patricians against him which turned into hate when he stormed and fulminated from the pulpit against the high-handed dealing of those who should give good example. And because the lord in his castle had a strangle hold upon the poor liege man, because the chatelaine in her laces dictated the policies of the poor hinds in their homespuns, and because the burghers were as haughty as the Jews were rapacious, an opposition to Albert, no longer secret, became manifest on all sides. It is not on record that anyone dared to oppose him to his face in any way. But he sensed the tense atmosphere and grew sad at heart.

At such times he would withdraw for prayer, thought, and writing to a villa at Donaustauff, belonging to the bishops of Ratisbon, about three miles from the city. Here he wrote, probably as an escape from harassing thoughts, his splendid *Commentary on the Gospel of St. Luke* which contains more references, even though somber and dismal ones, to current events than any other work from his pen. Then again he must have wandered lost in thought, through the groves till awakened from his daydreams—or was it nightmare?—by the cheerful song of the birds. Then, half blinded by tears, he may have strolled along the banks of the Danube till once more recalled to his senses by the white flash of fishes' bodies darting through the waters. In his works there are a few scattered remarks about such familiar and beloved sights at the episcopal villa. They form a kind of interlude, pleasant and refreshing, to the sad song he could not help but sing at the revulsion of popular feeling against him.

Whatever the accusations against him, Albert could not accuse himself of any remissness in the discharge of his duties. There is something touchingly self-revelatory in his commentary on the words of St. Luke, "Let him who is the greater among you become the least," written during the dark hours of misunderstanding and misprizement in the quiet shades of Donaustauff.

"Let him who is the greater among you become the least, let him who is the greater among you in ecclesiastical authority become the least, who is not raised to any dignity; for, says the Philosopher, 'no one will appoint young men generals of an army, because they clearly have not as yet experience.' 'Whoever shall humble himself as this little child,' it is said in St. Matthew xviii. 4, 'he is the greater in the kingdom of heaven,' because he is fittest to support the Church. Among the first Christians little regard was had to authority and importance, but all were intent on humility and the example of virtue. It was, moreover, this that our Lord desired when He said, 'Learn of Me, because I am meek and humble of heart.' Submit to My yoke, etc. Nothing is more easy than to lead inferiors with mildness and humility, as far as circumstances permit. But, when the irruption of evil constrains one to act seriously and with severity, the pastoral office becomes to a bishop, as of old to Moses, an insupportable burden, especially when he is unwilling to tolerate and protect evildoers, as certain Prelates are wont to do in these times, who act the part of Sardanapalus rather than that of Jesus Christ."[8] And Rudolf of Nijmegen says: "Would you learn the motives of this hate against Albert, search the Holy Scriptures and you will discover why a spotless lamb was a subject of horror to the Egyptians. The friends of pleasure were said to abhor the bishop because he was too severe; the sincere, on the contrary, because he was too mild. The true reason is that false and deceitful men detest the man of right and innocence."[9]

Albert turned to Rome in the spring of 1261, if we may believe the *Chronicle of Upper Altaich*. Perhaps on the road, he heard of the death of Alexander IV at Viterbo, May 25, 1261. According to the Altaich *Chronicle* he returned north with the papal taxes, fourteen years in arrears, which he handed back to the monastery.[10] Then, eager to lay

---

[8] Opp. XXIII, *Com. in Lucam.*

[9] Rodolphus de Novimagio, *Legenda* 49.

[10] H. Scheeben, *Chronologie*, 65-67.

down his heavy burden, he turned once more to the south. No assured date of his arrival at Viterbo, where the Pope then tarried, can be deduced from the documents of the time. It is certain that on May 11, 1262, Urban IV in a letter to the Ratisbon Cathedral Chapter had accepted Albert's resignation, for he commanded Leo Torndorf, Dean of the Chapter, to accept the episcopate despite his sworn oath to the contrary. It is, therefore, possible to place Albert's resignation in the winter, about November, of the year 1261.

Now the new Pope, Urban IV, was a great philosopher and it is the surmise of many investigators into the very sparse documents of the time that he prevailed upon the most renowned scholar of the day to remain with him at court, not so much as a confidential adviser as an intellectual companion. The Holy Father did not feel any too comfortable in his new post, far away from his own country and his books. Perhaps, coming from the North where Aristotle was more in favor among students than in the South, the Pope was glad to have at his side a kindred spirit, aglow with enthusiasm for the new study and better able than any living man to expound it and amplify it by observations of his own. Eckl and Grabmann, the best authorities on this hazy period of Albert's life, base their suppositions on the poems of one of the great singers of that day, Master Henry the Poet, who says that Urban forced the most renowned philosopher of the age to remain at his court.[11] Sufficient reasons can be adduced to show that Henry was not speaking of Thomas Aquinas.[12] The picture he paints of the nightly philosophical séances of the Pope and his guest look for all the world like a premature picture of the later Renaissance Attic nights. It is certain that Albert met Thomas during this time, probably at the Provincial Chapter at Orvieto, September 14, 1261. It was during this time, too, that Albert discovered the important treatise of Aristotle *De Motu Animalium*, which he forthwith began to expound to his indulgent friend and patron.[13] We are on certain ground again on February 13, 1263, when Albert was appointed papal nuncio to preach the crusade in the German countries.

[11] Eckel, *Urban IV und Deutschland* (München: 1917); M. Grabmann in *Historisches Jahrbuch* (1917), 315 sq.

[12] M. Grauert, Meister Heinrich der Poet in Würzburg und die römische Kurie (München: 1912); also Historisches Jahrbuch (1912), 936.

[13] F. Pelster, *Kritische Studien*, 87, 157 sq.

CHAPTER IX
HERALD OF PEACE

IT MUST have been some weighty reason, probably black reports about the reluctance of the people to volunteer for the crusade, which impelled Urban IV, on February 13, 1263, to appoint Albert his special Apostolic Nuncio to the German-speaking countries and Bohemia. The Pope must have known or heard favorable reports about Albert's mission to the Eastern peoples in 1255. This induced him to select for a dangerous and onerous task a man whose presence was sweet to him and whose years were piling up noticeably. The Pope realized that the work ahead of his chosen candidate would be very trying for, before Albert had left his side at Orvieto, he empowered him, March 10, 1263, to grant indulgences to all those who would lend a willing ear to his appeals. And, evidently, the Holy Father must have known the dexterity of his man for, before he so much as neared his destination, he sent a Brief empowering Albert to negotiate the appointment of a bishop to the see of Brandenburg. Albert was to see to the faithful execution of a matter which had long been hanging fire and had been the cause of much discord. So, some time after March 23, 1263, Albert turned his serene, untroubled, and imperturbable face in the direction of lands where he feared that nothing but thorns would be his harvest. Since on May 5, 1263, he executed a legal deed at Polling, lying between Weilheim and Murnam, we may be sure that he treaded his way, amidst many dangers, through Brenner Pass over the Alps.

Up to the present moment no document bearing upon Albert's activity as a preacher of the crusade has been discovered. But there is a long array of dry documents bearing witness to his willingness to be of help as peacemaker wherever he went, as also to the high esteem in which he was held by people and princes. And though it is not recorded we may be sure that he did not allow himself to be diverted from the work he had come to Germany to prosecute by any incidental offices he was called upon to exercise.

By way of Landshut, Freising, and Munich, he came to the

monastery of Polling, in Upper Bavaria, in May of the year 1263, granting an indulgence to all those who should visit the church and communicate. A few days later, May 10, we find him at Augsburg where on Ascension Day he granted an indulgence to all contributors to St. Catherine's Convent of Dominican nuns. Three days later, at Donauworth, he gave audience to six delegates conferring together in the dispute between Bishop Hartmann of Augsburg and Count Louis of Oettingen. The quarrel had embroiled the populace to such an extent that no impartial judge in the neighborhood was available. It was agreed between the contending parties that only a decision of Albert would reestablish peace. He decided in favor of Count Louis, and the delegates signed the instrument in the sacristy of Holy Cross Collegiate Church belonging to the Benedictines, in the presence of Prior Frederic and Brother Henry of Meure, both Dominicans, who had come to escort Albert to Würzburg. We may conjecture that the party passed through Ulm, Esslingen, and Gmund, and through the picturesque valley of the Rauen Alps, peopled with the fairies of German folklore.

As the Dominican church and convent were in process of construction, tradition says that Albert took up his abode in the Hotel von Wiesenfeld at Würzburg. Here his brother Henry lived and we can easily picture the warmth of the meeting. Here, too, Albert granted an indulgence to all who contributed to the erection of the Gate of Heaven Convent of the Benedictine nuns. Evidently he had had some opportunity to promote the crusade, for we find him going to the Franciscans for the purpose of selecting fit and capable men to continue the preaching of the holy war in the environs during his absence. Fleet of foot, he pushed on to Frankfurt where, on June 5, 1263, he granted an indulgence of forty days for all those who visited the Church of the Teuton Knights on the feasts of Our Lady, St. Elizabeth, Church Dedication Day, and on the octaves of all these feasts. Then passing through Würzburg once more, where he tarried long enough to grant an indulgence to all the contributors to the new oratory of the Augustinian Hermits, he reached Cologne on June 22. He granted indulgences to the benefactors of the Church of the Knights of St. John. He further effected a temporary reconciliation, a month later, between Archbishop Engelbert and the municipality—not so difficult a task for him as he had had dealings with both parties to the quarrel several years before, patching up a peace which proved as illusory as the present one promised to be, a suspicion which was amply borne out in the coming years. From the Abbess of the Convent of St. Ursula, Elizabeth von Westerberg, he received the gift of precious relics—some of the bodies of the virgins martyred in Cologne in Roman days whom legend numbered at "eleven thousand." He presented the relics of the bodies of St. Candida and St. Florina to the Dominican Church in Freiburg.

Then we lose nearly all trace of Albert till January of the following year when, by way of the northern route through Germany, he hastened to the Low Countries. On the way, at Magdeburg, he composed the dispute about the episcopal succession. On the last of October, in virtue of special powers given to him by the Pope, he designated Henry, pastor of Berges, as successor to the see of Brandenburg. This happy ending of a tedious and ticklish affair caused him a great deal of satisfaction, as is evident from the jubilant tone of his letter to the Premonstratentian superior at Havelburg to whom he communicated the news. During these weeks he exercised the good offices of a peacemaker between the Knights of St. John and Barnim of Stetten. Then, in haste, he descended upon Adelhausen, near Freiburg, tarrying just long enough to dedicate the parochial church. On February 20, 1264, he went by way of Strasburg to Speyer—resting place of the Emperors—where he granted an indulgence to those who assisted the Dominican nuns of Basel in erecting a convent. The same day he sought to elicit contributions from the faithful in behalf of the new church of the Dominican nuns at Klingenthal, near Basel, where shortly an unknown artist was to draw the most famous and realistic *danse macabre*, or Dance of Death, for which that age and locality would become renowned. On March 18, at Ratisbon, he presided at a trial between Bishop Leo of Ratisbon and Zachary of Hage. The latter pledged himself, under forfeiture of the tax exemptions stipulated at the time, to abstain from engineering the marriage of his children without the previous consent of the diocesan Ordinary. Three weeks later he was at Mainz, where he granted an indulgence to those who contributed to the erection of the Augustinian nuns' convent at Aldenburg. This is the last-known document to bear the signature of Albert as *Praedicator Crucis* or Preacher of the Crusade.[1]

[1] H. Scheeben, ***Chronologie***, *72-77.*

Pope Urban IV died October 2, 1264, and automatically Albert's appointment as papal nuncio to Northern Europe expired. It could not have been much before November of that year when Albert learned of the Pope's death, and he forthwith ceased his operations as nuncio. As he looked over the last two years the whole campaign must have appeared a very sorry and dismal affair. For despite the heart-rending reports about the complete collapse of what had been accomplished in the Orient in earlier days, the people of Europe could not be roused to the point of volunteering for the crusade. The whole movement had been too long drawn out to appease the craving of the people, who, then as now and always, were hungry for tangible results commensurate with the enormous sacrifices made by them in blood and possessions for the sake of the enterprise.

The people were too close to these titanic campaigns to see the cultural value of the crusades from which each participating nation had profited; too close to measure the constructive effects of these great undertakings which, in leading the sworn and born war lords abroad, gave the individual nations at home a chance to breathe and develop. Indeed, the conscience of Europe had been profoundly shaken since that day at Clermont, when the assembled thousands, with one voice, had signified their willingness to go to the holy wars in the Holy Land by shouting into the ears of the Pope the words, "God wills it." That great cry of a Europe united politically for a great spiritual ideal had been followed by a sober, fuzzy morning when, fatigued from the exertions of realizing a lofty universalist ambition, the people awoke to the sad realization of the teasing problems nearer home.

Pope Urban IV did not understand fully the change that had come over Christian Europe. In his rather sheltered life as a student in the Low Countries he had not had much chance to grapple, at close range, with the problems of a people newly conscious of the power and pride that come from total emancipation from the soil and the possession of independent wealth and ample opportunities of amassing it. How hard the Pope found it to disengage himself from intellectual pursuits as a personal pastime is clear from his stern, if friendly, pressure upon Albert to remain at Orvieto as a companion with whom he could informally exchange ideas—a preference, however, which he with laudable selflessness relinquished when, as Father of Christendom, he had sent his private intellectual fencing master to the turbulent, war-ridden peoples of the North to preach a crusade. Urban's call to Europe was the hollow cry of a watchman on the Tower of St. Peter to a people that, with its supreme interest in its own multiple affairs, had no understanding of the welfare and the common good of all nations. And his successor, Clement IV, a man who had been in close touch with the rough and stubborn actualities of the times, had no concern for the poor, gasping survivors of what had once been the Kingdom of Jerusalem. Under the circumstances Albert abandoned a tiresome trip to Rome to submit in person an account of his crusading campaigns. And we may take it for granted, seeing that the document has not survived, that Clement IV spent little time reading Albert's written report of an enterprise foredoomed in this Pope's eyes to be the failure it actually turned out to be.

Albert, a wiser man through the miscarriage of the crusade, withdrew before Christmas of 1264 to the convent of Würzburg, where his brother Henry resided.[2] If the people would not be taught a sane and safe internationalism, although members of a universal Church, Albert would not on that account be dissuaded from using his enforced inactivity in furthering the work of peace and in trying to set on foot proposals aimed directly against the exaggerated nationalism and jealous individualism which were the root causes of the almost constant and chronic disorders of the day and age. The long, tedious recital of his efforts during these years, taken together, form a wondrously beautiful picture of Albert's far-seeing political spirit which refused to be broken, disillusioned, and disenchanted just because it would persist in believing in the perfectibility of human nature and of political institutions, however slow-moving and embryonic. Albert never succumbed, as he had every reason to succumb, to political pessimism. He was essentially an optimist—perhaps just a few removes from an idealist. At a time when any other man would have eaten up his heart and confidence in human nature by useless and sour repining over his diplomatic failure, Albert resolutely turned to the work of doing whatsoever good could be done at home among the fractious lords. If the body politic could not be made over afresh nor ensouled with the authentic internationalist spirit, which, because fathered by the papacy, had worked veritable

---

2 *Ibid.*, 78-81.

miracles in the past, he would not disdain to patch up its lacerated members or sorely muddled head wherever he could. He would seek by sweet reasonableness to promote, within rational bounds, a nationalist spirit that was not too self-centered and hide-bound to take pity and have compassion on the peoples beyond its own narrow periphery. Albert's political theory of action was not cramped or constricted. His theory was essentially internationalistic because it was a conscious and conscientious reflection of the century-old papal policy of sane internationalism, binding, or seeking to bind, together the Christian states in Catholic amity and solidarity. Yet, seasoned diplomat and expert tactician that he was, Albert agreed that if the people refused to submit to such a major operation by the chief surgeon of the world—which was the medieval papacy—his would be the not inglorious part of performing minor operations made necessary by local or national malignant growths or bruises. Let us see, rapidly and cursorily, how he did this.

Together with Poppo, provost of the Würzburg Cathedral, Albert brought to a happy issue on December 4, 1264, the long dispute between the Church of St. John of Haug and the contentious nobleman, Godefried of Hohenlohe, over the respective rights of their provost of Hopferstadt and Rudershausen. He intervened the following years in the quarrel of the same parties of the first part and Irving, Bishop of Würzburg, respecting the rights of the provost of Koeningshoffen, Wolkshausen, Fichelsee, and Herschein. A few months later he arbitrated between the commander of the Knights of St. John, Ulrich von Velberg, and the proprietors of the manor of Wegenhein, who had erected stables at Würzburg shutting off the view of the city bank. (Even then there were such things as spite fences and buildings.)

But a quarrel of much more aggravated form was submitted to Albert for arbitration. The Würzburg merchants, proud of their wealth and strength, challenged the secular rights of the bishop and openly defied him. The counts of Henneberg effected a compromise with the bishop in 1261. The citizens promised to recognize and preserve intact the episcopal rights, authority, and immunities, to admit none to citizenship and to elect none to the Council without his knowledge and approval, to honor the face value of his coinage, to pay the customary dues to him, to respect and defend his possessions, as also those of the cathedral chapter and the clergy, and not to molest the Jews living under episcopal protection. But in 1265, the bishop, loyal to the measures of King Henry VII who forbade trade corporations throughout the Empire, blocked the aspirations of the bakers, butchers, and carpenters. As a result, they took possession of the city streets and works, drove out the Jews, expelled citizens and stirred up the populace, coined money on their own account, and surrounded the city walls with bastions in order to defend themselves against surprises. The mischief-makers demanded that the monks feed them and, this failing to be done to their satisfaction, stormed the monasteries, churches, and episcopal palace. Bishop Irving enlisted the services of Lords Conrad Trimberg, Hohenlohe, and Wenesberg, as well as other episcopal vassals, all of whom supplied knights and soldiers. Just then, however. Count Louis of Rieneck and Henry of Brauneck effected a reconciliation, largely through the intervention of Albert, whose name is first among the witnesses of the treaty. To him was given the authority to determine the amount of indemnity due the Abbot of St. Burckhard by the citizens. And this done, the twenty-four principal townsmen, selected as guarantors of the promises, signed their names to the treaty. The death of Bishop Irving, in 1266 caused the feud to break out once more, since the powerful Berthold of Sternberg, elected by one faction, took forcible possession of the episcopal palace, thus ignoring the valid claims of Conrad of Trimberg, the other contestant. The administrator of the diocese, Berthold of Henneberg, with the support of the citizens and the Lords, defeated Sternberg at Kitzengen on August 8, 1266, with a loss of five hundred men, among them several Canons. Conrad hastening to Rome for confirmation, died of fever on the way. Berthold occupied the see despite Henneberg's violent opposition. Albert tried at every juncture to pour oil upon the troubled waters, but it was plain that matters would have to run their appointed course. Yet he did establish peace between the Brother Hospitalers of St. John and Marquard, surnamed Caruso, a debtor of the hospital. A very short time after Albert supported Berthold, with whom he was on friendly terms, in the matter of taxes and rents.

About the beginning of the year 1267 Albert moved his residence to Strasburg, and in a very short time was besieged by the quarrelsome people and lords.[3] In July he blessed a chapel and altar in the Cistercian

[3] *Ibid.*, 81-93.

Abbey at Burtscheid, near Aix-la-Chapelle, and thence left for Cologne where, on August 4, he blessed an altar in St. Mary's Church. A few days later he issued a document in favor of the Teuton Knights. Now as it is scarcely probable that he should have come solely for this purpose, it is generally held that he intended to take up his residence in Cologne but was dissuaded from doing so by the internal state of affairs, which only a short time later came to a climax in the capture and imprisonment of Archbishop Engelbert of Falkenberg. He returned to Strasburg in the autumn of 1267, remaining till 1270, when he took up quarters in Cologne. Perhaps, he was prevailed upon to come to Strasburg by his friend Ulrich, who was head of studies in the Dominican College. Some documents of this time, in which Albert signed himself *lector*, or teacher, would seem to justify the conclusion that on the earnest solicitations of Ulrich, mayhap to inject something of his own infectious enthusiasm into the students who were distracted enough by the quarrel between the bishop and the city authorities in which Clement IV had to take a hand, the old man returned to his loved occupation of teaching and presiding at the public disputations of the students intended to test and perfect their argumentative skill.

But Albert's teaching must have been sporadic, for we find him on April 29, 1268, in Esslingen where he dedicated the Dominican church in honor of St. Paul and consecrated the main altar. Five days later he had already reached Schellstadt where he dedicated an altar in the church of the Knights of St. John, on June 4, and the following day at Colmar he granted indulgences for every visit to the church of the same Religious. Undoubtedly, he visited the convent of the Dominican nuns at Colmar who were already giving evidence of the high mystical experiences of many of its inmates. Without pausing to take breath he turned to Strasburg to consecrate an altar in the church of the Brothers of Penance. Before leaving the city he granted indulgences in favor of the Dominican Convent of nuns at St. Catherine's and granted a marriage dispensation in the case of Henry von Hohenlohe. Stopping for a short time at Villengen, in October, he granted there three different and specific indulgences in order to promote the works of religion. Then he pushed on to Rottweil to lay the corner stone of the Dominican church, blessed the cemetery, granted indulgences, and delivered a rousing sermon to the people. Either on the way to Rottweil or on the journey back to Strasburg he dedicated a church for the lepers at Adelhausen, near Freiburg; another at Rottenburg in honor of Our Lady; and another at Schlettstadt for the Knights of St. John. Returning to Strasburg he dedicated St. Peter's Church and, thereupon, in company with Albert of Havelburg and John of Freiburg, he went to Mechlenburg to settle a dispute between the Knights of St. John and Barnim of Pomerania, which had kept the city in a state of unrest for three quarters of a century. Albert came with special powers of absolution for the guilty party from Pope Clement IV and clear instructions how to deal in the case. Returning to Strasburg for the Spring Ember Days he ordained in the Dominican church one hundred and fifty priests, at the same time conferring other orders on four hundred more clerics. Toward the end of August he traveled to Basel where he dedicated the Dominican church and consecrated the main altar. A few days later, at Mülhausen, he granted indulgences in favor of the Knights of St. John. About this time he dedicated the church of the Dominican nuns at Colmar and another at Katharinenthal, near Diessenhofen. He consecrated, also, the altar in the Augustinian oratory at Mülhausen and another in a Minorite church at Colmar.

One would imagine that such persistent journeying and episcopal functioning, oftentimes entailing a late fast as in the case of consecrations, would have sapped completely the strength of this valiant and tireless old man. But it is at this period of his life that Albert's name was seriously considered for the professor's post at Paris. For things began looking very ominous for the Friars about 1268, when an able and slippery man, Gerard of Abbeville, dared openly to head the factions which had managed to exist after the condemnation of William of St. Amour by Alexander IV. The several attempts of William to smuggle, under a thin disguise, his *Perils of These Latter Times* into the Christian arena—which was the University of Paris—and the strangely lenient repulse his audacity met with at the hands of the Pope and the university, encouraged his secret followers and abettors, as also the inheritors of his splenetic spirit, to take the first steps toward launching a bitter onslaught on the Friars whose success, renown, and influence were increasing daily by leaps and bounds. Moreover, from an unexpected quarter, a favorable and favoring wind blew up for his cause. Just about this time, namely, Siger de Brabant forced himself upon the notice of the university by his undoubted gifts, which he employed to give a frankly pantheistic interpretation to

Aristotle.[4] Rendered reckless by his high repute for learning and emboldened by his success as a philosopher and interpreter of Aristotle in the sense of Averroes, he began to maintain positions which no other orthodox theologian would have cared to champion. Falling foul of some of the harder heads among the Friars—Albert, for instance, who had challenged him as far back as his Anagni days—Siger quite naturally ranged himself with the disaffected coterie at Paris. Together these two suspected factions constituted a great menace to the Friars and were in a position, posing as martyrs, to do them irreparable harm—at least such was the conclusion of the Dominican General, Blessed John of Vercelli. For from the memorandum book of the German Dominican Provincial, Henry of Minden, we can gather that the General was prepared to do the unheard-of thing of sending Albert back to Paris for a second time as professor. Evidently the danger was considered imminent enough to drive the General to set aside all precedents and consider something which had never been tried out so far in the history of the Order.

From the digest of letters passing between Henry and the General and from one excerpt from a letter of the General to Albert we can reconstruct the situation clearly and exactly.[5] Albert declared himself ready to go to Paris to teach as master for the second time. The General expressed his satisfaction over this to Albert, as is evident from an excerpt in Henry's memorandum book. But Albert had laid down the condition that he be supplied with an assistant, not indeed the bachelor who, in the ordinary course of events, would be present at Paris as teacher under him, but a helper or a secretary at his entire disposal. There must have been some reasons for placing this condition—perhaps Albert's eyesight was failing, as was his physical strength, for it is about this time that we first come across the information that he used a saddle horse on his journeys. John of Vercelli had counted on Albert's unconditional acceptance. When, however, the General found that he did not have time to interfere in the provincial's authority concerning a secretary for Albert, he hastily,

---

[4] P. Mandonnet, Siger de Brabant et l'Averroisme Latin (Louvain: 1908).

[5] H. Finke, Ungedruckte Dominikanerbriefe des 13. Jahrhunderts (Paderborn: 1891), 80-82; J. A. Endres, "*Eine zweite beabsichtigte Berufung Alberts des Grossen an die Universität Paris um 1298,*" in *Historisch-Politische Blätter (1913),* 749 sq.

and as a last resort, appointed Thomas Aquinas to this post, some time after the opening of the school on September 1.[6] Thomas's late arrival, we know, caused some unfavorable comment, as it was bound to do, seeing the many disgruntled and inimical followers of Siger and Gerard who were on the spot with eyes single for anything that might serve as a pretext for starting a commotion against the Friars in the university. The General, no doubt, relieved that he had found a man to fill the chair in Paris, thanked Albert in a letter of which there is a partial transcript in Henry's notebook.[7] In the meantime the provincial must have got the information to the General that a man had been found to assist Albert. Thereupon the General asked Albert to proceed from Strasburg to Cologne on important affairs for the good of the Order and the Church. The secretary whom the provincial had selected for Albert could have been any of the following men: John of Freiburg, Albert of Havelberg, Gottfried of Duisberg, Hugh of Lucca, or, probably, Reiner. Gottfried is called *minister* in the documents and, probably, acted in the same capacity of companion and valet to Albert as Reginald of Piperno to Thomas in his later years. He was the only one of these brethren who could not have been employed in teaching as he did not have the required grade of the lectorate. Thus having escaped the rigorous charge of a professorship at Paris, Albert went back to the banks of the Rhine. It was late in the August of 1270.

---

[6] A. M. Walz, *Delineatio Vitae S. Thomae Aquinatis* (Roma: 1927), 72, 74; M. Grabmann, *Mittelalterliches Geistesleben* (München: 1926), 148.

[7] *Nam in Argentinam venientes sicut Karissimus...* mihi significare curavit, fratis doctrina sacra reficitis cum earum profectu, promissione ordinis et vestrorum augmento. Finke, Ungedruckte, 51.

CHAPTER X
STATESMAN AND DIPLOMAT

When John of Vercelli asked Albert to go back to the brethren in Cologne "for their advancement" he cautiously intimated that he had been persuaded to do this by the earnest entreaties of the secular clergy. For Cologne was again in a state of great turmoil over the recrudescence of the old conflict between the archbishop and the citizenry. On two occasions in the past Albert had intervened, but the reconciliations had been ephemeral. At this time the archbishop had been in prison since October, 1267, and an interdict had been placed on the city on August 3, 1268. Five days later a strong protest had been lodged against this punitive measure, and in the interim the penalties for disregarding it were not imposed. But, unfortunately, matters had changed for the worse with the coming of the headstrong, tactless papal nuncio, Bernard of Casteneto who, after scarcely an investigation into the merits of the case, had ordered the clergy to leave the city within two months and had suspended all commerce in the city. As there was no immediate redress, nor hopes of it as long as the nuncio remained in authority, the clergy, willing to grasp at any straw, had turned to the Master General of the Dominicans with a plea for Albert's return as the only available peacemaker.

John of Vercelli was now face to face with a dilemma. As the man of God he was, he must have sympathized deeply with the people, who, without any great fault of their own, were deprived of the ministrations of religion; they were doomed, besides, to misery if the quarrel could not be healed. On the other hand, he knew enough canon law not to impinge or infringe upon the authority of the nuncio. Courtesy, at least, dictated that he, stationed so far away, should not presume to question the wisdom of his measures. Hence, John was so cautious and circumspect in his letter. He made it sufficiently plain that Albert was to go back to Cologne to render whatever services he could to the brethren, whether this be writing or teaching. But at the same time he hinted that the clergy were looking to him for some solution of the sorry state of affairs. Undoubtedly, the General knew Albert well enough to feel sure that he would take in the situation at Cologne at a glance and set measures on foot to alleviate the disturbed condition of affairs, without contravening in any way the express letter and spirit of the canon law of the Church.[1]

But before Albert reached Cologne from Strasburg the air had cleared. Engelbert was released from captivity on April 16, 1271; he laid down his conditions for peace with the city; he appointed a peace commission composed of his coadjutor, Bishop Winrich, Count William of Julich, Gerard of Landskron, and Albert. From the very sparse notices that have come down to us of this peace treaty, it can only be gathered that Albert confined most of his efforts to placating and mollifying the angered Engelbert, who was all for the strictest justice, perhaps retaliation and revenge. Albert held up before him the sorry spiritual condition of the people, making it plain that upon his merciful and forgiving attitude, whatever may have been the injustice he had suffered, depended a lasting and beneficent peace.

Naturally there was a lingering aftermath of legal proceedings following upon this treaty. Of the many cases brought to Albert one had reference to the quarrel between the Provost Wolfram and the Chapter of Kerpen, which was amicably settled on September 29, 1271. Another, dated about a month earlier, August 31, 1271, was an agreement he effected for Baron Gerrard von Werden. In the early part of October he opened before the eyes of the people the shrine containing the relics of St. Evergislus. At an uncertain date toward the end of the year he hurried to Utrecht to dedicate the Dominican Church, which through his good offices in 1248, had been transferred from an outlying, inaccessible spot to the confines of the city. Then he pushed on to the General Chapter of his Order in Montpellier. The sole reason that could have brought him to this convocation was the meetings of the board of educators who were to examine into the workings and effectiveness of the program of studies drawn up in 1259 at the Chapter of Valenciennes, in whose deliberations he played a preponderating part. Peter of Tarentaise, who was shortly to ascend the pontifical throne; Richard Kilwardby, who was to occupy the archiepiscopal chair of Canterbury; and Peter Conflеton, shortly to be

[1] H. Scheeben, *Chronologie*, 93-122.

titular archbishop of Corinth, were in attendance, and the discussions of these men of such varied interests and outlooks must have been extremely suggestive. Albert, we may be sure, argued long and eloquently in favor of Aristotle against such a redoubtable opponent as Kilwardby who was all for the Platonico-Augustinian movement and against Peter of Tarentaise whose mind and temper were distinctly legalistic. For the year 1272 there are only two documents that have reference to Albert's activities. In the case of Gerhard Gyr and the Abbey of Kamp he acted as the official witness, on August 12, and further witnessed in December to a bequest made to Abbess Geva of St. Cecilia's at Cologne.

But he was in no wise idle, as his correspondence with Ulrich of Strasburg attests. The letters which passed between them were many and confidential and it redounds to the credit of Ulrich, now Provincial, that he sought advice and counsel from an old professor who had always manifested affection for him and a deep interest in his grandiose plans.[2] The tenor of Albert's letters can be inferred from the jottings and notes which Ulrich made in his memorandum book. These are sufficient to prove conclusively that they were on terms of the closest friendship. Albert had, like all good men, a great capacity for friendship and he never reduced it to the miserable condition of a hardship. He knew what it was to be busy about a thousand things and hence did not require any crucifixion to the pen in the form of correspondence to keep up that loving understanding and surrender which are the very essence of friendship. It is to be doubted whether St. Thomas Aquinas and Albert ever exchanged epistolary confidences. Thomas was too absorbed in his work and by nature too reserved to have sacrificed the time and made the surrender. Albert was too courteous and too sensitive to foist himself upon any man, even upon an old pupil. But the friendship between the two was deep and lasting. Perhaps the initial exchange mutually made, when they first met, was so sacrosanct that it needed not to be fed by such poor makeshifts as epistles. But the bond between Albert and Ulrich was of another sort. Ulrich was essentially communicative, effervescent, though deep in his feelings. He could never forget what Albert meant to him and had done

---

[2] H. Finke, Ungedruckte, 80-82, n. 47, 50; L. Pfleger, "*Albert der Grosse und das Elsass,*" in *Archiv für elsässische Kirchengeschichte (1930), 1 sq.*

for him when, as a raw, callow youth, with high dreams and flaming enthusiasms, he had come as a student under the master's influence. And he never had reason to lower in his heart the pedestal on which he had placed Albert. It is an endless pity that only faint shadows of his correspondence, in the shape of digests of Albert's letters, are still visible, but what we see and what we can envision embolden us to believe that few recorded medieval friendships were nobler or more idyllic.

We know from the old chroniclers that during these comparatively hidden years of his life, Albert composed some of his greatest works; finished others that he had been forced to lay aside; retouched others with the wisdom that comes from past experience and is cast forward by the shining of the fires lit on the hills of eternity; made excerpts from his larger works to circulate among the people for apologetic purposes. There were heresies pullulating all over Europe, helped, on the one hand, in their malign growth by the chronic wars among the Christian princes which scandalized the simple children of the Church, and on the other hand, by the doctrinal and especially moral extravaganzas imported from the Orient by returning crusaders. Is it any wonder that the Church was assailed from within by many whose hearts were right but heads all wrong, or again by those whose hearts were groveling and heads haughty? Of these Albert had said years earlier in his *Commentary on St. Luke:* "Heretics resemble Sampson's foxes; like those animals, they all have different heads but are bound together by the tail, that is, they are always united when there is a question of opposing the truth." And his experience and observation, especially during these later years when duty carried him so much abroad, warned him to take nothing away from that sound historical apothegm. For these erring and stubborn children he circulated a golden little book, which in its way is a philosophy of Catholic history without aspiring to be such: *The Valiant Woman,* where with eloquence he discourses on the Church Militant, her gifts and economy, her marvelous organization, her sureness of her divine origin and mandate. There are echoes of St. Augustine's *City of God* in this inspiring and suggestive tract, the same penetration into the divine stuff out of which she was builded, the same understanding of her matchless spirit that cannot be quenched, the same adaptability to new exigencies without the surrender of antique loyalties, the same sweeping gaze over the vast expanse of the ages over which she stands, with light unfailing, as the guardian of truth and the sure white guide to the nations of the world.

At a period when men were too busy making history to take time to write it, Albert, with that capacious mind to which nothing seemed foreign or useless, grasped the truth that history can be made to bear witness to the Church. And while he would have certainly been a real curiosity, perhaps even a freak to his age, had he abandoned his chair of philosophy to become a rattler of dry dates and a mumbler of mere names, however great, he yet found a way of giving men the broad outlines of a philosophy of Church history that can afford to dispense with the peddling of dates in order to philosophize on the big movements toward the Church or away from her. He established, once and for all, that she is the only pivot of history because the one stable thing in a world of change.

The year 1272 probably saw Albert at Wimpfen for the laying of the corner stone for the Dominicans, an undertaking that had been opposed so long and bitterly that Pope Gregory X was impelled to empower Bishop Hildebrand of Eichstatt or Albert to break the opposition. Again we find him in September undertaking a journey to Nijmegen, on the pressing invitation of Count Reinold of Geldern, son of Count Otto II, to dedicate the Church of Our Lady and St. Stephen, which was in dependency on the Church of the Apostles in Cologne. He also consecrated two side altars in this church of Canon Regulars in honor of St. Nicholas and St. Catherine. As the old church outside the city was razed to the ground and the cemetery destroyed, Albert ordained that an annual procession of the Blessed Sacrament wend its way to the abandoned place in memory of the sacred things that had occurred on the spot.

Almost immediately on his return to Cologne he was prevailed upon to take a hand in the reform of the Sisters of St. Mary Magdalen, or White Ladies, as they were called.[3] For many years this local congregation had been in process of decay. It could scarcely have been otherwise, seeing the unsettled state of affairs in Cologne during the turbulent days of Conrad of Hochstaden and Engelbert of Falkenberg,

---

[3] *A, Simon,* L'Ordre des Pénitents de S. Marie Madeleine en Allegamne au XIII siècle (Fribourg: 1918), 69-130.

whose chief concern it had been to penalize the citizens for the rights they claimed as their own in virtue of immemorial concessions and agreements. That these and other pious women in the same deplorable state were not satisfied with their spiritual standing is clear from the almost universal movement among these small local communities to affiliate themselves with the rising Orders of the Mendicants and thus save themselves from utter collapse. Most of the local institutes which did not effect an absorption by the Friars fell into such monastic decay that they died out from sheer inanition or were mercifully suppressed by ecclesiastical authority. Dean Wittico, under whose spiritual direction and authority the White Ladies were constituted, opposed such a union as far back as 1266. He sought to reform the community. This reform was accepted in 1268. Wittico died shortly after and his work soon fell to pieces. The nuns were then placed under the spiritual care of the Dominicans and reorganized under Pope Nicholas IV. Provost Reimar of Aix-la-Chapelle, superior of the institute at Cologne, after consulting with Albert was willing to surrender some of his prerogatives. Attendance outside the convent at general chapters was no longer demanded. The dean could not give commands without prior consultation with the nuns. Visitations could take place only every three years and were to be conducted in person by the dean. Transfers of individual nuns to other convents, such, for instance, as the one in Freiberg in Saxony, which had incurred excommunication, were prohibited. The dean could not tax the convent for any reason, nor did the appointment of superiors or confessors appertain to him. This agreement, in October, 1274, soon effected peace and stability and the religious life in all its beauty thrived there, due to the common sense of Albert, who did not insist on the letter of the law nor browbeat the nuns with threats of excommunication, who did not flirt with the vague aspirations of the nuns on the one hand, nor, on the other, leave any opening or subterfuge for the high-handedness of the dean.

For Albert, in his seclusion at Cologne, this year opened inauspiciously with the death of Thomas Aquinas at Fossa Nuova, on March 7, 1274. Albert of Brescia, in the year 1300, related to Anthony of Brescia that on that day, at an early hour in the morning, as Albert sat at table with the brethren at Cologne, he suddenly burst into tears. The prior and the other brethren pressed him for a reason for this sudden outburst of tears. Albert replied: "Thomas, my son in Christ, the bright luminary of the Church, passes at this very moment from the world to his Lord."[4] And he wept and lamented much that his own earthly pilgrimage should be so long prolonged. Later biographers have been at pains to ascribe this instant knowledge to supernatural power. This may certainly have been the case, although absolutely speaking it is not necessary to go beyond the known and tested phenomena of telepathy. At all events, the Cologne brethren carefully noted down the hour of Albert's experience and, when the sad tidings came from Italy, proved to their own satisfaction that the hour agreed.

Brother Hugh of Lucca, who lived in close relationship with Albert at Cologne, was in a position to see how deeply the old man was affected by the demise of his favorite pupil at the very height of his career. In the process of St. Thomas's canonization, undertaken by John XXII, Bartholomew of Capua related under oath that he had frequently heard Brother Hugh say the following: "Whenever Albert heard Thomas spoken of he began to weep. He was, he would relate, the flower and ornament of the world. He could never hear his name pronounced without at once shedding tears. These constant tears affected the religious for they feared, considering Albert's great age, that they were the result of an enfeebled brain."[5] This, better than anything else, gives us to understand how intimately united in heart and mind were these two great wrestlers for the truth, and how Albert, far from being jealous at having been eclipsed by the labors of his disciple was proud of him as having wrought masterfully and well for the Lord, even as a father is proud of a son who has acquitted himself with distinction in some difficult task.

While Albert's heart was seared by the going of Thomas, he was far too human and experienced to hand himself over to useless grief and repining. He had learned, no doubt, as a young student, during his days of worriment at Padua, that the Italians, who understand the exquisite tortures of the human heart better than any other people, had recourse to what they picturesquely called the "solace of movement." And hence Albert welcomed the opportunity late in March to set his face in the direction of France, where Pope Gregory X had convened a Council of the Church to grapple with the problem of bringing the world to

---

4 *Acta Sanctorum*, Martii I, 714 sq.; H. Scheeben, *Chronologie*, 109.

5 *Ibid.*

Christ. The Pope still further entertained the hope that Michael Paleologus, King of Greece, weighed down by the difficulties surrounding him at home, would be willing to listen to the voice of Peter to return to Christian unity. Thus would be undone the evil of that fatal day when Photious questioned the teaching of the Church on the profound doctrine of the procession of the Holy Ghost from the loving embrace of the Father and Son in the divinely fecund life of the Blessed Trinity.

That Albert was at Lyons, which some modern authors dispute, is amply attested by Leo, Bishop of Ratisbon, who declared on June 24, 1274, that Albert at the Council of Lyons had granted an indulgence to all who would befriend the Dominicans at Ratisbon. Only recently a letter of Albert's, dated March 24, 1274, at Lyons, in favor of the Dominicans at Halberstadt, has been discovered.[6] Albert himself made a direct reference in his theological *Summa* to some point he had heard discussed at Lyons against the sophistries of the Greeks.[7] John of Vittoria speaks explicitly of his attendance there, and Rudolf of Nijmegen speaks of Albert's activities at Lyons.

The only reason for calling this in question arises from the fact that historians have found it rather difficult to assign any definite work in which Albert might have been engaged at Lyons. There is no doubt that as a bishop Albert had been invited. As the Greek errors were to be discussed at the Council, the Pope summoned Thomas who had written learnedly on the subject. As the question of the Mendicants would again come up for consideration, he had summoned St. Bonaventure, the very storm center of this unloyal quarrel in the Franciscan Order. Now Albert had spoken of the Greek false teachings on various occasions with great learning and penetration. And he had been the very champion of the Mendicants at Anagni. So it is fair to conclude that his presence as an adviser would be most welcome to the Fathers of the Council. Humbert of the Romans was in attendance at the Council and had furthered it in every way by writing his *Opus Tripartitum*, which might be looked upon as a tentative list of the

---

[6] *de Loe, "Albert der Grosse auf dem Konzil von Lyon,"* in *Beilage der Kölnischen Volkszeitung (July 16, 1914), 225 sq.; F. Pelster,* Kritische Studien, 174; M. Grabmann in *Speculum (1931),* fasc. 1.

[7] Opp. XVIII. fr. XVIII dist. CXXL.

subjects that should come up for consideration. If, then, the Pope had not directly invited Albert, which is not impossible, though no documentary evidence can be produced in support of this contention, a personal invitation by Humbert is not only not excluded but very probable.

Then, too, Albert may have been asked to go to Lyons by the city authorities of Cologne who were anxious for the removal of an interdict which still hung over the city. Perhaps, too, he determined to go on the invitation of the Electors of Cologne and Mainz who, on September 29, 1273, had elected Rudolf of Hapsburg as Emperor. And were not Rudolf and Albert friends of long standing? Had not Rudolf, after his coronation at Aix-la-Chapelle, stopped off at Cologne to see Albert? As it was of supreme interest to Church and Empire that peace reign between them, it is just possible that Albert was designated as an imperial diplomat to carry on negotiations outside the conciliar chambers for the papal ratification of Rudolf's assumption of the Iron Crown.

That no official standing in the deliberations of the Council was assigned to Albert is the undeniable testimony of history. But, perhaps, there was an invitation from John of Vercelli, the General of the Dominicans, who was much concerned about making a magnificent show of the Order's power and vitality. He convoked the General Chapter of the Order at Lyons during the deliberations of the Council. There were about fifty representatives from all the provinces. Besides, the *Francia*, or French Province, held its biennial Chapter at Lyons at the same time, at which there were at least one hundred Friars in attendance. Many of the more renowned professors of the Order were gathered together at Lyons to consider the question of studies. This is clearly shown by the extraordinarily large number of legislative ordinations of the Chapter on this point. Ulrich of Strasburg was certainly at Lyons if we may believe the provincial ledger where an entry for expenses is charged up against his name. Now the one reasonable explanation of his going was to share, as regent of the important House of Studies in Strasburg, in the deliberations of this pedagogical commission. So there can be no doubt in the face of these facts that Albert was present in the city of Lyons, if not at the Council. He left Cologne some time after March 7 in company with his companion and confessor, Gottfried of Duisberg. Perhaps Otto, the

Dominican Bishop of Minden, traveled also with Albert on the way out but not on the return journey, for he died in Dijon, November 17, 1275.

It is easy to imagine with what warmth Albert was welcomed at Lyons by the three Dominican cardinals and the thirty Dominican bishops. They all knew him by reputation; were followers of his teaching methods for the most part; were lost in admiration for his vitality and adroitness in handling affairs of moment. Perhaps, too, several of them, more fine-grained by nature and not too much absorbed by the business or excitement of the Council, remembered to say a word of sympathy to the old man in his hour of sorrow over the death of Thomas. Did Bonaventure, now Cardinal-Bishop of Albano, recall the day when, at Paris, they both had looked upon Thomas with wonder, asking themselves secretly: "What manner of man will this one be?" Would not such an evocation of the olden days have compensated Albert for the fatigues of the journey and requited Bonaventure for his labors at the Council, which brought about his death, dramatically, two days before its formal close? To go through the list of names of those in attendance is to recite the glories of the Church at that epoch—and Albert had been in touch, in one way or another, with the majority of these ecclesiastical leaders who, in answer to the Pope's call, had come to settle some of the vexing questions of the hour.

The imposing sights attendant upon the deliberations of the bishops of Christendom under the presidency of the Pope, passed rapidly before the dimming eyes of Albert. Because of his vast knowledge of the history of the Church and his deep understanding of the dogmas that were asserted with such truly Petrine tenacity, he understood the significance of what was taking place as few of the learned prelates present at the Council. Perhaps, he rejoiced inwardly that for once in his long lifetime he was free to sit back, unworried about the tasks assigned him for immediate dispatch, to enjoy the full beauty and sweet import of the divine pageant, the ineffable love feast between two parts of Christendom united for a brief space in the embrace of dogmatic unity.

But the chroniclers are one in asserting that though Albert did not engage in the proceedings of the Council, he did not hold aloof from the discussions of one kind or other which were incidental to it. When Rudolf of Nijmegen speaks of Albert's engaging in learned arguments about the Greek errors, he obviously cannot mean, so far at least as can be gathered from the Official Acts of the Council, that there was any question about these points after the arrival of the Emperor's ambassadors. For they declared themselves ready at once to recognize the Roman teaching on every point of difference. There may have been discussion before the ambassadors' arrival and the points they would be expected to retract may have been decided upon. This, undoubtedly, must have been a private argument, for the Pope was clear in his mind as to what he would insist upon. It is more probable that Rudolf was referring to the public disputations, agreed upon as a kind of distraction after the sessions of the Council, which theologians held as intellectual tournaments to refresh the minds of all participating, on the errors, real or imputed, of the Greeks. Perhaps theologians of Constantinople provoked discussion on the question of incontinency and defended its lawfulness by means of interpreters. This is the only explanation that can be read into Albert's words in his *Summa* and the only hypothesis that will save Rudolf's name as an accurate historian on this point.

The chroniclers are explicit in their statements about Albert's negotiations at the Council in behalf of the newly elected Emperor, Rudolf of Hapsburg. He had, indeed, been elected and crowned in the preceding September, thus forcing Alphonsus of Castile, who had never set foot in Germany, to withdraw his claims. But he had not been formally crowned by the Pope, a proceeding looked upon as necessary since that Christmas in the eighth century when Charlemagne had laid the foundations of the Holy Roman Empire of the West, of the German people, by receiving his mandate from the Pope. The question was discussed in a consistory, on June 6, at which many German bishops attended, as for instance, the archbishops of Mainz, Magdeburg, Cologne, Traves, and Bremen. The ambassadors of Rudolf appeared; pledged that their lord would observe faithfully the guarantees of Otto IV and Frederic II to the Holy See; promised that they would protect the Papal States and make peace with Charles of Anjou. It was at this consistory that Albert preached in favor of the Emperor on the text: "He shall send them a savior and a defender to deliver them" (Isa. xix. 20). Peter of Prussia,[8] who is thoroughly acquainted with the details of

[8] Petrus de Prussia, *Vitae*, Chap. XLL

the Council, can be trusted when he says that Albert painted vividly the virtues and capacities of this founder of the House of Hapsburg; how he had a determination to restore order and justice in the state after a deplorable interregnum; to establish once more peace between the Church and the Empire and to rescue the Holy Places from the Mohammedans. Rudolf had given proofs of his valor, love of justice, and piety. This latter quality was evident from his conduct at the coronation at Aix-la-Chapelle when, in the absence of the imperial scepter, he had seized a crucifix in its place amid the hearty acclamation of the people.

Albert, who was the spokesman of the German bishops, pleaded mightily and not in vain. The Pope was deeply impressed and declared openly against Alphonsus whose refusal to make a renunciation of his claims had prevented Rudolf from enjoying his crown in peace. Gregory X conveyed the news to Rudolf that he, with the cardinals, recognized him as King of Rome, adding: "We notify you to prepare yourself to receive from Our hands the imperial crown when We shall command you—which We trust will not be long." This letter was dated September 7, 1274. Shortly another papal letter to the new king commanded him to go to the nearest frontier and to apprise the Roman Curia of it. This occurred the following year, when Rudolf with his entire family and many German princes repaired to Lausanne. Here he swore to defend the rights and possessions of the Holy Roman Church. Here also, he with his nobility, took up the cross against the Mohammedan.

Albert's plea had not been in vain. His frank espousal of the first king of a new line helped the German people to appreciate one who was as ideal a ruler as any who ever sat upon the throne. That Rudolf was not ungrateful for Albert's mediation is plain from his loving references to him in a royal letter to an unknown person.[9]

---

[9] J. Gerbert, *Codex Epistolaris Rudolphi, I.* Cf. Gerbert, *Romanorum regis* (Typis. S. Blasiensis, 1772), 27; de Loe, in *Analecta Bollandiana* (1900), 305, n. 187.

CHAPTER XI
FRIEND OF GOD

RUDOLF OF NIJMEGEN tells us that Albert recited the entire Psalter each day, slowly and thoughtfully, so as to extract from each one of the one hundred and fifty psalms its full dogmatic and devotional savor.[1] Now just as the psalms kept alive among the Jews the immemorial hopes for the coming of the Messiah, so they fired Albert's heart with love for Him who had fulfilled the promises in an unspeakably tender way in the sweet condescensions of the Blessed Sacrament. And his piety was realistic enough not to attempt separating Mary from Jesus.

No medieval schoolman wrote more extensively than Albert on the Blessed Eucharist and the Blessed Virgin. Few, if any, grew quite so lyrical, intimate, and compelling as Albert; for few, if any, had made larger room in their devotional life for the Blessed Sacrament and the Mother of God. In the most unexpected places in his voluminous works he stops for a digression which often assumes the proportions of a small dissertation or treatise on both these subjects. And there can be no doubt that, at the end, when the habits of a lifetime are likely to assert themselves most strongly and spectacularly, during a period of almost unintermittent interruptions, he recouped and steadied his spirit by writing his incomparable work on the Sacrifice of the Mass and on the Holy Eucharist and by revising and enlarging his book of thirty-two sermons on the same Sacrament. These three works are of capital importance in the history of the liturgy in the Middle Ages.[2] Rudolf of Nijmegen says: "In the books which Albert wrote toward the close of his life on the Mystery of the most Holy Sacrament of the Altar he no longer appears a mere mortal, but as one filled with the Holy Ghost and fed with celestial bread; he might be likened to the beloved disciple reposing on the breast of Jesus and contemplating at leisure those awful mysteries." And another contemporary, Bernard of Castres,

---

[1] Rodolphus de Novimagio, *Legenda* 20.

[2] C. Callewaert, Liturgicae Institutiones (Bruges: 1925), 77: "*De officiis et sacramentis ecclesiasticis scripserunt multi: alii dogmaticas praesertim quaestiones tractabant, inter quos eminet sane B. Albertus Magnus qui in exponenda liturgia missae interpretationem symbolicam rejicit et litteralem docte et pie defendit.*"

adds a few welcome details: "Brother Albert, Bishop of Ratisbon, so illustrious in sacred and human science, left to the world many and varied works for the exposition of the Holy Scriptures and other doctrines. To enumerate them would be too laborious a task. Toward the end of his life, when preparing for his passage from time to eternity, he wrote a book on the profound mysteries of the Sacrament of the Altar. He clearly shows the sweetness which inundated his soul when studying the Holy Scriptures, the purity of his faith, the liveliness of his hope, and the ardor of his love for God."[3]

In his work on the Sacrifice of the Mass Albert is at his best. The wondrous array of his learning is charged with the scalding unction of his glowing heart. The book seems to have been conceived and penned near the altar, in the soft light of the sanctuary lamp, so reverent is the tone throughout, so hushed the clangor of earthly interests, so surcharged with high feeling and virginal longing his every thought. Each sentence is written in starlight and the eternal tears of love. Indeed, Albert is always the expert theologian, familiar with the most sententious sayings of the Fathers and schoolmen on the subject, conversant with the mind and heart of the Church as she observes the divine etiquette which the King has established for His earthly courts.

Thus it comes that Albert weaves into his text historical facts and explanations that not only help us to understand the gradual growth of the liturgy but the spiritual significance of its smallest rubric. The bursting words of the liturgy are tapped for their strong sap of dogma and the meaning behind each rubric is, as it were, compared with the rubrics that angels observe before the great White Throne upon which the Lamb who was slain for us sits in the eternal Session at the right hand of the Father. Albert writes as if he saw. There is something stupendously awful about his remarks, like the words of a man who has looked death in the eyes. His every sentence pulses with life, vibrates with vitality. He gushes forth reasons of all kinds, mostly drawn from the rich literature of the Church on the subject, many drawn from the innermost caverns of his own adoring heart. If Albert had written no other line outside this book his name would be worthy of remembrance as one—a modern Moses—who, taking off his shoes in deepest awe, had drawn close to the Burning Bush on the Altar,

[3] Rodolphus de Novimagio, loc. cit.

stealing thence a flame to enkindle cold hearts. Like a child lost in wonderment before some masterpiece of art, genius, or nature, he asks questions which because of the fire within his heart are no longer puerile, misplaced, or irrelevant. He dissects and applies to the Mass the six motives why the patriarchs of old sighed for the coming of the Messiah. He discusses why the Kyrie is sung in Greek and not Latin; why a particular language is made use of; why the Councils of the Church—Constantinople, Nice, Antioch, and Ephesus—legislated so minutely on the subject; how Gregory the Great reduced to order the many customs of a local kind which, in every corner of the world, where the Mass was known, threatened to smother under a blanket of accidentals the substantial action; why the priest turns about, not all during the Sacred Action, as in Apostolic times, but only at the *Dominus vobiscum*, toward the people for whom the Mass must be a real social action; how the sequences arose at a time when men learned to sing in the consecrated Latin tongue because the heart within them would no longer be still; why the people stand at the Gospel and the Credo; why, like a procession of witnesses from the tomb, mentioned in turn by name, the Apostles and saints of the early Church, some wearing white garments, others with robes dyed in the carmine of Tyre and Bosra, pass through the Canon; why the living are recalled by name in the presence of Him who has their names written on the palm of His hands; why the dead who have died in the Lord are resurrected from the graves of our dark memories before Him who is the Resurrection and the Life eternal; why the Host is broken and a part of It dropped into the chalice; why the priest kisses the chalice at Communion time; why he communicates himself with two parts; why the Postcommunion is a real psalm of joy. And at the end of this superb hymn of the Eucharist Albert humbly remarks: "Such are, rapidly and in a few words, the thoughts we have tried to express on the Sacrifice of the Mass, leaving to more cultivated minds to write new and more sublime things concerning it."[4] Probably Albert knew before he died that one man had written better than even he on this subject, none other than his pupil, Thomas Aquinas, whom none has here excelled. But would Thomas ever have become the lutanist of the Eucharist without the long lessons he had had in the school of Albert—lessons

[4] Opp. XXXVIII, 1-199.

which for all we know, just because they were verbal and, therefore, more easily improvised, may have contained more fire than is locked up in this burning book? Aside from Thomas, the ages have produced nothing so redolent of the altar, so mellow with the "little red lights" of the sanctuary, as this masterpiece of the great master.[5]

In that work Albert promised his readers another, a fuller book, on the Eucharist, and in keeping his promise he tells us frankly what he had in mind to do: "Since there are many special difficulties touching the most Holy Sacrament of the Altar, we have reserved this subject to the last, in order to speak of it at leisure. And as we frequently apply to the Eucharist, in the Mass, the terms grace, gift, nourishment, communion, sometimes sacrifice, and often also sacrament, we shall divide the subject matter into six points, and examine all that is possible to be said on each of them according as God may be pleased to enlighten us."[6]

With the matter thus clearly divided for us, we are prepared for a systematic treatment which shall leave no detail out of count. And the fullness of the work is one only of its wonders. There is a lucidity and beauty of thought, a profundity of insight into the divine purposes of the Sacrament, an overpowering erudition culling the best sayings of the Fathers on the subject, a richness of allegorical reasoning and moralizing, an inventiveness in the comparison of types and antitypes, and a beauty and almost disarming simplicity of language that make this a real armory of Eucharistic dogma and erudition. The types, the matter and form, the institution and the effects of the Eucharist are set forth so extensively as to forestall some of the subtleties and inanities of future scholastics. But Albert was so impressed with the immensity of his task that he apologizes humbly in this wise: "A host of things which the human mind cannot grasp still remain hidden in the secrets of God; it behooves us to leave them to the light of the Holy Ghost, to the fervor of piety, without discoursing longer on them." And then, at the end, as if utterly disgusted interiorly with his work, he writes: "See what we have felt it incumbent on us to write concerning the most Holy Eucharist, for the honor of our Lord Jesus Christ; but how many beauties may still be found therein! Should the reader meet with

---

5 A. Franz, *Die Messe im deutschen Mittelalter* (Freiburg: 1902), 469 sq.

6 Opp. XXXVIII, 192, 432.

anything in our words which is not agreeable to him, let him refer it to our ignorance. Although what we have said has no claim to depth, he will nevertheless meet with much useful teaching therein. Amen."[7] One day Albert's favorite pupil, Thomas Aquinas, will feel just like his master after writing about the Eucharist. But with the flamboyant temper of the South he will take his book, not as Albert did to the bar of human opinion, but to Jesus Himself for approbation. And in his childlike faith he will hear in Naples from the altar: "Thou hast written well of Me, Thomas." But how well would Thomas have been able to write without the Eucharistic training given him by Albert?

But this belated disciple of the Unseen Master, walking with Him daily on the way to Emmaus for the breaking of the Bread, "felt his heart burning within him," and so ran to the city to tell those busy about many things that he "had seen the Lord." In order to enkindle the hearts of the people with love of the Eucharist, Albert prepared thirty-two sermons which have within them a living flame. No preacher could read them and be quite the same ever again. It is a Eucharistic repertoire where every aspect of the question is touched upon so directly and impressively as to make forcible speakers out of the poorest human stuff. Albert explains his purpose in publishing the sermons in this wise: "Out of all that we have said, established, and proved by the most lucid passages of Scripture, there have sprung, with God's help, a multitude of sermons. Sometimes one, sometimes another, or at least one portion or other of these homilies will, according to time and place, serve to confirm faith in souls, or to perfect life and piety in them."[8] He divides the matter into seven sections which set forth each portion of the doctrine in a complete and continuous whole. He treats in turn of the end of the institution of the Sacrament as a commemoration of Christ's sufferings; a sacrifice and a spiritual food; the form under which Christ left this Sacrament; the wonders of divine power gleaming forth in the Eucharist; the dispositions necessary for its reception, such as faith, purity, and devotion; various ways of receiving it, sacramentally (as do the unworthy who possess it without the effects of grace), spiritually (like the devout who cannot receive it in reality); and sacramentally and

[7] *Ibid.*, 432.

[8] Opp. XIII, 699-797; G. Meersemann, *Introductio*, 113-116.

spiritually combined; the effects of the Sacrament are twelve, to offset the twelve evils of life: temptations of the devil, resistance of the passions, the stains of the heart, the offense of God, the feebleness of self-knowledge, feebleness of love for one's neighbor, the loss of interior sweetness, weakness in safeguarding good, the cause of eternal death, the rapid disfigurement of a virtuous life, exile in the midst of earthly miseries, the conversion of all matter into ashes on the last day. Finally, Albert treats of the merit, utility, and sweetness of the Precious Blood and how it deserves to be remembered, respected, and desired by men—this last subject a favorite one in those violent days when men, conscious of their guilt, sought to arouse themselves to sorrow and conversion, not so much by a contemplation of Christ's mercy, as by a pondering upon His bitter sufferings in which there was health abounding.

What strikes us in a careful study of these three Eucharistic works is the astounding fullness and variety of knowledge Albert possesses on the subject. In this respect he has displayed far more extensive erudition than Thomas Aquinas, who seems to have focused the bright light of his mind on finding reasons and arguments for bolstering up our faith in this august mystery. No doubt, in other places Thomas does discover an attitude toward the Eucharist which does not appear so clearly from Albert's treatment of this dogma in the eighty-four wonderful questions which have been rightly considered the highest flight of his genius. If Albert falls behind his pupil in this respect, it must be insisted upon that there is in his works a breath of personal devotion, an appeal to the unwavering voice of the Church, a utilization of those familiar arguments and objects which bring the Blessed Eucharist up to the very portals of the soul. The general impression of this Eucharistic cycle is very much like that produced upon an unexperienced man when a wise old pedagogue, out of the fullness of his thoughts, study, and experience, lets gush forth the Niagara of his knowledge on his favorite subject or dogma, to sweep him along despite himself. One admires and wonders at the reasoning acumen of Thomas and never more so than when he treats of this Sacrament. One loves Albert for treating the subject the way he did. He does not require you to bend yourself to hard thought in order to know and understand what he is saying as Thomas does. He beguiles you along the way with arguments you can understand without much labor, pointing out hidden meanings of the thousands of things to be seen and heard and experienced in this pleasant and refreshing sanctuary spot; and then smiles benignantly when you cast yourself down and adore. Thomas has eliminated almost everything but pure reasoning from his workshop, except for the stately magnificence of his liturgical Eucharistic writings—Albert's workshop is like an inviting porch affording a view down the centuries to the Upper Chamber where Jesus did the ineffable thing of changing, for the first time, bread and wine into His Body and Blood. And if in the marvel of the vision you cannot hear reverberating so distinctly as in Thomas's laboratory the words of the Master, it is because your ears are filled with the music of the Catholic centuries and your eyes are holden by the star dust which Albert has raised by the rush of all nature to the feet of its God and by the dust clouds swirled up by the throngs he makes to fall down in loving adoration upon the ground of this daily Bethlehem.

A young man could never have written of the Eucharist as Albert did. There is, in his approach to the subject and his handling of it, too much of the psychology of the human heart, too great a reservoir of reverence for the teaching of past ages, and too great a pride in the good sense and uprightness of average men who honored themselves by loving Jesus in His Eucharistic disguise. Without seeking to be comforting Albert puts a soothing hand on your troubled spirit. Without aiming at edifying you by what he says he makes you fall in love with Jesus for the sheer pleasure of it all. Without an attempt at forcing the consent of your mind he evokes the affection of your heart. Here is the manly but tender mysticism of the North, without rhapsodies and apostrophies, without hesitations and inner debates, without half loyalties or divided attachments. Man here is face to face with the Man—the Ideal Man dreamed of by Plato in *Phaedrus*, and Aristotle in the *Nicomachaean Ethics*, and Virgil in the *Fourth Eclogue*—*Ecce Homo*—in the ***Häuschen***, or Little House, as the artists of Nurnberg, contemporaries of Albert, in their holy loving familiarity with the Great Guest, called the humble place of His tenting with poor travelers in this miserable world. Albert is astounding in many places in his many tomes: he is overpowering on every page of his Eucharistic works.

This frankly Eucharistic crusade made Albert tremendously popular with the people who, with their unerring Catholic instinct, always take to their heart of hearts every priest who labors at increasing love toward Him who rewards His own, even in this present time, with spiritual delights and consolations. But Albert was not satisfied. From the testimony of Peter of Prussia we know that he composed many Eucharistic prayers for general circulation among the masses. Unfortunately, all but three of these popular prayers have been lost, of which one reads as follows:

"Hail, Salvation of the world, Word of the Father, true Host, Living Flesh, integral Deity, true Man. May we, incorporated in Thee, merit to be offered to Thy Divine Majesty, near Thy Body which is at the right hand of the Father. May we, united with Thee, be sharers of a blessed eternity, partakers in Thy bliss and beneficiaries of Thy Incarnation; for Thine is the glory of all ages."[9] Rudolf of Nijmegen vouchsafes the further information that Albert composed several liturgical Offices of the Blessed Eucharist which either have not come down to us or have not yet been discovered.[10] This is very probable, for in the Eucharistic renaissance which marked the thirteenth century, as a consequence of the institution of the Feast of Corpus Christi, there are records of many men who were thus engaged—St. Bonaventure, for instance, and then Pope Urban IV, who, as a simple professor in his native land, had written an Office for the diocesan celebration of this carnival of the Lord at the request of St. Juliana of Mont Cornillon. It has been established beyond the peradventure of a doubt that St. Thomas relied upon an old Eucharistic Office, used among the Cistercians, in the composition of his own superb work. Perhaps it is not too rash to maintain that the Angelic Doctor, not feeling that it was necessary to go so far afield for models, laid Albert's Office under contribution or, perhaps, drew from it suggestion and inspiration.

The second characteristic devotional practice of Albert's spiritual

---

[9] Petrus de Prussia, Vita ad finem.

[10] Rodolphus de Novimagio, *Legenda* 61-62; G. Meersemann, *Introductio*, 123; Karl Richstaetter, S.J., points out (*Illustrious Friends, of the Sacred Heart*, St. Louis, 1930, 113-121), that "it is precisely as a keen observer of nature that the blessed man has become of importance for the devotion to the Sacred Heart. In commenting on the passage in St. John's Gospel, which says that on the opening of the Lord's side Blood and Water flowed forth, he notes the marvel that the Sacred Blood could flow, although generally when the body has grown cold it ceases to circulate and stops flowing. This thought was now taken up by the mystics, and also by David of Augsburg, and directed to the Sacred Heart of the Savior."

life was his tender love of the Mother of God. There is nothing quite so attractive about the character of Albert, and of his piety, too, as his love for the Blessed Virgin. Just as a thoroughly corrupt man has a low estimate of woman, so a poor Christian has a mean devotion, if any at all, to the Blessed Mother. Devotion to Mary is the test of Catholic piety. And if, despite all the weakness and violence of the Middle Ages we find them full of chivalric, sometimes mawkishly sentimental, respect for women and a genuine and spontaneous love for Mary, we may be sure that cynicism and moral perversion could have no chance to eat at their fundamentally sound heart.

Now Albert is in no respect so much a man, a typical child of his age, as in his love of Mary. There is a childlikeness and a very freshness of the morning of life about his devotion to her. Rudolf of Nijmegen says: "Albert was so devoted to the holy Mother of God that he could not conceal her praises, and he, moreover, appended to all his works something in praise of his beloved Lady, or closed his studies with a song to her glory. He composed many sequences in honor of the glorious Virgin which are as remarkable for their depth of meaning as for their harmony and interior spirit.

In the convent garden and elsewhere he delighted to sing them with intense sweetness, devotion, and enthusiasm. His sighs and tears would often interrupt his song, and thus disclose his fervor, love, and ardent piety."[11] Now, surely, the man who hunts out quiet lanes for solitary walks with an unseen presence, who is ravished out of himself by the speechless eloquence his inner ear is listening to, who sighs for the day when the veil will be torn away for him to see in wonder the one whose beauty he has long contemplated, who weeps like a homesick child for the mother's embrace and kiss, and the folding to the big mother heart, surely, such a one is madly in love.

And need we wonder that he preached the beauties of this Mother wherever he went. Albert had a distinctly social purpose in mind in preaching Mary. Europe was then rough with the boisterousness of its healthy, unspoiled youth. It was willful, stubborn, spiteful, cruel, like any child that has gone beyond bounds. It must be tamed by a penance that saves itself from cruelty through devotion to her who is sweetness and tenderness. Chivalry simpered off into sentimentality and thus

---

[11] Rodolphus de Novimagio, *Legenda* 22.

became a snare. It was not ensouled and informed with religion. Devotion to Mary, however, is chivalry at its best, purified and sustained by the true religion and by the authentic example of Jesus, on which it is based. If Albert's preaching struck home to the hearts of the people surely, directly, and unfailingly, it was because without saying so to the masses, it gave them in abundant measure what their Catholic piety, chilled momentarily by the conditions of the times, made it impossible for them to put into intelligible words.

And just because there was an ideal which the people longed for without knowing how to ask for it, there lay at the very core of medieval mirth and gayety an infinite wistfulness, a kind of subtle loneliness and poignancy, a sorrow all-pervading and all-consuming to which, like a wise physician, Albert applied a soothing salve in such words as these: "Mary became without sorrow, in solitude, the retreat of the Word, the nuptial bed of the Eternal Betrothed, the palace of the Son of God and of the Great King, the tent of the Holy Trinity. Let us, then, praise her frequently and wisely. Frequently, that she may never be separated either from our hearts or our lips, as Isaias says: 'Sing well, sing many a song, that thou mayest be remembered' (xxiii. 16). Wisely, that our praises may be sincere, lest she one day say of us: 'This people honoreth Me with their lips, but their hearts are far from Me: they praise Me without reason.' Wisely, in such a manner that he who praises may resemble her who is praised, and that this praise may be the faithful expression of the heart. How, indeed, can the voluptuous praise the Virgin? How can the proud man praise her who was humble? How can the cursed praise her who was loaded with heavenly blessings?"[12]

Here, then, was a hero, an ideal within reach of men who were dreaming dreams of big deeds and achievements. Mary was no longer far off but so very near that she cast a glory and a glamour over the most prosaic and workaday tasks of life. Is it passing strange, therefore, that Albert's Marian sermons are one long litany of the honorable titles which the Catholic heart has blurted out in the transports of its joy over finding her? Is it childish that by asking all kinds of minute questions about her nature, endowments, prerogatives, offices, and interventions in the affairs of men, these sermons familiarized the

[12] Petrus de Prussia, *Vita*, 193.

people with her who achieved the dreams they were cherishing? Is it reprehensible that in speaking to a young, ardent, and romantic people these sermons should embody strange tales and impossible stories drawn from the monotonous life of the masses? Is it dramatic pose that at the end, as if in sheer exhaustion from the effort of praising her in a fitting way, these sermons should die out in something like a jangle, a prayer like this: "Enlighten my understanding, give me a right conception, a vigorous mind, true knowledge, a firm faith with corresponding speech, which will convey grace to my hearers; speech which will tend to the establishment of the Faith, the edification of holy Church, and the honor of the sacred Name of your Son our Lord Jesus Christ; speech which will not fail to proclaim your praises and to declare your mercies. May this speech, O Mary, tell again and again that you cease not to load with the gifts of your mercy an unworthy sinner like myself, and to manifest through his mouth the prodigies of your omnipotence."[13]

Albert's Marian sermons exercised a tremendous influence on all people in quest of an ideal. They were forthwith translated into German, even into some of its rich and picturesque dialects. They were cut up in pieces and circulated among the people as bookmarks, and even mottoes for the walls of homes. If there is such a tender note in the German mystics, such a marked devotion to the joys and sorrows of Mary, such an echo of sweet songs as one remembers from the golden age of childhood when one believed all because one saw all and felt all as an immediately present and intimately personal experience, it is in great measure due to the bewitching and seductive joyousness or plaintiveness of Albert's Marian sermons.[14] They appealed to children because they breathed love; they were drunk up by sinners because they distilled mercy; the ignorant understood them because they abounded with new visions of a fresh world. The piety of the ages fed upon them to good effect, especially when it sought more substantial food than mere pious fancies and sentimental exaggerations. Our own day is returning to them for suggestion and inspiration in such new phases of Marian devotion as her physical

---

[13] *Ibid.*, 90.

[14] B. Greith, *Die deutsche Mystik im Prediger-Orden* (München: 1871), 137-146; F. Le Bachelet, in *Dictionnaire de Théologie Catholique* (1923), VII, 1040-1050; 1055-1066.

mediation in the affairs of men.[15] If devotion to Our Lady is to escape from some of the prettiness introduced by leaders who repose more faith in pious reflections than in dogmatic statements, Albert can well be taken as a guide and master. His *Mariale* is an encyclopedia of dogmatic teaching, patristic erudition, historical facts and anecdotes, expressions of personal devotion, and pious reflections on Our Lady. In two hundred and thirty questions, all clearly and logically divided up, he covers the whole field with surprising clearness and originality.

But he was not satisfied with such a formal heralding of Mary's greatness and nearness to us. She obsessed his thoughts. No matter how deeply he had plunged into the depths of philosophical investigation, no matter how high he had soared into the dazzling light of theological speculation, Albert can always pause to gaze upon the bright, untroubled face of Mary. In his masterful *Commentary on the Sentences of the Lombard* there is a fund of dogmatic and ascetical thought on Mary. He had inserted in his unedited book *De Bono sive de Virtutibus* a beautiful little treatise on Mary's virginity.[16] An unpublished *Commentary on the Hail Mary* puts him in the company of those great saints and thinkers of all Catholic ages who have seen in this prayer the best prayer after the Our Father which it is given man to utter.[17] He has written more on Our Lady than any single scholastic. And he has written better on Mary than any man of his age, probably as well as any man in any age. And he discovers to us the spirit and purpose in all he said and wrote about the Blessed Virgin in these frank, manly words:

> "It is written (Eccles. xxiv. 29-31): 'They that eat Me shall yet hunger: and they that drink Me shall yet thirst. He that harkeneth to Me shall not be confounded: and they that work by Me shall not sin. They that explain Me shall have life everlasting.' It is in hope

---

[15] G. Esser, "*Die Gnadenfülle der Allerseligsten Jungfrau Maria nach der Lehre des sel. Albertus des Grossen,*" in *Theologisch-Praktische Quartalsschrift (1881), 273-288; H. Albers, "La Mediacion de la S. Virgen segun el B. Alberto Magno," in* La Vida Sobrenatural (1929), 244-264; 312-325; 370-377; (1930), 15-23; 171-176; J. M. Bover, "*La Mediacion universal de la Santissima Virgen en las obras del B. Alberto Magno,*" in *Gregorianum (1926), 511-548.*

[16] *M. Grabmann,* L'Influsso di Alberto Magno sulla Vita Intellettuale del Medio Evo (Roma: 1931), 56.

[17] *Ibid.*, 57.

of these promised riches that we undertake this work; otherwise we should be too much exalted above our narrowness of mind and knowledge. But we know that God's arm is not shortened, and that everything, on the contrary, is possible to him who has faith. The work that we are entering upon portrays the beginning of our Lord's Incarnation and the mystery of our Redemption. We undertake it for the praise and glory of the most illustrious of all creatures, the honor of the incomparable Virgin Mother of God, full of faith in her special help and mercy, who is the surest anchor of our hope. It is from her that we expect the happy completion and reward of our task. It is she who guides our wills, who determines us to write, and who knows our intentions. We implore, then, above all, the mercy of God, the Father Almighty, who dwells in the inaccessible abode of the Divine brightness, to dispel, by the splendor of His light, the illusions of error, deceits of falsehood, the desire of vainglory. May He vouchsafe to enable us to see what is right, and to declare what is true regarding the Mother of mercy and of truth itself. We also pray those who read this book not to attribute to our presumption anything which, through its novelty, may be a scandal to them, but rather patiently to bear with the seeming exaggerations of our unbounded devotion. God forbid that we should exalt the glorious Virgin through falsehood, or that we should use emphatic language to speak new and abstruse things to the educated, and to seek thereby, not the glory of the incomparable Queen of Heaven, but our own gratification. We are desirous only to render ourselves useful, through these unpretending pages, to simple and untaught people, like ourselves. Having nothing more worthy to offer to our beloved Sovereign in our misery and ignorance we shall be exceeding glad if they who are more gifted would take occasion to speak of her and to proclaim her praises."[18]

Thus, in the acute realization of his own unworthiness to sing the praises of Mary, Albert discovers to us how near he had drawn to the heart of the "handmaid of the Lord."

Now, as Mary did not hesitate or blush to serve actively in the house of St. Elizabeth, proving thereby that she considered herself the

[18] Opp. XX.

servant of God's servants, so Albert was not content to have his devotion to Mary to consist merely in pious sentiments or ineffectual words. Hence he fostered the custom of erecting altars of the Blessed Mother in the sanctuary of the home and of placing her picture or statue at the crossroads to remind the traveler of the land beyond the stars; he encouraged the practise of pilgrimages to the shrines of Mary which dotted the fair surface of the fatherland; he suggested a more universal imposition of the name Mary on children at baptism, following in his exhortations the line of argumentation which St. John Chrysostom had used with such good effect centuries before; he stressed the need, and as bishop legislated in favor of a more intense observance of the Marian feast days; he sought to spread wherever he went the custom of fasting, or at least of abstinence, on Saturdays in honor of Our Lady.[19]

And he did not exclude St. Joseph from his Marian devotion, following in this an instinct of his Order. Hence, when centuries later Isidore of Isolanis, O.P., wrote the first systematic theological treatise on the spiritual prerogatives of the Foster Father he frequently invoked the authority, words, and example of Albert. All the historians of popular devotion to St. Joseph, especially J. Seitz, insist that the Office in honor of St. Joseph which Albert is known to have composed, although it has not as yet been rescued from the libraries, exercised a great influence upon the liturgical honors paid to the Foster Father of Christ in the Occidental Church, which in this matter was centuries behind the Oriental Churches.

---

[19] "*Quia tunc* (feria 4 ante Pascha) venditus fuit Dominus, ideo in jejunio quod fit in honore passionis post sextam feriam (in qua crucifixus est Dominus) secundum locum tenet quarta feria in qua traditus et venditus. Sed qui jejunat in honore Virginis matris sabbato, jejunat congruentius: quia illa die ceteris dubitantibus, fides in ea stetit; et ideo in sabbato inolevit consuetudo solemnizare de Gloriosa Virgine." Opp. xxl, 154.

CHAPTER XII
MARTYR OF THE PEN

NO MEDIEVAL schoolman wrote at greater length and on more diverse subjects than Albert. He stated in scientific terms and tried to reduce to a system everything that was known to his contemporaries of the Christian Occident. He introduced to the West much knowledge and erudition which so far had been jealously guarded by the Muslims in Spain. His body of writings is the most colossal encyclopedia ever undertaken and carried through by a single individual. The Paris edition of his works, published in 1890 and following years, fills thirty-eight quarto volumes, in double column, of several hundred pages each. Since that time several works, not included in the Paris edition, have been discovered and published separately.

Many treatises incorporated in the Paris edition are not from Albert's pen. Up to the present time the authorship of several of these works has been established in favor of some other writer. There are other works in the Paris edition which are undoubtedly spurious, others uncertain.

But by way of compensation there are fragments, sometimes treatises of Albert's works, in some of the big collections of other medieval authors—as, for instance, the *De Fato* included among the works of St. Thomas Aquinas.

There are at the very least ten quarto volumes of unedited works by Albert in various libraries of Europe;[1] in other words, more than four thousand closely printed pages in double column. Scholars are busy today ferreting out these supposedly lost works of Albert. Not all the works mentioned in the catalogs of Albert's productions have been discovered, or else they have been discovered in part only. There are other scholars engaged in editing works of Albert about whose existence in manuscript form there was never any doubt. Much

[1] G. Meersemann, Le Opere Edite e Inedite del B. Alberto Magno (Memorie Domenicane), (1931), 431, says: "*Tuttavia quel cumulo di volumi non comprende tutta la grande opera albertina, ma a quei volumi editi, dobbiamo aggiungere per lo meno 10 volumi inediti.*"

research is necessary to gather the sermons of Albert written in the vernacular and the many prayers he composed for the people.

A splendid survey of the present state of Albertinian investigation is the learned work by G. Meersemann, *Introductio ad Opera Omnia Beati Alberti Magni* (Bruges: 1931). It is final as far as it goes and affords us a good idea of what remains to be done before we can hope to possess everything Albert wrote. Since the short time of its appearance several discoveries of new and reputedly lost works of Albert have been made.[2]

The Goerresgesellschaft, or Society of German Catholic Savants, at its annual convention at Cologne, in 1931, undertook a critical and definitive edition of Albert's complete works, setting aside for this purpose a fund of money and gathering together a corps of specialists.[3] This edition will be carried on along the lines and in the spirit of the *Monumenta Germaniae Historica*, which has been in course of publication at government expense for more than one hundred years. Each member of this body of editors will make it his life's work to study, compare with existing manuscripts or editions, annotate, illustrate, and explain at least one of Albert's works. Carl Jessen, in 1867, afforded a model in his critical edition of Albert's *De Vegetalibus*. And Hermann Stadler, in 1916, published a critical edition of Albert's *De Animalibus*, in which the use of various kinds of type shows in an instant just what parts of the work are original contributions of Albert's, what other parts, even sentences, are paraphrases of Aristotle by Albert or are borrowed verbatim from other writers. If the final edition follows the style of typography and the critical norms of Stadler, the learned world will be in a position some day to judge justly the stupendous literary output of Albert.

The chronology of Albert's work is, perhaps, one of the most teasing of interesting puzzles in the contemporary literary world. At the present time there is great confusion in this field of investigation. But the difficulties are not insoluble. For we are fortunate in possessing a catalog of Albert's works dating back to within a few decades of his death, the so-called *Catalogue of Stams*, discovered about forty years ago

---

[2] G. Meersemann, "De S. Alberti Magni Postilla super Jeremiam inedita," in *Angelicum (1932), 1-20; M. Grabmann,* L'Influsso di Alberto Magno sulla Vita Intellettuale del Medio Evo (Roma: 1931), passim.

[3] M. Weiss, "*Rückblick auf den 15. November, 1930,*" in *Archivum Frat. Praed., (1932), I, 437-469.*

in a Swiss Benedictine library by Father Henry Denifle, O.P., the internationally known medievalist. This official catalog is supplemented by others dressed by half a dozen writers of the thirteenth and fourteenth centuries. Father Franz Pelster, S.J., and Dr. Heribert Scheeben have devoted years of labor to the task of bringing a little order and light to the task.[4] But much remains to be done, and necessarily so, for otherwise we shall never be in a position to follow the intellectual growth of Albert's mind, nor the development of his teaching, nor the literary influences to which he was submitted. Until we are absolutely clear on these matters there must needs be gaps in the story of Albert's life, as also uncertainties in the history of his mental growth and literary productiveness. As matters stand at the present moment, we are safe in adopting the tentative chronology of Mandonnet.[5] Albert's books on the natural sciences were composed in the period of years from 1240 to 1256. His *Commentary on the Sentences of Peter Lombard* falls certainly between the years 1247 and 1249. His *Summa Theologica*, especially the latter part of what was actually written by Albert, must be dated after the year 1274, for he speaks in this work of a condemnation pronounced at the Council of Lyons at which he was present.

Perhaps the best, quickest, and surest way of arriving at a just appreciation of the tremendous literary output of Albert is to divide up his known works (whether edited or unedited) into two series or categories—the profane and the sacred writings.

PROFANE WRITINGS

The profane writings of Albert contain a course on philosophy in forty-five books. In this first peripatetic course he explained the doctrine of Aristotle for the purpose of making the Stagirite accessible

---

[4] *M. Weiss,* Primordia Novae Bibliographiae B. Alberti Magni (Parisiis: 1905); de Loe, "*De Vita et Scriptis B. Alberti Magni,*" in *Analecta Bollandiana (1902),* 301-371; P. Mandonnet, Revue Thomiste (1897), 95-106; F. Pelster, "*Zur Datierung einiger Schriften Alberts des Grossen,*" in *Zeitschrift für katholische Theologie (1923), 475-482; H. Scheeben, "Les Ecrits d'Albert d'apres les Catalogues," in* Revue Thomiste (1931), 37-68; M. M. Gorce, ibid., 69-78; H. Scheeben, "*Die Tabulae Ludwigs von Valladolid im Chor der Prediger-Brüder von St. Jacob in Paris,*" in *Archivum Frat. Praed. (1932), 223-265; G. Meersemann,* Introductio ad Opera Omnia B. Alberti Magni (Bruges: 1931).

[5] P. Mandonnet, "*Albert le Grand.,*" in *Dictionnaire de Théologie Catholique.*

and understandable to the western world—*Latinis reddidit intelligibilem.* There is no doubt that in Albert's time certain texts of Aristotle were known to scholars. But these texts had been tampered with by the Muslim commentators in Spain. Hence, their use in Christian schools was forbidden by the Council of Sens in 1210, and five years later by Robert de Courcon, who had been sent to Paris by the Pope to look into this very matter. In 1231 Pope Gregory IX renewed the prohibition with the reserve "until these works are expurgated of all the errors they contain contrary to the Christian faith." On this occasion the Pope appointed a Commission of three men to procure a correct text, but they never put their hands to the difficult task.

Scholars had tasted enough of Aristotle to whet their curiosity. In face of the papal prohibition there was nothing to do but read Aristotle secretly. It was forbidden to mention his name from the pulpit or in the classroom. But there was nothing to prohibit professors giving an outline of his thought, refuting his errors, utilizing his methods. Indeed, this artful dodge was resorted to in many schools. But it was a subterfuge fraught with many dangers for those who were being prepared to be the intellectual leaders of the time. Since the texts of Aristotle were rare and expensive, since the copies in circulation were horribly vitiated by the errors of Arabian commentators, since the Christian professors possessing these versions were careful not to be seen reading them publicly, much less circulating them among their students, it is easy to see that it was next to impossible to hope for a correct or emended reading. Students, on the other hand, could not control the exposition of Aristotle's thought put forward by professors. The professors, who either did not understand the Stagirite or did not own a copy of his works, were practically safe, as far as their students were concerned, in giving what was or purported to be the genuine and authentic mind of the great philosopher. It is only on this assumption that we can satisfactorily explain the unchallenged entrance into Christian schools of forms of Aristotelianism which were the boldest travesty of the Greek's thought. The interpolations of the Muslim commentators were proposed to students as integral parts of the original text. And even the wary and suspicious students could not "check up" on their professors because they possessed no texts. Even if they were fortunate enough to lay hand upon one, they dared not admit or confess it openly, for fear of the consequences provided for by the papal prohibition. It was, forsooth, a delicate and dangerous situation. Aristotle enjoyed little chance of being fairly and honestly expounded by Christian masters. The secrecy to which students must perforce resort in order to arrive at the true doctrine of Aristotle begot a sneaky, furtive, double-faced temper and attitude toward all learning. And a dishonest scholar is a social menace, because a poisoner of the springs of knowledge at which all are asked to drink.

Albert set out to render Aristotle intelligible to the West in the face of much opposition in his own Order, as a careful reading of *The Lives of the Brethren* clearly shows. For the frequent mention of apparitions to the brethren, in which they were warned against following the new learning, was nothing else than a subtle campaign against Aristotle and the introduction of his methods into the schools. But Albert was not deterred by these whisperings among his own, nor yet by the frank opposition of that body of scholars who stood pledged to the Platonico-Augustinian system of teaching, represented in Paris by Stephen Tempier and at Oxford by Richard Kilwardby. The safety of learning and the integrity of teaching methods were at stake. Albert saw the need of interpreting in an impersonal way the books of the Stagirite. It was of supreme moment, not to give his own interpretations of any body of knowledge, but to offer the authentic doctrine of Aristotle which had suffered so much at the hands of those Muslim commentators who, while they did not respect the texts of his works, arrogated to themselves the exclusive understanding of his thought. It was difficult to supply correct and amended texts, though Albert did busy himself in trying to find the best transcriptions available.[6] He was nevertheless forced to use texts which had been distinctly tampered with. In rejecting interpolated readings and inserted comments, Albert displayed a really astounding critical sense—no medieval scholar, not even the Bishop of Lincoln, Robert Grosseteste, can compare with him.[7]

[6] *Quae diligenter quaesivi per diversas mundi regiones, Miner.*, III, tr. 1, Chap. 1.

[7] *Quod de actore quidam quaerunt, supervacuum est, et nunquam ab aliquo philosopho quaesitum est, nisi in schola Pythagorae; quia in illius schola nihil recipiebatur nisi quod fecisset Pythagoras; ab aliis autem quaesitum non est; a quocumque enim dicta erant recipiebantur, dum probatae veritatis haberent rationem. Causa etiam efficiens extra est, et ab ea neque habet res firmitatem neque infirmitatem, sed potius a ratione dictorum.* (*Comment. in Perihermeneias Arist. in principio.*) For other examples of this same spirit in Albert, see *De Somno et Vigilia (III, tr. I, Chap. 12);* De Causis (in principio); *De Animalibus (in fine)*; VIII *Physic*, (tr. I, Chap. 14); IV *Metaph. (tr. III, Chap. 2);* Summa Theol. (tr. 1,

There is something undeniably uncanny about Albert's manipulation of these faulty versions. But most of his fine critical sense is expended in paraphrasing the words of Aristotle in a Christian sense, emending or else interpreting in an orthodox way, not only the Greek but also his unscrupulous commentators. This task of emending the Stagirite's thought was done with a reverence which shows the natural probity of Albert's mind as well as his preoccupation to safeguard the claims of Catholic teaching.

Never has an author been treated with more honest understanding. Never has an author been approached by a disciple more concerned about reproducing faithfully his authentic thought. It has been frequently admitted by scholars that from Albert's paraphrase we could build up with astonishing fullness the philosophic doctrine of Aristotle.[8] And if those who were using Aristotle for their own ends in the thirteenth and subsequent centuries persisted in calling Albert "the ape of Aristotle," they were unwittingly bearing witness to the fidelity and success with which he had accomplished the work he had set out to do. For Albert made Aristotle speak his own language and discover his own thought. And in his great commentaries, where we find little treatises, or *digressiones* as they are called, where errors are corrected, he taught the pagan professor to talk as a Christian. This adaptation, this working over his thought into a Christian text which could be used with safety in any school, is one of the finest specimens of scholarship ever vouchsafed to man. Taken alone, this achievement would entitle Albert to a prominent and permanent place in the history of thought and science. He preserved the Stagirite from the perversions of those who posed as his intellectual friends and heirs. He made Aristotle greater than he had ever dreamed of being or becoming—an unbaptized Father of the Church.

Following the divisions of Aristotle, Albert divided philosophy into the following three parts:

I. *Rational* philosophy, or dialectics, comprising eleven books in which the mental operations were discovered from every angle.

II. *Real* philosophy, or speculative or theoretical philosophy, which

---

ques. 4, art. 5); De Natura et Origine Animae (tr. 1, Chap. 2).

[8] M. Grabmann, "*Ist das philosophische Universalgenie bei Heinrich dem Poeten Thomas von Aquin?,*" in *Historisches Jahrbuch (1917), 316 sq.*

was subdivided into three sections: (A) Physics, in twenty-two books; (B) Mathematics, comprising books on arithmetic, music, geometry, and astronomy, none of which have been printed in either Jammy's or Borgnet's editions of Albert's complete works; (C) Metaphysics, consisting of thirteen books of paraphrase, to which are added treatises on *De Causis Procli* and on *De Natura Deorum* which are not found in the printed editions.

III. *Moral* philosophy, consisting of Albert's commentaries in forty-five books on Aristotle's treatises on *Ethics, Economics,* and *Politics.* Albert is at his best here, especially as regards the orderliness of his procedure, his keen insight into psychological questions of conduct, and his stern insistence on logical methods in order to discover a rational basis for all problems of morality.[9] In reading over these commentaries one senses a kind of lurking affection in Albert for this part of Aristotle. Not only are the commentaries fuller and more all-embracing in outlook, more profound in thought, but there is present a note of immediacy and actuality which may have been induced in Albert by a sight of the social disorder encircling him, which literally clamored for norms and formulas, for self-discipline and self-government; in other words, for personal morality, ethical principles in commerce and statecraft. Albert maintained here, as everywhere else in his paraphrase of Aristotle, an admirable and marked impersonal tone and attitude, vouchsafing rarely an opinion of his own, which, no doubt, he felt he was not called upon to do since this adaptation was intended for professors who were supposed to be familiar with the main features of the Greek's thought. But in reading these commentaries one senses that for all his aloofness and detachment Albert never lost sight, for so much as one moment of the times in which he lived and the social conditions among which he worked.

But Albert also prepared a second course of philosophy, intended mainly for students. The fragments which have so far been discovered would appear to be the notes, or *reportata*, of the students who sat spellbound at his feet, taking down his lectures. Albert was good-hearted enough to look over these extensive notes, to make sure that

---

[9] Odon Lottin, "*Le Rôle de la Raison dans l'Ethique d'Albert le Grand,*" *in* Alberto Magno. Atti della Settimana Albertina (1932), 153-177; A. M. Rohner: "*Kommentar des hl. Albertus Magnus zur Einführung in die Politic des Aristoteles*" in *Divus Thomas (Freiburg: 1932), 95-109.*

his students were reporting his lectures adequately and faithfully. Recently such a body of notes in the handwriting of St. Thomas Aquinas, with corrections and additions by Albert, was discovered. These lectures were intended to show his eager students how to apply the Aristotelian method which he had preconized and sponsored. He analyzes with fine precision and acuteness the text of Aristotle. He delivers his own judgments on what the Stagirite taught. He shows how to lay under contribution for Christian purposes the immense riches of the Greek philosopher. Although only a very small part of this course of philosophy has been published by Monsignor A. Pelzer and Father Franz Pelster, S.J., we do possess sufficient excerpts of Albert on the *Nicomachaean Ethics* to be convinced that a just appreciation of his philosophical eminence must depend upon a conscientious study of this course. The remaining lectures of Albert, which are so indispensable for an appreciation of his own insight, penetration, and originality, are being searched for diligently at the present time. There are enough hints in the catalogs of manuscripts in some of the older libraries of Europe to give grounds for hope that sooner or later we shall be in possession of all, or the greater part, of this extremely valuable corpus of his philosophical teaching.[10]

SACRED WRITINGS

The sacred writings of Albert fall into three large categories and comprise the bulk of his literary output.

I. *Biblical Writings.* A rather full knowledge of the Bible was presupposed on the part of every medieval ecclesiastical student, since the Scriptures were rightly looked upon as the chief source of theology. Every theological professor began his career by expounding the Bible

---

[10] *Drei ungedruckte Teile der Summa de Creaturis Alberts des Grossen (Leipzig: 1919); M. Grabmann,* L'influsso, 35-40; A. Pelzer, "*Le Courts inédit d'Albert le Grand sur la Morale à Nicomaque,*" in *Revue Néo-Scolastique (1922), 333-361; 479-520; M. Grabmann, "Die Stuttgarter Handschrift des ungedruckten Ethikkommentars Alberts des Grossen,*" in *Ethik und Leben (Münster: 1931), 55-65; F. Pelster, "Alberts des Grossen neu aufgefundene Quastionen zu den aristotelischen Schriften,*" in *Zeitschrift für katholische Theologie (1922), 332-334; F. Pelster, "Der Tractatus de Natura Boni,*" in *Theologische Quartalschrift (1920), 64-90; F. Pelster, "Neue philosophische Schriften Alberts des Grossen,*" in *Philosophisches Jahrbuch (1923), 150 sq.; A. Birkenmajer, "Zur Bibliographie Alberts des Grossen," ibid. (1924), 270-272.*

during several years, when he was referred to as the *lector sacrae paginae*. His auditors were known as the *Biblici*.[11] Now, most of the Biblical teaching consisted in a search for the various meanings of the inspired words: the literal, the allegorical, or the moral sense, as they were called. There was no concern about textual criticism of the Bible and those cognate and auxiliary sciences of history, chronology, and comparative religions, which arose later on as there was need to refute heretics who assailed the revealed word of God.

Albert wrote extensive commentaries on the Four Gospels, on the Apocalypse, the Psalms, Job, Daniel, the Twelve Minor Prophets, Baruch, and on the eleventh chapter of Proverbs which he published under the name, *The Valiant Woman*. His unedited commentaries are upon the Canticle of Canticles, Isaias, Jeremias, Ezechiel, and the Epistles of St. Paul.[12]

Except in the case of the Psalms, Albert abandoned the moral interpretation of the Scriptures, preferring an exposition of the literal sense of the text. He rarely used the allegorical sense, though he showed in *The Valiant Woman* what we might have expected from him in this respect. Frequently, whenever occasion presented, he inserted dogmatic dissertations into his commentaries, as might be suggested by the text he was explaining. These are done with fine artistry and a masterful insight into the dogmatic content of the words of the Scriptures. In this respect he was surpassed by few men of his age. He used and perfected the method which his friend, Hugh of St. Cher, had introduced into the schools. For he was the first to divide and subdivide the text for the sake of clearness. What Albert accomplished in the field of Biblical interpretation proved of immense service to St. Thomas Aquinas, who built upon the exegesis of his master and stamped it with the mark of his own genius. Albert holds an intermediate place between Hugh of St. Cher and St. Thomas which is sufficient distinction for any scholar. Emil Michael is not afraid to declare that

---

[11] H. Denifle, "*Quel livre serait de base à l'enseignement des maîtres en théologie dans l'Universitié de Paris,*" in *Revue Thomiste (1894), 149-161.*

[12] A. Vaccari, "*S. Albertus Magnus Sacrae Scripturae Interpres,*" in *Alberto Magno, Atti della Settimana Albertina (Roma: 1932), 127-152.*

Albert was the greatest German exegete of the thirteenth century.[13]

II. *Theological Writings.* The theological works of Albert fall into two classes, according to the method of teaching then in use in the schools. Since the eleventh century the *Sentences* of Peter Lombard had been the ordinary handbook of theology. This work consisted of a long catalog of the dogmas of the Church which were commended to the acceptance of students by proofs based on the teaching magisterium of the Church and the dogmatic decisions of the Councils. It was an extremely dry presentation of the truths of the Faith, legalistic and formalistic, with scarcely an appeal to the reasoning powers of men. Only an age profoundly impressed by the authority of the Church could have relished this method of teaching. Its effect upon teachers was deadening. For, as a rule, the man who could juggle with greatest ease and dexterity the largest number of texts was looked upon as the outstanding theologian of his school or country. He was seldom expected to adduce reasons for his belief which would satisfy the mind. To have asked him to do so would have exposed both professor and student to the suspicion of disbelieving or misbelieving a dogma of the Faith.

Now, Albert was a match for any scholar of the day in his wide familiarity with the riches of ecclesiastical tradition. Few, if any men, could compare with him for erudition and ability to quote at will the Fathers of the Church, the schoolmen, and the sacred and profane writers of all ages.[14] It would seem that he never forgot what he had read, or if he did he always remembered where he could find what he needed or was looking for. Even though Albert's show of erudition never sounds like the empty parading or obtrusion of his astounding riches of patristic and ecclesiastical lore, there is none the less noticeable a kind of intellectual impatience in his very act of unlocking the doors of the past. He was, in the fullest and best sense of the word, a man of his day, conscious of its needs, ambitions, and desires,

---

[13] *E. Michael,* Geschichte des deutschen Volkes, III, 214-222. *Man lerne die Sprache der Scholastik verstehen und man wird überrascht sein von dem Scharfsinn Alberts, von der Sicherheit mit der er seinen Stoff bemeistert, und von der Fülle der Ideen, welche auf wenigen Blättern niedergelegt sind. Vorzüge, denen gegenüber Sonderlichkeiten in der Entymologie und allzu peinliche Unterabteilungen, die auf einen minder denkkräftigen Geist störend wirken, wenig ins Gewicht fallen.*

[14] F. Pangerl, "*Studien Uber Albert den Grossen,*" in *Zeitschrift für katholische Theologie (1912), 536-549.*

cognizant of its ways of thinking and its sly attempts at imitating the methods of men who were admired for breaking away from stereotyped forms and disciplines. Nor did he frown upon this new spirit that was bound, sooner or later, to invade the theological schools. Hence, we find him making room, cautiously and sparingly, for the new methods in one of his earliest works, the *Commentary on the Sentences of Peter Lombard.* And for this very reason it will ever occupy an important place in the history of Christian thought, not so much, if at all, for what it says, but for what it dares to allow the new learning to suggest timidly, almost surreptitiously. In this work we see the first streaks of a light which one day he will let shine in all its radiance. Albert was feeling his way, testing the temper of his students, preparing their minds for what he would yet dare to do in the teeth of those who were satisfied to mumble the *dicta* of the past instead of stammering in the precise and sharp-cut terms of the present.

Albert's commentaries on the pseudo-Dionysius contain his teaching on mystical theology for which he had a decided bent. He has the unique distinction of being the only man of his age to write a complete commentary on these four most abstruse books of the Christian inheritance. St. Thomas never ventured to grapple with more than one book of the pseudo-Dionysius and no scholar will think the less of him for that. Most of Albert's speculation in mystical theology remains unedited.[15] What we do possess in printed form of his Dionysian commentaries, and the many dissertations on mystical theology which he managed to weave in his other theological works, prove beyond a doubt that he was one of the leading mystical writers of his age, exercising an undeniable influence upon Tauler and the school of mystics along the Rhine who shaped the mind and heart of Thomas à Kempis.[16]

Two handbooks of theology were composed by Albert. The first was never completed by him. Though the three parts of which it was to have been composed were written out in rough draft, it was never actually worked over into a systematic whole. The work is known as the *Summa de Bono seu de Creaturis.* It was discovered by Grabmann in

---

[15] G. Thery, "*L'Authographe de S. Thomas conserve a la Biblioteca Nazionale de Naples,*" in *Archivum Frat. Praed. (Roma: 1932), I, 15-86.*

[16] *C. Greith,* Die deutsche Mystik im Prediger-Orden (Freiburg: 1862), 42, sq.; C. Bäumker, Der Anteil des Elsass an den geistigen Bewegungen des Mittelalters (Strasburg: 1912), 28.

the Marcian Library at Venice, in 1917. The sections *De Resurrectione* and *De Sacramentis* are scattered throughout his other works.[17]

His second theological work, the *Summa Theologica*, was written by Albert toward the end of his life and only partially finished. It was intended for those students who could not procure original texts and yet were desirous of a sound grounding in theology. In this volume he does not quote authorities verbatim but expounds their teachings in his own way of thinking and argumentation.

III. *Devotional* writings from the pen of Albert treat of the *Sacrifice of the Mass*, the *Holy Eucharist*, *Sermons on the Sundays and Festivals*, an exposition of the Our Father in the *De Forma Orandi*, the famous work on the Blessed Virgin, *De Laudibus Mariae*, and numerous sermons in German of which only two so far have been edited.[18] He composed also many prayers which, despite their simplicity of language, are filled with profound theological thought and redolent of the liturgy. Thus he appended a prayer based on the Gospel of the day to each of his Sunday sermons, and he embroidered a prayer on each of the invocations of the Litany of the Saints. He breathed a liturgical breath into each of the propositions of the Lombard's *Sentences.* He wrote and circulated widely, prayers in honor of the Most Blessed Sacrament, the Holy Spirit, the Blessed Virgin, prayers before and after Mass, all of which render impressive, even if they do not rehabilitate, his definition of theology as a *scientia quae secundum pietatem est:* a science intended to foster piety.

In addition to all these systematic works Albert wrote small but not negligible dissertations on such vexed philosophical subjects as *De Unitate Intellectus contra Averroistas* and *De Quindecim Problematibus.*[19]

The works about whose Albertinian authorship there is dispute are many and important. If we possess such numerous uncertain works it must evidently be due to the fact that men were convinced of Albert's immense literary productivity and thought there could be no end to it. And authors who wished to find a ready reception for their books were

[17] G. Meersemann, *Introductio*, 127; M. Grabmann, *L'lnflusso*, 35, 74.

[18] de Loe, Alberts des Grossen Homilie zu Luc. XI, 27, zum ersten Mal herausgegeben (Bonn: 1916); P. Strauch, Kölner Klosterpredigten des 13. Jahrhunderts (Norden und Leipzig: 1911), 21, 48.

[19] A. Masnova, "*Alberto Magno e la polemica Averroistica,*" in *Alberto Magno Atti della Settimana Albertina (Roma: 1932), 43-62.*

shrewd enough to attach his magic name to them. The process of determining the authenticity of these uncertain works will be a long one and may save for him—as Dr. Heribert Scheeben professed to be able to do[20]—such spiritual classics as *The Paradise of the Soul* and *On Union with God* which some modern critics ascribe to other writers.

But the absolutely certain works mentioned above prove beyond the shadow of a doubt the literary fecundity of Albert, his encyclopedic interests, his profound scholarship, his scientific temper, his matchless originality, and his infectious piety. Like a deep, capacious basin Albert's mind received the knowledge of all past ages. He did not allow these waters to grow muddied or stagnant. Stirring them by his powerful intellect in the sunlight of Catholic truth he made men see new flashes, irridescent rainbows and refracted glories of which his predecessors had never dreamed. But what is more, his apostolic zeal pulled out the plugs of his native modesty and humility so that the waters of knowledge, human and divine, stored up within his mind, might gush forth to water and fructify that garden which we call the Catholic Church.

---

[20] *H. Scheeben, "Les Ecrits,"* in *Revue Thomiste* (1931), 36, n. 3.

CHAPTER XIII

PIONEER SCIENTIST

THE MIDDLE AGES gloried in the possession of two great gifts which they tried their best not only to appreciate justly but also to utilize largely.

The Greco-Roman culture having survived, even if in an attenuated form, the cataclysm of the break-up of the Roman Empire brought about by the migration of the Northern peoples, did impress mightily and solicit subtly the medieval man. Brought face to face with civilized ways of thinking and acting, he blushed for his own native savagery of thought and conduct. Thus when Charlemagne sought to lead his people to a higher tableland than that afforded by Germanic dreams, he could do no better than speak of the Holy Roman Empire of the West.

The second great possession of the medieval world was the Catholic Faith which the average man valued highly, not only for its own intrinsic worth and beauty, but also for the cultural advantages it had conferred and promised to continue to bestow upon the peoples which then constituted Europe. Had there been no such thing as an international and supranational agency in the medieval world, Europe would have soon lost everything cultural it had inherited from the past, had acquired laboriously, and was bestirring itself in countless ways to make its own more completely in the various departments of life and activity.

For the normal state of Europe was one of chronic warfare, an unintermittent struggle of the various racial elements and peoples to build up a stable form of government, an absolute absence of articulateness and independence among the masses, an arrogant attitude of the nobles especially those who had distinguished themselves for military prowess. There was only one class of men free from the obligation of war and the worries of daily existence—the priests who had the time and found the means to devote themselves to the constructive works of peace, chief of which was education. As we look back upon the vivid picture of those ages we find the priest everywhere. But the truth is that he *was* everywhere where there were hopes for better things and efforts for a higher life than those conditioned by war. We may think with superficial readers of history that medieval Europe was priest-ridden. But the fact is that if it took Europe so long with all the priests it had to smother its ambitions for war and its liking for the ways of the camp, it would have emerged sooner, with less haltings and relapses if there had been a larger number of them about their business of peace and social reconstruction. Had there been fewer priests in that day, surely the savage princes would have succeeded more grimly in choking the higher aspirations of the masses, and the rough people of the hamlets and countryside would have strangled more effectively all attempts at just and orderly self-expression.

Now this point is very important when considering the study of the natural sciences in the Middle Ages. The average man then was either a warrior, or a farmer, or a fisherman, or a huntsman. The warrior knew only the profession of arms and the fine art of looting and destruction. He cared little about the utilities of peace. On the other hand, the farmers and fishermen and huntsmen were in constant communion with the mysteries and wonders of nature. If anyone of this class did not sink entirely into darkest superstition, it was because, when face to face with what was inexplicable to him, he turned instinctively to the one man in the community who was fitted by education to give a rational answer and solution.

Now the priest, besides being a fairly well-educated man, was by profession the man of God, intermediary between the Creator and the creature, conversant not only with mighty workings of grace in human hearts but also with the interposition of Divine Providence in human lives and human affairs. The pagan gods, who had been identified with every natural thing, had been finally driven out by the Catholic Faith of the Middle Ages, and so the medieval man could enjoy the beauties of nature without exposing himself to the danger of becoming a pantheist or an idolator. As God had not been carted out of His own creation it was the priest's business to make the illiterate people see a vestige of His passing and power in every created thing. He would speak in the language which men knew and understood.

And hence it came that the Catholic Faith was linked up with the actions and interests of the people's daily lives, that every created thing took on a voice to speak of the Lord's love of His own. Faith dominated the medieval world. Europe might present the picture of a camp, but it was a camp with a shadow of the cross falling across it. Thus the crusades were martial expeditions, but with a holy and spiritual purpose in view. It was the medieval bishop, on the steps of his cathedral church, who dispensed justice gratis to the people who did not always or even generally find it at the courts of justice of the princes. The fairs were held in the broad piazzas before the churches, on the feast days of saints, under the kindly eyes of the clergy, for else the violent passions of man would have sought satisfaction in unspeakable places and in debauching ways. The building of churches was a collective act of the people, anxious to have a rendezvous where they could enjoy the democracy of the faith in their father's house without being treated as step children, as was so often the case in the baron's castle. Art became etherealized because it spoke of the true home beyond the stars whither all were supposed to be tending over the selfsame way of the cross. And in line with every department of medieval life, learning, even of the most secular kind, could not get away from the sanctuary where it had been born and where, in the incense-laden air, it had grown strong and had been allowed and encouraged to exercise its muscles.

Hence, it is easily understood that, when the clergy explained the phenomena of nature, there was always a hint of the spiritual about their answer. For this world came from God and its mysterious workings were but a faint picture of the wisdom divine which held this sphere on its appointed way and endowed it with powers which the mind of man must needs study in order to ascertain the range of all its wondrous fecundity of operation. When minds worked slowly the priest wisely adapted his teaching to the capacity of his pupils. If the main business of life was to know God, then the utilization of the natural sciences for this sovereign duty was as sensible as inevitable. This had been done from the very first days of Christianity after the example of the good Master who had spoken to the Apostles in parables which they generally understood. Paul speaks of the athlete's stadium and the runners, and there were no purists of language nor narrow-minded sportsmen who found fault with him for using such explanations. And when the author of *Physiologus* made use of the knowledge of the natural sciences of his day to exemplify religious truths or drive home spiritual lessons there were none to cry out about the prostitution of secular learning to spiritual ends. This book became so popular at once with preachers and people that it served as the basis for whole cycles of naïve stories, fables, and myths about birds and trees and snakes and flowers. There was no longer any danger of turning men's minds from God by such symbolism, such spiritual etymology and Catholic mythology. The people may or may not have believed the stories; but they did get the obvious lesson intended. Hence, medieval Gothic cathedrals would not be the exhaustless storehouses of spiritual teaching perpetuated in stone had it not been for the large vogue among the people of investing created things with a spiritual meaning and significance which the ordinary man did not miss. If this symbolism did nothing else it surely did arouse and feed the Christian imagination with images that did not carry with them a horrible connotation of war, sin, and meannesses of every sort. It drove out ugly remembrances—nightmares—of battle fields and brothels, and sent through the emptied corridors of man's memory sacrosanct images of Christ, His Blessed Mother, and the saints who lived in a world of man's creation, indeed, but a world filled with the incense perfume of the sanctuary, the perfume exhaled by flowers which, just because they were tended by loving, consecrated hands in cloister garths or cathedral closes, had a symbolical language of their own. Medieval poetry was made possible by such means, indifferent often about the grammarians' rules, but solicitous always about the heavenly Master's nearness and the sweetness of His tarrying with man. And stone never came so near human speech as when every block from foundation to pinnacle found a tongue to speak a language all its own.

This, then, being the medieval attitude toward the natural sciences and the fine arts, and this the end to which they were frequently put, we must be prepared to find in Albert many things which to this age seem trivial, childish, far-fetched, perhaps even tendentious. We shall never evaluate at its proper worth the scientific work of Albert if we do not keep in mind the mental attitude of the people and the method of treating subjects which obtained in his day. With all his medieval traits and symbolical preoccupation with created things, Albert did put forth an effort to be really scientific, and in doing so did discover in an eminent degree the genuine qualities of a scientific mind and temper.[1]

It was in response to a judicious estimate of the possible harm to which the method of teaching then in vogue might eventually lead in the schools and among the people which first turned Albert's attention to Aristotle and his commentators. The great professor, who made it his business to see for himself how currents of thought had developed in the past and how they had worked out in the schools, was not ignorant that the study of natural sciences had practically remained at a standstill for centuries. Scarcely any progress toward a deeper understanding of the phenomena of nature had been made in three hundred years. And where an interest in this direction had been manifested it had been accompanied by a pantheistic strain. Bernard of Tours, Amaury of Beur, and David of Dinant by their rationalizing teaching had broken down in the schools the congenital horror of the schoolmen for pantheism. And like every system of thought that had once flourished and after being replaced had got a fresh breathing space, this new rationalistic and rationalizing doctrine would not scruple about the means it resorted to to reestablish itself, wash its face, if not in the schools, then at least before the unthinking mob which could be made to applaud what it admired, even if it did not understand. Exiled philosophers are as wily as exiled princes when once they have been readmitted to their own land. Moreover, the returning crusaders had brought home with them from the Orient

---

[1] S. Dezani, "*I Parva Naturalia del B. Alberto Magno,*" in *Memorie Domenicane (1931), 420-425.* Dotato di un deciso talento per la ricerca naturale, di uno schietto e forte sentire, di un amore grande per la bellezza della natura, di un inesauribile stimulo alla sintesi della verità sparse, ed a porre tutte questi doti, di uno straordinario patrimonio di osservazioni ed esperienze personali, nonchè di uno spirito di intuizione da cui si sprigionano spesso lampi di genialità Alberto Magno si accinge a scrivere quelle opere di scienza naturale, le quali, se per cinque secoli non stupirono quasi che per la loro mole, da un secolo in qua stupiscono spesso lo studioso moderno per la ricchezza dei loro dati, per la logica dei procedimento scientifico e per la divinazione di leggi che la scienza moderna non ha fatto che confermare e completare.

Da tutte le opera sulla natura di Alberto Magno balzò poi evidente la constatazione che alia sua mente si erano già nettamente disegnati i mezzi della scienza sperimentale e la sua meta: l'experimento ed il raziocinio; il progresso umano verso Dio. Ed Egli proclamò che il compito della scienza non e già quello di racimolare semplicemente le cose narrate e scritte, ma di ricercare le cause dei fenomeni naturali. Alla autorità del 'magister dixit' Egli sostituisce, ovunque è possibilia, quella dell 'osservazion e dell' esperienza persoanale, e quello del Beato non e l'osservazione fortuita e fortunata ma bene spesso l'osservazione ricercata e continuata talora per anni.

much recondite learning which they showed off with gusto amid the plaudits of the poor yokels of the countryside and the insular townsmen. Then, too, the Arabian and Jewish commentaries, being introduced stealthily from Spain, were filled with much information which was looked upon as scientific, probably because it was so new and dressed out in such high-sounding terms. Men are always interested in their health and these Muslim commentators of Aristotle volunteered to cure bodies while helping the mind. It is on this assumption that we can in great measure account for the quick and glad reception of the vitiated teaching of Aristotle in the Christian schools. The pantheistic Christian philosophers had prepared the minds for the reception of such bold theories.

Now Albert saw the twofold danger—the breaking down of academic morale by the followers of Bernard of Tours with their pantheistic doctrine and the enthusiastic welcome extended the rationalizing commentators of Aristotle. A corrected text of the Stagirite, with a frankly Christian interpretation, would cut the ground from under the feet of the pantheistic European philosophers and would drive out in confusion the discredited Muslim commentators.

In other words, Albert realized that it was supremely necessary to get at the true thought of Aristotle about natural phenomena and, in the next place, to build up a hierarchy of the natural sciences in such a way as not to exclude the almighty and omnipotent power of God. While admitting always and everywhere the overshadowing concern of God in His own creation "it is necessary," Albert said, "to establish every experiment not in one way only, but according to all the circumstances."[2] In these words Albert betrays the true scientific temper.[3] Possessing this critical bent of mind and a profound and extensive knowlege of phenomena, Albert was prepared to outline a classification of the natural sciences which is not only the finest exhibition of his own scientific and constructive spirit but also one of the most monumental syntheses evolved by human genius.

So Albert in giving an explanation of Aristotle's *Physics* divides up

---

[2] *De Causis et Proprietatibus Elementorum I (tr. II, Chap. 9).*

[3] *Lynn Thorndike, A History of Magic and Experimental Science (Oxford: 1923), says: "Coming back from the opinion of others concerning Albert to his own attitude towards natural science, it is to be noted that, while he may make all sorts of mistakes judged by modern standards, he does show unmistakable signs of the scientific spirit," (II, 535).*

the *philosophia realis* into metaphysics, mathematics, and physics. He plunges directly into his subject by taking exception with Heraclitus, who taught there could be no science of physics. In another digressive expository chapter on Aristotle, Albert considers the subject of physics; namely, the body *mobile.* Then he gives the divisions of composite bodies. He takes issue with the ancients upon the real constitutive element of things and next reasons out the true notion about matter. The second book of Albert's *Physics* treats of nature, especially as considered in motion, when studied in mobile or composite substances. Then came treatises on movement, place, time, and eternity. Because, in Albert's scheme, the soul precedes the science of animate bodies, he next dwells exhaustively on the soul and its powers. Thence we pass on to the study of minerals and other topics of physics. These topics are followed up by paraphrases on Aristotle and original digressions, often assuming the proportions of little treatises on sense perception; on memory and recollection, sleep and waking, movements of animals, age, youth, decrepitude, respiration, life and death, nourishment and nourishing foodstuffs; on place, the properties of the elements; on the air, vapors, and vegetables—surely a range of subjects wide enough for the most encyclopedic mind. Every scientific question that could agitate the medieval mind comes up for discussion. No human interests, especially as they are affected by men or affect men, are here overlooked.

Just where and in what spirit his vast fund of knowledge was accumulated Albert himself indicates in these words: "When there is question of faith and morals Augustine enjoys the greatest authority; of medicine, Galen and Hippocrates; of natural sciences, Aristotle."[4] Wimmer says: "Albert has studied and described the entire cosmos from its stars to its stones."[5] And Henry Osborn Taylor states: "The writings of Albertus Magnus represent, perhaps more fully than those of any other man, the round of knowledge and intellectual interests attracting the attention of western Europe in the thirteenth century."[6] Lynn Thorndike speaks of him as "the dominant figure in Latin learning and natural sciences in the thirteenth century, the most

---

[4] *Opp. XXVII, 247, 11, Sententiarum, dist. 13, art. 2.*

[5] *J. Wimmer,* Deutsches Pflanzenleben nach Albertus Magnus (Halle: 1908), 7.

[6] H. O. Taylor, *The Medieval Mind* (New York: 1918), II, 453.

prolific of its writers, the most influential of its teachers, the dean of its scholars, the one learned man of the twelfth and thirteenth centuries to be called the Great."[7]

Albert's Scientific Spirit

There are sufficient indications in Albert's work to guarantee the statement that from his earliest youth he was deeply interested in the natural phenomena which he beheld about him. It was not the mere idle curiosity of a lad in search of new sights. The fact that the students at Padua, as he implies in the passage previously quoted, looked to him for an explanation of the death caused by poisonous vapors issuing from a well, proves that his explanations were more than the glib remarks of one who wished to shine among his fellows.[8] Again, no mere idler would have remained quiet for a space of two hours, as he tells us he did, to see the battle of an eagle and a swan. If his observations on the course of fishes are to be dated from the days of his youth it shows plainly that Albert was sufficiently interested in the matter to study closely and long. And when he put forth such herculean efforts to introduce a true text and Christian version of Aristotle, it was never at the expense of personal observation of natural phenomena. He tells us that in scientific matters one could not expect to investigate everything in person, though if this were possible, it would be the ideal method of procedure. Since, however, it is out of question, the next best thing is to base one's theories on the observations of men whom one has no reason to suspect of lying or chicanery. If, therefore, he chose Aristotle as his guide and authority in the sciences, it was because he had reason to conclude, owing to the instances when he had tried out and tested the Greek's sayings by his own observations, that the Stagirite was faithfully reporting his own observations and those of his pupils. Hence, it is unjust to identify Albert's scientific doctrine absolutely and exclusively with what Aristotle had said. Albert put it down as a fundamental principle, which he carried out frequently in his own case, that when Aristotle's findings were in contradiction with one's observations, the only honest

---

[7] *Op. cit.*, 523.

[8] *H. Stadler, Albertus Magnus als selbstständiger Naturforscher (Mainz: 1906), 95-114.*

and sensible procedure was to hold to one's own opinion. Albert did subject Aristotle's scientific statements to scrutiny. Thus he rejects Aristotle when he says that lunar rainbows appear only every fifty years, since he himself had witnessed two in one year. This is one case only out of many where he proves his contention that even Aristotle is fallible; God alone is infallible.[9]

He insists that the purpose of the natural sciences is not served by blindly accepting the sayings of others, but that there is imperative need to go in search of the causes behind the natural phenomena.[10] He allows that much time and labor must be expended in making such personal observations.[11] The examination must be made on divers occasions under various conditions and circumstances. Only thus can one arrive at a true and adequate knowledge of the causes of natural phenomena. It will not do, therefore, to say with Taylor: "His *digressiones* usually discuss abstract problems as, for instance, whether beyond the four elements any fifth principle enters the composition of animal bodies."[12] Again Taylor complains: "He corrects few ancient errors, either anatomical or physiological and his own observations, occasionally referred to in this work, scarcely win our respect... On the whole, Albert's merit in the province of zoology lies in his introduction of the Aristotelian data and conceptions to the medieval Latin West."[13] These broad statements of Taylor are in utter conflict with the method of procedure to be followed in the natural sciences as put down several times in the most explicit words by Albert. They are in conflict, too, with Albert's own career of observation, kept up during the periods of

---

[9] *W. Kraft, Albert der Grosse und seine Stellung zur Wissenschaft seiner Zeit (Elberfeldt: 1876), 105-116; G. von Herding, Albertus Magnus (Münster: 1914), 40.*

[10] *Earum autem quas ponemus, quasdem quidem ipsi nos experimento probavimus, quasdam autem referimus ex dictis eorum quos comperimus non de facili; aliqua dicere, nisi probata per experimentum. Experimentum enim solum certificat in talibus, eo quod de tam particularibus naturis sillogismus haberi non potest (De Vegetal., VI., tr. 1, Chap. 1); A. Mansion, "L'induction chez Albert le Grand," in Revue Neo-Scolastique* (1906), 115-134.

[11] *Multitudo enim temporis requiritur ad hoc ut experimentum probetur, ita quod in nullo fallit; unde Hippocrates in medicinalibus loquens: 'Vita brevis, ars vero longa, experimentum fallax, judicium difficile est.' Oportet enin experimentum non in uno modo, sed secundum omnes circumstantias probare, ut certe et recte principium sit operis* (*Ethic.* VI, tr. 2, Chap. 25).

[12] *Op. cit.*, II, 459.

[13] *Ibid.*

life when he was engaged in important ecclesiastical business. On this point Thorndike says:

"Albert's work on plants does contain, however, many passages in which he recognizes experience as a criterion of truth or gives the results of his personal observations. Such passages occur especially in the sixth book where he tries to satisfy his student's curiosity, but we may first note an earlier passage where he recommends 'making conjectures and experiments' in order to learn the nature of trees in general and of each variety of tree, herb, fruit, and fungus in particular. Since, however, one can scarcely have personal experience of them all, it is also advisable to read the books which the experts (*experti*) of antiquity have written on such matters. But a mistrust of the assertions of others often accompanies Albert's reliance upon personal observation and experience. Like Galen in his work on medicinal simples, he explains in opening his sixth book that merely to list the names of plants found in existing books would fill a volume, and that he will limit his discussion to those native varieties 'better known among us.' Of some of these he had personal experience; for the others he follows authors whom he has found unready to state anything unless it was proved by experience. For experience alone is reliable concerning particular natures. He cautions in regard to a tree which is said to save doves from serpents, 'But this has not been sufficiently proved by certain experience, like the other facts which are written here, but is found in the writings of the Ancients.' Of another assertion he remarks, 'But this is proved by no experience'; and of a third he says, 'As some affirm, but I have not tested this myself.'

"Personal observation and experience are equally, if not more, noticeable in Albert's work on animals. He proposes to tell 'what he knows by reason and what he sees by experience of the natures of animals'; he adds that science cannot be attained in all matters by demonstration, in some cases one must resort to conjecture. After listing various remedies for the infirmities of falcons from the work on falconry of the Emperor Frederick, he concludes: 'Such are the medicines which one finds given for falcons and the experience of wise men, but the wise falconer will with time add to or subtract from them according to his own experience of what is beneficial to the state of health of the birds. For experience is the best teacher in all matters of this sort.'

"In the treatise on animals as in that on plants Albert's allusions to experience occur mainly in the last few books where he describes particular animals. Here he often says, 'I have tested this,' or 'I and my associates have experienced,' or 'I have not experienced this,' or 'I have proved that this is not true.' Like Alexander of Neckam he rejects the story that the beaver castrates itself in order to escape with its life from its hunters; Albert says that experience near his home has often disproved this. In discussing whales he restricts himself entirely to the results of his own observations, saying, 'We pass over what the Ancients have written on this topic because their statements do not agree with experience.' According to Pouchet, Albert gives even more detailed information concerning whales than do the Norse sagas, and also includes animals of the north unknown to classical writers. He occasionally reveals his nationality by giving the German as well as the Latin names of animals, and he displays an acquaintance with the fauna of surrounding countries such as Norway, Sweden, Bohemia, and Carinthia. He asserts that there are no eels in the Danube and its tributaries, but that they abound in the other rivers of Germany. He tells us of observing the habits of eagles in Livonia, or supports the account in Solinus of a monstrous beast with fore legs like human arms and hind legs like human legs by stating that he has seen both male and female of the species captured in the forests of Russia (Sclaviae). Of his wide travels and observation of natural phenomena we shall meet with other examples as we proceed.

"Albert has not only observed animal life widely, he has also performed experiments with animals as he apparently did not do with plants. He and his associates, for instance, have proved by experiment that a cicade goes on singing in its breast for a long time after its head has been cut off. He also proved to his satisfaction that the turtle, although a marine animal, would not drink sea water, unless possibly fresh water which flowed into the sea, by experimenting with a turtle in a vessel of water. He had heard it said that the ostrich eats and digests iron, but the many ostriches to whom he has offered the metal have consistently declined it, although they would devour with avidity stones and bones cut into small bits. Crude experiments these may be, but they are at least purposive."

On the subject of minerals Thorndike says:
"Albert's general attitude toward past authorities and present experience remains the same in his treatises on minerals. He will give the names of the important gems and state their virtues as known from authorities and experience, but he will not repeat everything that has been said about precious stones because it is not profitable for science. 'For natural science is not simply receiving what one is told, but the investigation of causes in natural phenomena.' Concerning the metals, too, he intends to state 'rationally either what has been handed down by the philosophers or what I myself have experienced.' He adds that once he wandered far in exile to places rich in mines in order that he might test the natures of metals. 'And for this same reason I investigated the transmutation of metals among the alchemists, in order that I might observe something of the nature and characteristics of the metals.' In a later chapter he alludes to workers in copper 'in our parts, namely, Paris and Cologne, and in other places where I have been and seen things tested by experience.' *Fui et vidi experiri,* such is Albert the Great's peaceful paraphrase, probably unintentional, for warring Cæsar's *Veni, vidi, vici.*"[14]

It is evident from all this, then, that Albert did possess a scientific and critical spirit of no mean degree and that he exercised it to good advantage during all his life. That he did not completely surmount the popular notions of the time need not be wondered at. He is as free as any of his contemporaries, indeed much more free, of a credulous and easily fallible spirit. Alluding to the observation that "science ceased to have a history in the Middle Ages," Mr. Arnold Lunn observes: "a general statement of this kind, can, of course, always be challenged. It is possible to cite instances of acute scientific observation, pregnant with hints of future discovery, in the works of scholastics such as Albertus Magnus. But an age must be judged by its master energies and the intellectual energies of the Middle Ages were devoted not to science but to philosophy."[15] If Albert, when introducing the purely

---

[14] *Op. cit.,* II, 539-541.

[15] Alfred Lunn, *The Flight from Reason* (New York: 1931), 46.

speculative philosophy of Aristotle to the Western world, did not stand below him but beside him, correcting him, criticizing him, amplifying him, then he assumed a much more critical attitude toward the Aristotelian teaching when there was question of the natural sciences which, in the last analysis, depend chiefly upon observation and experimentation. Nowhere does Albert appear so majestically the teacher as in his treatment of Aristotle's teaching on the sciences.

Albert, of course, found a personal satisfaction in the composition of enlightened and critical commentaries on Aristotle's *Physics.* Only a deep enthusiasm could have carried him through the gigantic task of dealing with all the then known sciences. In treating of the natural sciences, he was not under the compulsion of producing classroom work, in the shape of notes or lectures, as was the case with his theological works and, later on, after the change in the Dominican curriculum of studies, with his philosophical treatises. For after the change in the Dominican course of studies, at the Chapter of Valenciennes, scientific studies were officially provided for. Indeed it is true to say that for a time before this they were frowned upon by the legislators of the Order. There was even a secret opposition among the brethren against studies which some foolishly imagined were useless and out of joint with the priestly ideal. Yet despite this large wing of antiscientists, many deeply admired the work of Albert and were eager to profit by his observations and researches. Hence, there is a fine note of courage underlying his endeavor to supply these enthusiasts with books which they so much desired. There was no personal ambition or hope of personal advantage. Quite the contrary. The Chapters of the Order passed legislation directly under the nose of Albert which he could not fail to see was directly aimed at him. Probably, in his generous way, the veteran and seasoned professor smiled quietly to himself, hoping the while for the break of a better day when men of large vision would be able to understand that a knowledge of the natural sciences, far from injuring the philosophical and theological labors and outlook of the brethren, would promote it in an undreamed fullness. It is no wonder that the hidebound and retrograde may be found among legislators who by the very nature of their position and tasks must be conservative. Albert did not suffer from mental astigmatism when he shared in the legislative deliberations of the brethren. He tells us in his preface to the *Physics:*

"Our intention, in treating these questions of natural science, is to oblige as far as we can the brethren of our Order. For many years past they have asked us to write a book on the phenomena of nature which may supply them with a complete course of the natural sciences, and afford them suitable helps in studying the works of Aristotle. Although sensible of our incapacity for such an enterprise, we could not resist their entreaties. Overcome by the solicitations of some of them, we accepted the task. We have undertaken it above all for the glory of the Omnipotent God, the Source of wisdom, the Creator, the Preserver and King of nature, and also for the benefit of the brethren and all those who shall read this book and be desirous of acquiring the natural sciences. Our method in this work will be to follow the order and mind of Aristotle and to add what is necessary to his explanations and arguments, without, however, referring to the text. Besides we will make additions in order to discuss doubts and to supply what remains doubtful in the teaching of the Philosopher. Because of his short exposition we will divide the entire book into chapters. Where the title indicates the subject matter clearly, it is a sign that we have taken over the chapter from the works of Aristotle. However, where an addition is made in the words of the title we have made our own additions in order to complete and clarify what has been said. Proceeding in this way we shall give as many books as Aristotle under the same title. Here and there we shall add to the unfinished works, or to the interrupted or lost works which Aristotle either did not write or which, if he did write them, have not come down to us. Whenever this happens we shall indicate it in the following treatise."[16]

Albert enlightened the natural sciences by his observations, and kept them within the bounds which Thomas Aquinas did so much to render impregnable. Thorndike says:

"Thomas, however, did no such important work in natural science as Albert. His commentaries upon Aristotle follow the text closely and do little more than expound it; they are not full of long

[16] *Physicorum I, tr. I. Opp. III, 251.*

digressions and additions, as Albert's are. Thomas did not found an experimental school and had not himself devoted the long years of personal experience and observation to nature that his master had. And he seems to have had the less original and observant mind of the two. But his wide reading, his clear thinking, his well-ordered classroom presentation of material and arguments, and his broad yet moderate views insured his instant and permanent success in the field of theology, where the paths were already well trod, and it only remained for someone to put everything into as perfect and final a form as possible. In natural science, on the other hand, the labor that awaited men was not merely the lucid combination of Aristotelian and Arabic thinking with previous Christian thought, but the pioneer work of personal observation and experiment and the far more difficult combination of these with existing theories. Aquinas was a perfecter according to the standards of his own age; Albert sometimes was a pioneer in the spirit of the new age of science."[17]

ALBERT'S EXPERIMENTAL SCHOOL OF SCIENCES

In his book *On Vegetables* Albert tells a story from which we may conclude that he carried on or directed experimentation. It is so naïve that we shall here quote it: "An emerald was recently seen among us, small in size but marvelous in beauty. When its virtue was to be tested, someone stepped forth and said that, if a circle was made about a toad with the emerald and then the stone was set before the toad's eyes, one of two things would happen. Either the stone, if of weak virtue, would be broken by the gaze of the toad; or the toad would burst, if the stone was possessed of full natural vigor. Without delay things were arranged as he bade; and after a short lapse of time, during which the toad kept its eye unswervingly upon the gem, the latter began to crack like a nut and a portion of it flew from the ring. Then the toad, which had stood immovable hitherto, withdrew as if it had been freed from the influence of the gem."[18] Evidently Albert had been tricked by some magician or prestidigitator. But it almost smacks of the modern

---

17 *Op. cit.*, II, 601.

18 *Op. cit.*, II, 546 sq.

laboratory to find the toad a chosen specimen for this experiment.

In his *Meteorology* Albert, after refusing to subscribe to Aristotle's statement about the moon rainbows, remarks that "truthful experimenters have found by experience" that rainbows have actually appeared twice in the same year. He sees no reason why they should appear only twice in fifty years and goes on to say that: "those facts which have been adduced against his statement have been experienced beyond a doubt by myself and by other reliable investigators associated with me."[19]

The chapter headings of this portion of Albert's treatise suggest an antithesis between the ancient and the modern experimenters: "*Of the Iris of the Moon and what Ancients have said of it and what Moderns have Tested by Experience*" clearly indicates the existence somewhere of a school of experimentation or observation. And the same would seem to appear from the title of another little tractate: "*A Digression Stating Seneca's Views concerning Virgae and Experiments with Certain Arcs seen in Modern Times.*"

That Albert busied himself with chemical experiments is plain.[20] He says that such experiments, if abuses and superstitious practices are guarded against, "are profitable. This is a splendid and most infallible kind of investigation because by the proximate cause of a thing the thing itself is known and there is little doubt about its accidentals."[21] In that age such tests were frequently and generally spoken of as implying the practise of magic. Though there may have been much humbuggery and superstition practised in this connection, it is nevertheless plain from Albert's condemnation of sinful magic, or superstition, that he made a clear distinction between what was lawful and unlawful. Having settled his mind on the subject he proceeded like a scholar with his investigations and experiments. Hence, it need not cause us great surprise if we find in the collection of his works some that bear the malodorous imputation of alchemy. If, for instance, transmutation of metals was the chief ambition of these medieval

---

[19] *De Meteor.*, IV, 8-26.

[20] *De Mineral.*, III, 1.

[21] Omnis autem acceptio quae firmatur a sensu, melior est quam illa quae sensui contradicit; et conclusio quae sensui contradicit, est incredibilis; principium autem quod experimentali cognitioni in sensu non concordat, non est principium, sed potius contrarium principio (*Physicorum*, VIII, tr. II, Chap. 2).

alchemists they do not appear in ragged robes to our contemporary minds; for the greatest living physicists today change into copper, lithium brought under the influence of radium emanations. While, therefore, much doubt has been entertained about the transmutation of metals, and while Albert has been dubbed a magician for holding the possibility of such a change, we, who have seen it accomplished in our own day, can well afford to exonerate Albert from the charge of dark practices which enemies of the Church have tried to pin on him for the sole purpose of discrediting her. In order, then, to establish the thesis that Albert established a school of experimentation and carried on in the sight of his pupils tests of an elaborate kind it may be permitted to adduce this long quotation from Lynn Thorndike, Professor of History in Western Reserve University, in his monumental *A History of Magic and Experimental Science:*

> "The author also strikes an experimental keynote for his work, stating that after seeing so many fail he has decided to write true and approved works and the best which all the philosophers have to offer, works, furthermore, in which he has labored and which he has tested by experience, and he will write nothing but what he has seen with his own eyes. After suggesting a derivation for the word 'alchemy' and a theory for the origin of metals and 'proof that alchemy is a true art,' the author lays down eight precepts for alchemists to follow. The alchemist should work silently and secretly or he may be arrested as a counterfeiter. He should have a laboratory, 'a special house away from the sight of men in which there are two or three rooms in which experiments may be conducted.' He must observe time and seasons; the process of sublimation, for instance, cannot be successfully performed in winter. He must be a sedulous, persevering, untiring, and a constant worker. In his operations he must observe due order: first, *contributio*; then *sublimatio*; third, *fixio*; fourth, *calcinatio*; fifth, *solutio*; sixth, *coagulatio*; processes which are further explained in chapters 30 to 35. All the vessels which he uses should be made of glass. He should fight shy of princes and potentates, and finally, should have plenty of money. Chapters four to eight then deal with the subject of furnaces, and chapter nine tells how to glaze clay vessels.
>
> "In the tenth chapter, besides discussing what are the four

'spirits' of metals which dye or color, the author states his opinion as to the extent to which metals can be transmuted. He believes that metals can be produced by alchemy which are the equal of natural metals in almost all their qualities and effects, except that the iron of alchemy is not attracted by the stone adamant, and that the gold of alchemy does not stimulate the human heart or cure leprosy, while a wound inflicted by it swells up as one made by natural gold would not do. 'But in every other operation, hammering, testing, and color, it will endure forever.' In the two following chapters the author discusses what the elixir is and the kinds of medicines.

"A number of chapters are next devoted to description of various minerals, chemicals, dyes, and coloring matter, such as mercury, sulphur, orpiment, arsenic, salts of ammonia, common salt, various other salts, azure, minium, ceruse, and so on. We are then instructed in various processes, such as whitening quicksilver or sulphur or orpiment or arsenic, the making of powders, solutions, and distillations, leading up finally in the last two chapters to two brief recipes for the making of the precious metals. The general plan of this treatise is one to which many conform; it is noteworthy for the absence of mysticism and magic procedure."[22]

Evidently Thomas Aquinas was more or less familiar with the views, perhaps the experiments, of Albert. In his account of magic in the *Summa Contra Gentiles* and *De Potentia* he seems quite willing to accept the attitude of St. Augustine and Porphyry which Albert had made his own. As Thorndike says, "Aquinas accepts the essential features of the previous theological definition of magic as Albert did in his theological treatises." He says, for instance, "Natural things have certain hidden powers whose purpose cannot be assigned by man" (*Summa* II, 96, article 2). He also speaks of alchemy "as a true but difficult art" (Meteorology III, 9) and distinguishes between the illicit magic and the "occult works of nature."[23] He addressed a brief treatise to a "certain knight" on the subject, and in answering certain objections of the Master General, John of Vercelli, blandly states that

---

[22] *Op. cit.*, II, 572-573.

[23] *Op. cit.*, II, 602.

some of the inquiries had nothing to do with the Faith but were purely physical. Incidentally, too, while teaching under the eyes of Albert, Thomas may have received inspiration and encouragement to write at Paris a treatise on irrigation and mechanical engineering. For the professors, on hearing of his death, wrote to the General Chapter of the Order on May 2, 1274, to send them these and other unfinished works which he had composed while in their midst, and which in consequence they felt it their right to inquire after and beg to have.[24]

And whence, if not from Albert, did Ulrich of Strasburg draw his knowledge of mathematics and the art of clockbuilding which he exemplified in the Cathedral of Cologne? Where did Dietrich of Freiburg, another close friend of Albert, receive the encouragement to observe the phenomena of nature which led him eventually, between 1304-1319, to put forth his "Theory of the Rainbow," which the noted meteorologist of Hamburg, Hellman, declares "is the greatest achievement of its kind in the West during the Middle Ages," or, as Max Jacobi puts it, "we have to thank him for the first correct design of the path of the ray as it enters and leaves the little sphere" of the raindrop. Thomas of Catimpre, who is in great part responsible through his peddling of the gossip of the schools for the odium of magic attaching to Albert's name, followed the great professor's lectures at Cologne and in his works retails many of the scientific theories of Albert. Vincent of Beauvais, who is the first Frenchman to utilize Albert's works, takes one hundred and sixty-eight quotations from his *De Anima* for the *Speculum Naturale*; that is, about one third of this compendium of medieval knowledge.[25] Another French Dominican, Durandus—J. Koch would have him to be Durand of St. Pourcain[26]—utilizes the natural science of Albert. Radulf Brito, of the Paris University, speaks of "*Albertus et sequaces*," which proves conclusively that he had established a school of interpreters of Aristotle. Baumgartner points out that Dante's cosmographical ideas originate rather with Albert than Thomas.[27] There can be no doubt,

---

[24] H. Denifle, *Chartular. Univ. Par.*, I, 504-505.

[25] *L. Leiser, Vincenz von Beauvais als Kompilator und Philosoph (Leipzig: 1928), 61-69.*

[26] J. Koch, *Durandus de S. Porciano, O.P.* (Münster: 1926), 180.

[27] *M. Baumgarten, Dantes Stellung zur Philosophie (München: 1921), 27-47; P. Toynbee, "Some Unacknowledged Obligations of Dante to Albertus Magnus," in Romania (1908), 296-298; 492-517; G. Busnelli, "L'Origine dell'anima razionale secundo Dante e Alberto Magno,"*

therefore, that during his lifetime and immediately after, Albert did have a large following of students who had learned from him the experimental method in the natural sciences. He was called in one of the contemporary catalogs the "*doctor expertus*,"[28] which proves that men at large knew that he carried on experimental work. And this justifies Thorndike in saying:

"Thus while Albert of course believes that the statements of many of his authorities are based upon experience, he seems to feel that he and his associates have founded an important modern school for the investigation of nature at first hand. We may choose to regard it as a mere school of observation, but he dignifies its members by the title *experimentatores.* Again, therefore, we may admit that Pouchet was not unjustified in associating Albert with the modern experimental school."[29]

Perhaps the origin of the University at Cologne must be sought in the Albertinistic School, where the principles of Albert were given preference over Thomas's. We know that one hundred and forty years after Albert's death the university was constituted formally with full papal approbation. But just as the universities of Paris, Bologna, and Oxford had their origins in the monastic schools, so the one place where we should look for the assiduous cultivation of learning in Cologne during the period was precisely the Dominican school where Albert's name was kept fresh, where his ideals were carried through to startling discoveries, and where his fame continued to act as an incentive for a long line of scholars formed either directly or indirectly by his scientific spirit and experimental methods.[30] The origin of the Albertinistic School—the *Albertinisti*—has not been written, but we may expect shortly a preliminary study by Father G. Meersemann, O.P., whose name is so well known in all investigation having reference to Albert's many works.[31] This will be a glorious page in the history of scientific investigation, for we know this much that for centuries the Cologne University did shed luster upon the city on the Rhine and the

---

in Civiltà Cattolica, LXXX (1929), 289-300; LXXXI (1929), 97-107; 336-417.

[28] *F. Ehrle, Die Ehrentitel der scholastischen Lehrer des Mittelalters, 38, 42-44.*

[29] *Op. cit.*, II, 548.

[30] *M. Grabmann, Mittelalterliches Geistesleben (München: 1926), passim.*

[31] G. Meersemann, *Introductio*, 4, note 2.

Church Universal. If at the Council of Constance its professors, for political reasons easy to be understood, cast in their lot with the opposing faction, though they did submit when obedience was demanded, it must be to the eternal credit of the university that at the Reformation it became one of the staunchest of defenders of the Church, producing that doughty philosopher, John Eck, and drawing upon the professorial body some of the vitriol of John Reuchlin in his famous *Letters of Obscure Men.* Albert's spirit abided in the university for three centuries, radiated thence as far as Poland, where it persisted into the early eighteenth century. Having gone down in death after the Reformation, the University of Cologne came back to life in our own age—largely through the farsightedness of those great contemporary theologians, Cardinals Fischer and Schulte—as the Academy of Albert the Great.

It is a significant fact that the scientific reputation of Albert was rehabilitated by Humboldt, de Blainville, Pouchet, and Meyer precisely at a time when the world was ringing with the discoveries of Darwin, Spencer, and Haeckel, blatantly advertised on all sides as the death blow of revealed religion through the findings of modern science. And in our own day, when newer so-called sciences have been ushered upon the stage to take the place of the older ones, which have been battered rather pitifully by serious and honest investigators, it is worth keeping in mind that Barbado in his *Introduccion a la Psicologia Experimental* has shown conclusively that some of the pivotal points and problems of experimental psychology were envisaged, sometimes with surprising similarity of terminology, by Albert and his disciples.

Chapter XIV

ALL-SEEING NATURALIST

ONE of the inevitable results of the assiduous cultivation of the history of the various natural sciences, so characteristic of all scientific research today, is the rehabilitation of Albert's good name as a scientist. Scholars in goodly numbers are again thinking it worth their while to seek to evaluate his original contributions to the various sciences and to insist upon his towering position in the story of their development. While it is true that for centuries Albert did occupy a leading rank among the makers of science, it is also well known that he was ruthlessly pushed aside when the sciences had freed themselves from the influence of the Church and churchmen. An age which sought to establish a frank enmity between science and religion could not be expected to treat gently a man who was first and foremost a churchman to his finger tips without on that account feeling himself called upon or compelled to foreswear scientific research. And it was an easy matter to besmirch and belittle the scientific achievements of Albert because of the legends which a bedazzled age had attached to his name, in wonderment over his advanced ideas and novel experiments, as also because of the inevitable handicaps under which he worked and the prejudices against which he had to battle in order to accomplish as much as he did. If the first three centuries following Albert's death exaggerated most extravagantly his scientific attainments and achievements, then the next three hundred years unduly belittled them. Only since 1853 have scholars made a serious attempt to be fair and just to him. This is primarily due to F. A. Pouchet who turned the tide by his *Histoire des sciences naturelles au moyen age, ou Albert le Grand et son epoque considéré comme point de depart de l'ecole experimentalle.* While this important work has in the course of time been corrected in many respects and amplified with new historical data, while many of its secondary positions have been shown to be untenable the unassailable fact remains that its main contentions have not been set aside, even by so chronically prejudiced an authority as the anonymous author of the article on Albert in the *Histoire Litteraire de la France.* This writer had evidently been incensed by the extravagant claims of M. H. de Blainville, in his *Histoire des sciences de l'organization,* published from his notes, with additions, by F. L. M. Maupied (Paris: 1847). Subsequent scholars like Balss, Stadler, Wimmer, Jessen have supplemented and corroborated the main contentions of Pouchet. At the eightieth convention of the Society of German Naturalists and Physicians at Cologne, on September 31, 1908, Herman Stadler held up Albert to modern investigators as a model of what a true and conscientious scholar should be. Father Eric Wassmann, S.J., whose name will be remembered forever in the history of entymology for his epoch-making discoveries in ant life, remarked that this was the first time on record to his knowledge that a medieval churchman had been proposed as a model scientist to modern savants of any and every or of no shade of religious thought and belief.[1] Naturally, this tardy rehabilitation of a medieval monk and scientist aroused the vehement anger of men like White and Draper who, in challenging the claims put forward for Albert and other churchmen, only succeeded in betraying their own woeful lack of historical knowledge, erudition, and fair-mindedness.

It is worthy of remark in this connection that of all the scholars who in the past seventy-five years have studied the scientific attainments of Albert, Catholic students have been the most cautious, reserved, and modest in their claims and conclusions. They have taken nothing for granted. With laudable wisdom they have abstained from making panegyrics on Albert's character and from turning to apologetic uses his great achievements in the realm of medieval science. They have acted on the assumption that Albert is his own best justification and that, with all his scientific shortcomings, he was sufficiently in advance of his age to merit respectful consideration from all subsequent times. This admirable historical attitude is probably due in great measure to George von Hertling who, in his *Albertus Magnus. Ein Beitrag zu seiner Würdigung* (2d. edition. Münster: 1914), laid down historical norms to be followed in dealing with Albert's scientific labors

---

[1] E. Wassmann, "*Zur neuen Ausgabe der Tiergeschichte Alberts des Grossen,*" *in* Stimmen aus Maria-Laach (1912), 383.

which are a model of their kind for exacting criticism and rigorous scholarship. And the several scholars who have studied the philosophical and theological aspects of Albert's many-sided activity have been ensouled with the principles which von Hertling demanded of all those who essayed to delve in this field where exaggeration seems almost inevitable. Much of the same fine critical spirit—despite occasional betrayals of ignorance of Catholic dogma and regrettable lapses into anti-Romanist terminology—pervades the latest and most erudite study on *A Comprehensive History of Experimental Sciences* by George Sarton (Washington, D. C.: 1931), of the Carnegie Institute, where Albert appears with laudable and well-merited frequency in the large section devoted to medieval experimentation.

It must suffice to point out briefly, rapidly, and summarily, under special rubrics, the outstanding achievements of Albert in the various sciences he touched, and to indicate those points in which he outran his day and anticipated our own. In quoting the approving words of modern historical investigators we shall give the preference to those who, not being members of the Catholic Church, cannot be suspected of any undue sympathy for her attitude on the relations of science and faith and for Albert himself, who vindicated that attitude so magnificently.

BOTANY

In his *De Vegetalibus* Albert followed what he thought was a genuine work of Aristotle, but which, in 1857, was allocated to Nicholas of Damascus by Ernest Meyer. After following the pseudo-Aristotelian text for eight chapters Albert abandoned it because, as he said, he found it untrustworthy. Albert's first book, in six chapters, deals with the question of plant souls. The second book has to do with a classification of plants in which he comes very near modern times in the norms he lays down for distinguishing one plant from another. The third book discusses seeds and fruits. The fourth book follows the pseudo-Aristotelian text very closely. The fifth treats of the medicinal properties and effects of plants. The sixth describes trees in alphabetical order. The last book is a treatise on agriculture. Albert is the first European to mention and describe spinach,[2] the relation of

[2] J. Wimmer, Deutsches Pflanzenleben nach Albertus Magnus (Halle: 1909), 61.

grapes to the vines and leaves, the distinction between buds and flowers, the influence of heat and sunlight on the bark of trees. He anticipates Knight by centuries in holding that sap is odorless in the root but fragrant in the trunk and branches. He is the first man to refer scientifically to the rarity of duplicate leaves. He established the difference between thorns and thistles.[3] He had clear ideas on grafting—his remarks on the subject anticipate Luther Burbank. Ellison Hawks says: "His description of the apple, its three coats, the five-chambered core, the floral receptacle above the seed with testa and two hemispheral cotyledons is far superior to anything in any earlier writer."[4] Ernest Meyer, as early as 1836, said: "We do not find a botanist before Albert's time who can be compared to him with the exception of Theophrastus whom he did not know; after his time no one investigated the nature of plants more intelligently and fully until Conrad Gessner and Cisalpin."[5] Carl Jessen remarks: "Albert was the first man to describe German flora in a scientific way."[6] Remembering the ignorance about botanical studies in the Middle Ages, Hawks declares that "there was one man—Albertus Magnus—who did something to arrive at a scientific study of plants as living things. This had practically been at a standstill since the days of Aristotle."[7]

ZOOLOGY

George Sarton writes: "The best parts of Albert's works are the botanical and zoological books. The zoology was based on Michal Scot. It is divided into twenty-six books, of which the first nineteen are a paraphrase of Aristotle's treatises. Books twenty to twenty-six contain new matter, partly derived from personal observation or from direct information. Books twenty and twenty-one deal with generalities; book twenty with the nature of animals' bodies, their structure and forces;

---

[3] H. Stadler, *Albert von Cöln als Naturforscher* (Leipzig: 1909), 61.

[4] Ellison Hawks, *Pioneers of Plant Study* (London: 1928), 106.

[5] E. Meyer, *Geschichte der Botanik* (Königsberg: 1857), 9-84.

[6] Carl Jessen, *De Vegetalibus*. Einleitung V.

[7] Ellison Hawks, *op. cit.*, 102; K. Sudloff (*Kurzes Lehrbuch der Geschichte der Medizin*, Berlin: 1922) says: "The works of Albert on flora and fauna are epoch-making. He is the first who has treated these matters scientifically—in botany since the time of Theophrastus, in zoology since the time of Aristotle."

book twenty-one with perfect and imperfect animals and the causes of their perfection or imperfection (this is a kind of comparative psychology); books twenty-two and twenty-six are devoted to the description of individual animals, these being introduced in each chapter in the alphabetical order of their Latin names. These books were a sort of appendix to the *De Natura Rerum* of Thomas of Cantimpre, who had sat at his feet in Cologne. Book twenty-two, *gressabilia* (i.e., quadruples; our mammals, excepting bats, whales, and seals); book twenty-three, *volatilia* (i.e., birds and bats); book twenty-four, *aquatica* or *natalilia* (i.e., fishes, whales, seals, cephalopods, shellfishes, water snails, and other aquatic animals); book twenty-five, serpents (i.e., snakes, lizards, salamanders) including the varieties of snakes discussed in Ibn Sina's *Quantum*; book twenty-six, *vermes* (i.e., worms, insects, toads, frogs and snails). Many of the animals were here described for the first time."[8]

In the introduction to the critical edition of the *De Animalibus*, Stadler pointed out that Albert knew and described one hundred and thirteen kinds of quadrupeds, one hundred and fourteen birds, one hundred and thirty-nine aquatic animals, sixty-one serpents and forty-nine worms. He was the first man to mention the weasel, two kinds of martens, and the arctic bear. He was also the first to give the German names to the chamois, the ermine, and the fitchen or polecat. He has the distinction of first insinuating that the peculiarities of cats are due in great part to climatic conditions. He discovered the similarity between the teeth and claws of cats and lions. His brief treatise on falcons was an improvement on the classic work on the same subject by Frederic II. His veterinary erudition was remarkable for the age, so much so, indeed, that several anonymous writers on the same subject, by appropriating Albert's name, obtained instant success for their books. Thus many of the chap-books on "the white and black art of man and beast," circulating to this day under the name of Albert, while not due to his pen are an outcome of the authority he enjoyed among simple hostlers and veterinary doctors. He set the fashion of departing from the custom of the "bestiaries" where moral reflections are made *apropos* the habits and peculiarities of animals. He was one of the first founders of the science of animal anatomy and animal psychology.

[8] George Sarton, *op. cit.*, 938-939.

Lynn Thorndike says: "Albert has not only observed animal life widely, he has also performed experiments with animals as he apparently did not do with plants... Crude experiments these may be, but they are at least purposive."[9] Stadler points out that from Albert's treatises one could reinhabit German forests with animals found therein.[10] And Wassmann and Balss prove that his name cannot be overlooked in the history of evolution.[11] Balss also insists that in his remarks about the various kinds of squirrels in various countries which he had visited, the foundations of comparative zoology were laid. George Sarton remarks: "He had had and improved many opportunities of observing things in the course of his long travels as provincial of his Order (the Dominican rule obliged him to travel afoot). He observed animals in the Danube region, in the vicinity of Cologne, Augsburg, Worms, Treves in Friesland, Holland, Brabant, Italy... He also collected information from the many people of all classes he came across in the course of his missions."[12]

Entymology

Stadler remarks that "Albert showed an especially keen interest in insects,"[13] and this can be adequately proved from a study of his works, especially what he had to say about ants, spiders, and bees. No medieval man described so minutely and intelligently the life of these insects.[14] What Fabre's classic descriptions are to our days, that Albert's pictures of insect life were to Europe for three hundred years. He studied the anatomy of bees as none of his predecessors had. Jessen declares that he was the first to point out the belly marrow and structure of their feet and proboscis. In his botanical works he added supplementary data on these points as also keen observations regarding crabs and scorpions. Stadler insists that Albert's researches into the life and habits of ants was the finest achievement in this field

---

[9] Lynn Thorndike, A History of Magic and Experimental Science (Oxford: 1923), II, 541.

[10] H. Stadler, op. cit., 66.

[11] E. Wassmann, Die moderne Biologie und die Entwicklungstheorie (Freiburg: 1904), 11; H. Balss, Albertus Magnus als Zoologe (München: 1928), 141.

[12] George Sarton, *op. cit.*, 939.

[13] H. Stadler, *op. cit.*, 8.

[14] H. Balss, *Albertus Magnus von Cöln als Zoologe* (München: 1928), 115, 116.

during the entire Middle Ages.[15]

ICHTHYOLOGY

From his experience in Dominican refectories, where fish fare was almost perpetual, Albert could not remain indifferent about fish. From his youth he had been fascinated by their idiosyncrasies. He was the first to designate and describe the spolke; to call attention to the teeth of the carp; to reject the myths about griffins; to laugh at the common belief that pelicans feed their young with their own blood; to disprove the beaver's self-castration, the incombustibility of salamanders, and the birth of barnacle geese from trees. He was far ahead of his age in his knowledge of oysters and, probably, one of the first to suggest oyster beds, as we know them today. He knew the habitat of various kinds of fish, especially eels and salmon.[16] No medieval man wrote more extensively on this point. He was one of the first men to point out the distinction between fish and amphibians and how to establish it from the peculiarities of their anatomical structure. No preceding writer had as much to say, nor said it so engagingly, on whales and whale hunting.[17] He was the first to describe accurately the Greenland whale. From what he saw in Friesland, where he participated in a whale hunt, he knew the properties and uses of blubber. Even as a bishop in momentary retirement at his villa, Donaustauff, Albert did not lose interest in the denizens of the deep.[18] Despite his many intellectual pursuits and social cares he found time to reveal himself a premature Isaak Walton.

ORNITHOLOGY

Since in Albert's time Germany was rather sparsely settled and since, as a consequence, the many large forests were alive with birds, we need not be surprised that he devoted much time to their study and

---

[15] H. Stadler, *op. cit.*, 8.

[16] H. Stadler, Zur Tiergeographie Deutschlands im Mittelalter (München: 1908), 72.

[17] *De Animalibus (ed. Stadler), 310, 861.*

[18] J. Endres, "*Albertus Magnus und die bischöfliche Burg Donaustauf*," in *Historisch-Politische Blätter (1912), 832.*

to a description, in alphabetical enumeration, of their habits and peculiarities. Stadler says: "Now I could enumerate the entire German feathery kingdom which Albert knew: three (or rather four) species of swallows, five species of finches, three kinds of woodpeckers, besides the black, gray and green mocking birds, and two kinds of sparrows."[19] But this enumeration is obviously incomplete, for he knew and described at least six species of eagles, three kinds of peacocks, five kinds of wild geese and three of wild ducks, four kinds of gold finches, two kinds of falcons besides three pure and three mixed species. It must be borne in mind that these are only the birds with whose habits Albert was familiar. Since, for some inexplicable reason, legends of a moralizing or symbolical purport have attached to birds more numerously than to any other category of the animal kingdom—for which reason, no doubt, birds are at home in the decorations of Gothic cathedrals, as the sketches in the notebook of Villard de Honnecort, the greatest medieval architect, bear witness—Albert, with his sharp eye for their characteristics and his critical sense, puts himself to great pains to reject the statements of the Ancients, especially Pliny.[20] He rejects the fable of the one-eyed peacock, the peacock with one web foot, the peacock which weeps tears of blood. He will not admit that ostriches eat iron. He is the first German to mention the black stork, the best beloved of German birds. He discovered that swans sing in pain and not for the purpose of driving off pursuers. He knew more than any of his predecessors about eagles and none of his contemporaries were so uniformly correct in describing their habits. He loathes buzzards—probably he learned their rapacious ways on the hunt. With his love for the hunt he is a veritable mine of information on wild geese, ducks, and partridges. He sniggers at Hermes for holding that a rooster lays one egg before dying, from which the sun hatches a serpent, though this supposed prerogative of the rooster was stoutly maintained at Paris up to the late sixteenth century. He almost grows lyrical over the nightingale, which even then played a large part in the folk song along the Rhine. Albert's love of birds must have been generally known, for some of the earliest representations of him—even

---

[19] *H. Stadler, op. cit.,* 69.

[20] F. Strunz, Albertus Magnus Weisheit und Naturforschung im Mittelalter (Vienne: 1926), 150.

in Paris where birds have been proverbially rare—show him surrounded, like another *Poverello* of Assisi, with the most varied specimens of these songsters. He was familiar with the anatomical peculiarities of birds, from personal experimentation, as Vassalius suggested centuries later. Franz Strunz points out that Albert was the first to speak intelligently, with understanding wisdom and childlike simplicity, about the sex life of birds.[21] And Balss suggests that what Albert says about the life of a brood of birdlings in the nest is one of the most incomparably beautiful pieces of writing of that epoch.[22] There are echoes of Albert in so late a book as Thompson's *Ten Commandments Amongst Animals.* Emile Male, in his superb book, *The Religious Art of the Thirteenth Century,* does not forget to suggest how much the ornithological teachings of Albert contributed to the dazzling splendor of the medieval Cathedrals,[23] while Louis Gillet, in his *L'Art Religieuse et les Ordres Mendiants,* gives even higher praise to the bird lore of Albert.

COSMOGRAPHY

The average medieval man knew intimately his own little patch of ground. He entertained the most fantastic ideas about the far-off lands, concerning which the returned crusader or warrior spoke freely and extravagantly on every street corner or in every wine shop. In answering the many questions about these unknown parts of the world and exploding the tales about the wonders to be found in them, Albert was not only meeting a very urgent need of his day but also keeping alive an interest in exploration. He adopted Aristotle's teaching, with many reservations, in his *De Coelo et Mundo* and *De Natura Locorum,* where are to be found jumbled together elements of physical geography, mineralogy, metallurgy, astronomy, and in fact of all the sciences that had to do with the earth and the sky. He accepts Aristotle's theory about the rotundity of the earth, adding a mathematical argument of his own which is stronger and more

---

[21] F. Strunz, op. cit., 146, "*Auch das Geschlechtliche im Leben der Tiere und Menschen verliert vor einer solchen unverhohlenen, lieben Wahrhaftigkeit und ehrfurchtvollen Naturnahe alles Peinliche... In Albert ist der arglose, unbefangene Sinn des Kindes und doch des Weisen.*"

[22] H. Balss, *op. cit.*, 104.

[23] H. D. Taylor, *The Medieval Mind* (New York: 1918), 108, note 2.

convincing than any alleged by the Greek. He also invoked the argument from gravitation for, he says, since all parts of the earth converge to the center, there can be no doubt about the world's sphericity. Contrary to the opinions of Lactantius and St. Augustine he holds that there is an inhabited, or at least an inhabitable, land at the antipodes. Answering those cocksure writers who flippantly said that, if such a continent existed, the position, motion, and action of the sun must necessarily be inverted, Albert boldly proclaimed that right and left, upper and lower, Orient and Occident, are relative terms and that, therefore, the order of the heavenly motion on the supposed continent would be identical with that in Europe. In answer to the second facile argument that, since there is four times more water than land, more than half of this continent would be submerged in water, Albert insisted upon the many causes which might diminish the volume of water or the facility with which the water can transform itself, as for instance, by evaporation. In reply to the third stock objection that the supposed continent would be useless, since no one could go to it or across over to Europe from it, Albert shrewdly parried that it would be illogical to hold that no one lives there or might possibly live in that torrid zone. "I believe," he says, "that it is difficult to cross to those regions but not impossible. The difficulty about the entire matter arises from the large sandy wastes bleached by the sun. It is for this reason that there is so little communication between men south of this region and ourselves who are in the north."[24] This cosmographical teaching was traditional in Dominican schools for centuries and scarcely any otherwhere. Hence it comes that Albert's theories were taught to Dante by his Dominican professor, Fra Remigio de Girolami, and that they appear prominently in the tenth canto of the *Paradiso*.[25] This also accounts for the reverential mention of Albert by the great Florentine poet.

So, too, the man whose name was attached to the western hemisphere, Amerigo Vespucci, got his cosmographical ideals at San Marco, Florence, from his uncle, the Dominican George Anthony Vespucci. That these ideas were in the air when Columbus was seeking

---

[24] De *Causis Elementorum*, II (tr. 1, Chap. 3).

[25] M, Grabmann, "*Fra Remigio de' Girolami, O.P.*," in *Scuola Cattolica (1925), 267-281, 347-368.*

support for an expedition to the Indies is plain from the poem *La Sfera* of Leonardo Dati, which reproduced faithfully the teaching of Toscanelli, the friend and correspondent of Columbus.[26] No wonder Diego Deza, the Dominican confessor of Isabella, faithful to the Albertinian tradition in the Dominican schools, took up the case of Columbus with the queen, about the year 1485. No wonder that Columbus whose set of Albert's works, annotated in his own handwriting, is still preserved in Seville, found a hearing, sympathy and shelter at St. Stephen's Convent, Salamanca, where the question of an expedition to the Indies was once more agitated after having been shelved for the seven years following the first junta of learned men at Santa Fe in Spain. And only a few months before his death the discoverer wrote to his son Ferdinand begging him to convey to the gracious queen the information that, but for the goodly offices, interest, and learning of Diego Deza, she would not have been able to add the jewel of the Indies to her crown. Mandonnet, who has written an exhaustive study on the subject, remarks with justice: "Thus it is a true title of glory for the two men who dowered the Middle Ages with the most solid speculations and the most positive teaching, that they were the first and most powerful patrons of those cosmographical ideals which conspired in preparing the *milieu* in which the genius of Columbus developed and in which would emerge the project of the discovery of the Indies."[27] And, later on, repeating what Humboldt had suggested earlier in his *Cosmos*, he says: "Nearly everything true and fluid which fifteenth-century science possessed came from antiquity by passing through the Middle Ages by way of Albert the Great above all others, who was the first man to introduce the Latin world to the scientific riches of the Arabs. The Dominican school, faithful to peripatetic philosophy, preserved the traditional teaching without difficulty and at the time of the discovery of the Indies it had denied nothing elementary in its teaching."[28] Perhaps there is something reminiscent of all this in the words of Pope Clement VIII who, in canonizing St. Rose of Lima, the first American saint, remarked that the

---

[26] *P. Mandonnet,* Les Dominicains et la Découverte de l'Amérique (Paris: 1893), 31-34; J. M. Schneider, "*Aus Astronomie und Geologie des hl. Albert des Grossen,*" *in* Divus Thomas (Freiburg: 1932), 41-68.

[27] *Ibid.,* 37-38.

[28] *Ibid., 95.*

Dominican Order seems to have received from God "the mission of watching over the two continents of the western hemisphere and the Philippines."

Albert's curiosity about the physical constitution and conformation of this world extended in all directions and we find him speaking with originality on all phases of cosmography. In establishing the rotundity of the world he speaks in the plainest terms of the Suez Canal as it was built in our own age.[29] Emil Michael sees in his cosmographical doctrine a very clear adumbration of Laplace's theory.[30] As regards the movement of planets, he suggested theories that were put forth later on as practicable and workable. It is no wonder that Albert's influence on Copernicus has often been pointed out. There is still preserved a well-worn set of Albert's works, filled with original notes by that indomitable investigator.[31] His influence on Keppler cannot be denied, and the researches of these two together cleared the way for Newton and his immortal laws. Nor is it unlikely that Newton harked back to Albert, for there are points of view and modes of expression in the great Englishman which sound like echoes of the medieval scientist. If another Englishman, Locke, spoke about the *tabula rasa* and primary and secondary qualities of things, it has been shown that this terminology had first been used with a fixed philosophical meaning and connotation by Albert.[32]

Alexander Humboldt called attention to the fact that Albert had sketched a workable theory of zones in connection with, and growing out of, his treatise on climatology. Better than most of his contemporaries Albert indicated the effects of temperature on flowers, beast, and men. He was far in advance of his age in explaining rain, dew, and snow. His acquaintances, Konungo Skuggsja or Peter of Dacia, the Dominican, and Matthew Paris, for all their remarkable work which shows the influence of Albert, were resigned to follow him

---

[29] *P. Gerard, "La Cosmographie d'Albert le Grand d'après l'observation et l'expérience au moyen âge," in Revue Thomiste (1904), 466-476; (1905), 147-173.*

[30] E. Michael, *Geschichte des deutschen Volkes* (Freiburg: 1903), III, 450.

[31] *M. Grabmann, L'Influsso di Alberto Magno sulla Vita Intellettuale del Medio Eva (Roma: 1931), 114.*

[32] *C. Bäumker, "Zur Vorgeschichte zweier Locke'scher Begriffe," in Archiv für Geschichte der Philosophie (1908), 296-298; 492-517; (1909), 380, 497.*

when speaking of winds, currents, tides and floods, and earthquakes.[33] He stands alone in his day for his vivid and accurate description of volcanic eruptions.

CHEMISTRY

Though the knowledge of chemistry was very rudimentary in the Middle Ages and hampered by the most grotesque experiments, Albert was familiar with many chemical processes and their operations such as distillation and sublimation, purification of gold and silver by cementation and the use of lead. He knew that mercury may be successfully distilled without loss of weight. He recognized that wine, when heated, gives off a substance "supernatant" and "inflammable." He taught that cinnabar is produced by the union of mercury and sulphur; that sulphur attacks all metals but gold; that pure arsenic is produced by heating two parts of soap with one part of orpiment (arsenic trisulphide); that the nature of arsenic is metallic; that nut galls are a source of tannic acid; that the compounds which he called *marchasita* include iron, zinc and copper pyrites and other sulphides of metallic luster. According to Professor Florian Cajorie, of the University of California, he knew as early as 1250 that gunpowder could be prepared from sulphur, saltpeter, and charcoal. He introduced the term *vitroleum* to designate sulphate of iron. In a recent issue of *The Laboratory*, published by the Fischer Chemical Company, of Pittsburgh, it was shown that Albert knew the color reaction between gall nuts and vitriol.

Professor John M. Stillman, of Stanford University, writes in *The Story of Early Chemistry* (New York: 1924): "Of the great value of the work of Albertus Magnus in helping to spread the knowledge of chemistry of his time there can be no doubt... He presents this knowledge with a clearness and directness that characterizes him as one of the ablest thinkers of his century—this very clarity of expression—free from intentional secrecy or mystification—must have given his works an important value in helping to lay the foundations for sane and sensible points of view, in a time when, according to the writers of the times, fraud, charlatanry and imposture in alchemy were

[33] G. Sarton, op. cit.

very prevalent."

In order to show the style used by Albert in his descriptions and also to furnish examples of his general attitude to the subject of chemistry and to alchemy as well, we are quoting directly from Stillman's translations: "Those who operate much in copper in our region, namely in Paris or Cologne and in other places where I have seen them at work, convert copper into brass by powder of a stone called *calamina.* And when this stone evaporates there still remains a dark brilliancy turning slightly to the appearance of gold. But that it be rendered paler and thus more like the yellowness of gold, they mix with it a little tin by reason of which the brass loses much of the ductility of the copper. And those who wish to deceive and to produce a brilliancy like gold retain the stone (*calamina*) so that it remains longer in the brass in the fire (or furnace) not quickly vaporizing from the brass. It is thus retained by *oleum vitri* (liquefied glass), for fragments of glass are powdered and sprinkled in the pot (*testa*) upon the brass after *calamina* is introduced, and then the glass so added swims upon the brass and does not allow the stone and its virtue to evaporate, but turns the vapor of the stone back into the brass, and thus the brass is long and strongly purged and the feculent matters in it are burned away. Finally, the *oleum vitri* vaporizes the virtue of the stone, but the brass is made much more brilliant than it would be without it. He who desires to simulate gold still more completely repeats these operations of heating (*optesim*) and purging of the melted glass frequently and mixes with the brass, silver instead of tin, and thus it is made so red and yellow that many believe it to be gold itself when, in truth, it is still a kind of bronze (or brass, *aes*)."

"Besides we have never found an alchemist so-called, operating generally (*in toto*) but that he colors with a yellow elixir into an appearance of gold and with the white elixir colors to the resemblance of silver, seeking that the color may remain while in the fire and may penetrate the whole metal, just as the manner of working it is possible to produce a yellow color, the substance of the metal remaining. And here again it is not to be maintained that several kinds of metals are contained in one another. It is from this and similar things, that is demolished the dictum of those who say that any kind of metal you please is contained in another."

Albert's description of *nitrum,* which in his time, as also in that of the ancients, meant carbonate of sodium or potassium as contained in plant ash is here described by him: "Nitrum is thus called from the island of Nitrea where it was first found. The Arabs call it baurac. It is a kind of salt less known than *sal gemma* (rock salt) transparent but in thin plates. It is roasted in the fire, and then, all superfluous aqueous substance being given off, it is burned to a high degree of dryness ('*efficiter siccum magis combustum*') and the salt itself is rendered sharper. The varieties are distinguished according to the localities where it is formed."

Tuchia, a name applied to a more or less impure sublimate of zinc oxide is described by Albert in the following paragraph: "Tuchia, which has frequent use in the transmutation of metals, is an artificial and not a natural mixture, for tuchia is made from the smoke which rises and is solidified by adhering to hard bodies, when brass is purified from stones (minerals) and tin which are in it. But the best kind is that which is sublimed from that (that is, re-sublimed) and then that which in such sublimation remains at the bottom is *climia*, which is called by some *succudus*. There are many kinds of tuchia, as it occurs white, yellow, and turning red. When tuchia is washed, there remains at the bottom a sort of black sediment of tuchia. This is sometimes called *Tuchia Irida*. But the difference between succudus and tuchia is as we stated, namely because tuchia is sublimed and succudus is what remains at the bottom unsublimed. The best is volatile and white, then the yellow, then the red; the fresh is considered better than the old. All tuchia is cold and dry and that which is washed is considered better in those operations (that is, in above mentioned transmutation of metals)."[34]

J. W. Mellor, in *A Comprehensive Treatise on Inorganic and Theoretical Chemistry* (New York: 1922), accentuates not only the original contributions of Albert to chemistry but his undoubted influence on St. Thomas Aquinas.

> "Albertus Magnus especially studied the union of sulphur and the metals; and like the Arabian Rhases, he considered the metals themselves to be compounds of different proportions of the three principles or elements: arsenic, mercury, and sulphur. Sulphur, said

[34] J. M. Stillman, *The History of Early Chemistry* (New York: 1924), 165; passim.

he, 'blackens silver and burns the metal on account of the *affinity* which it has for these substances.' The term affinity was thus used for the first time to designate the unknown cause of chemical action. Silver was supposed to be the metal most closely allied to gold, so that he considered the transmutation of silver into gold would be the easiest to realize. Albertus Magnus knew how to separate the noble from the base metals by fire, and how to separate gold from silver by *aqua regia.* Some suppose the treatise ascribed to Albertus Magnus to be spurious. The canonized scholar, Thomas Aquinas (1225-1274), was a pupil of Albertus Magnus. It has been said that while the master was a student of nature and philosophy, the pupil was a student of man and society. Both are considered to have excelled as exponents of theology rather than as students of natural science. From the little knowledge that is available concerning the alchemical labors of Thomas Aquinas he would appear to have been particularly attracted by the action of mercury on the metals—tin, lead, etc.—and he applied the term *amalgam* to the liquid or paste which is formed when these metals are opened up with mercury."[35]

But not only on Thomas Aquinas did the powerful influence of Albert react. Besides Dietrich of Freiburg and Ulrich of Strasburg, who could not deny their dependence on Albert, there were John Glogan, Joachim de Gostnum, Michael of Breslau, and Stanislaus Rozycki, who gave Poland the best scientific books in their day, all filled with the

---

[35] J. W. Mellor, *A Comprehensive Treatise on Inorganic and Theoretical Chemistry* (New York: 1922), I, 46. "Sulphur he describes as *substantia uniformis in partibus suis*, which might well mean that it was an element in the modern acceptation of the term; that is, a substance which is chemically indivisible into other substances. If this be so, it must be admitted that St. Albert, and not Lavoisier, was the first to recognize the elementary nature of sulphur. He also mentions different kinds of sulphur, and the passages suggest that some at least of the allotropic modifications of this element were known to him." H. Casey, "The Scientific Work of St. Albert the Great," in *Irish Ecclesiastical Record* (1932), 378-387. "Methods of dialysis, and in fact the phenomenon itself, are usually considered as discoveries of Thomas Graham, who flourished during the first half of last century... But anyone who wishes to take the trouble of reading the nineteenth chapter of the *Libellus de Alchimia* will find therein an excellent description of dialysis, written at least six hundred years before Graham's discovery of it. St. Albert employed the method of dialysis through a semipermeable membrane, for the purification of different salts, and with no small success" (*ibid.*).

audacious spirit of Albert and his suggestive and inventive temper. But before them there appeared in Germany Albert of Orlamund, whose *Philosophia Pauperum* was a favorite textbook with a frank bias for physical sciences; Conrad Summerhard, for whose book on science Wimpheling wrote some of his bombastic verses to serve as an introduction; Conrad of Halberstadt, an authority on gems and metallurgy; John Weiss, the best scientist of his day, and Konrad von Meyerberg, whose scientific attainments were the wonder of his age. These and scores of lesser students were outspoken advocates of Albert's scientific methods and devotion to the natural sciences.[36]

By a strange paradox, when men began tiring of natural philosophy and sought peace of mind in the study of theology, it was John of Dambach who, in his *Consolatio Theologiae*, gave birth to a big literature known as the *Trostbücher*.[37] And his favorite author was Albert, not Thomas Aquinas. In these books of consolation intended for worn-out, jaded, or disappointed students and scholars, the last flickerings of Albert's scientific influence upon the ages must be sought. And just as in Albert's work there was always a preoccupation to lift man's mind to God through the natural sciences, so in these *Trostbücher* the knowledge of created things is made to subserve the purposes of theology. Albert could not have desired a finer consummation for his own study of nature nor the impetus he gave to the study of the natural sciences.

---

[36] *M. Grabmann, L'Influsso, passim.*

[37] *A. Auer,* Johannes von Tambach und die Tröstbücher vom 11. bis 16. Jahrhundert (Münster: 1928).

CHAPTER XV
EXPERIMENTALIST, NOT MAGICIAN

ANY study of Albert's interest in medicine, as it was understood in those days, must necessarily bring up a discussion of magic for which he was extravagantly praised by his contemporaries and just as violently condemned by later writers. In the thirteenth century, medicine and magic were interchangeable terms. But later generations took a different view. Appraising his medical knowledge, which must be considered rather full for that time, and taking cognizance of his constant effort to increase his store of knowledge by experiments, they beheld in all his experimentations nothing but black magic, with its more or less frank trickery, mountebankery, and mystification.

At the outset, it must be insisted upon that from his youth Albert had had a decided tendency for medical studies. To prosecute these in something like a scientific way he passed on to Padua. Northern Italy, at that time was the favorite rendezvous of all of those who, while wishing to be more than mere blundering homeopaths, still did not care to go or could not afford to go to the medical schools of the Muslims in Spain. Salerno had established a reputation in medical teaching. In Albert's time Bologna was already beginning to usurp this hegemony. Did Albert on his visits to Bologna prefer to seek out for discussion the medics or the juriconsults who swarmed about the city? carried on for the practical end of discovering remedies of a homely kind for the people. The herbalists were, to all practical intents and purposes, unlicensed physicians familiar with the curative properties of herbs and flowers, something like the medicine men of our own Indians, though, of course, on a higher grade of expert knowledge. The medieval peoples were exposed to the diseases common in their respective lands, diseases which, while they appeared frequently, were all the more ravaging because of the peoples' utter disregard for sanitation and other prophylactic measures. There were, too, the scourges brought back from the Orient by the crusaders. Many of the plagues which periodically visited Europe in the Middle Ages can be traced to the custom of bringing back from the East the unembalmed corpses of the crusaders. In devoting so much time to the study of the physiological structure of plants and animals, Albert was trying to keep pace with the new mania for a knowledge of anatomy and for dissection, against both of which clinical operations Frederick II, in 1241, legislated very stringently but to no very good effect. For the need for just such study was made imperative by the many cripples of one kind or other produced by the almost unintermittent wars of the times.

If Albert gave a decided medical turn and tone to many of his sermons, betraying as he does in doing so a rather full knowledge of the commoner sicknesses of the day, their symptoms, effects, and medication, it was in no wise repugnant to the people or contrary to the practise of many preachers. The people looked upon their priests as the best-educated men in the town, and were willing to accept medical advice of a rudimentary sort from them. And the preachers knew full well that any show of interest on their part in the bodily health of the masses would be the surest way of opening the doors of the peoples' hearts. Monks were pharmacists, dentists, nurses in that day without any lowering of their ecclesiastical influence or standing. And itinerant preachers, like Albert, did not count it beneath their dignity to gather wherever they went homely recipes that would drive away ills of the body.

In all his works Albert scattered medical lore, such as it was, with a free hand. His *De Animalibus*, similar to if not actually based upon the *Anatomia Vivorum* of Richard of Wendover, is in many respects a first attempt at a comparative anatomy in which the organs of beasts are compared with those of men. He was attracted to Aristotle, among other reasons, for his due consideration of the human body and medicinal lore. And since the Jewish and Arabian commentators upon Aristotle had produced the best medical theory up to that time, Albert perused with special interest the works of Maimonides and Sina Quariam, which Gerad of Cremona had put within reach of the West in a Latin translation. By such careful study Albert arrived at a fairly thorough knowledge of man and beast. Thus he was more than passably familiar with the diseases of horses. He wrote so well on the diseases of falcons that there was circulated under his name for a long time a handbook on the subject which, because of its simplicity, must have been written by some unknown farmer or hostler who sought to get a large popularity for his manual by attaching Albert's name to it. This thing precisely was done in the case of Frederick II's book on falconry which Albert used largely.[1]

Albert's method was conditioned, to a great extent, by the state of knowledge in his time. George Sarton, in his *Comprehensive History of Experimental Science*, says that "we must bear in mind, for the sake of fairness, that medical progress as we are able to register it today, year after year, was entirely impossible and unthinkable until relatively recent times."[2] The only alternative for a man like Albert was to try out his recipes and remedies on any willing patients who offered themselves or could be persuaded to use them, and if the simples proved successful, to adopt them for general use and commendation to others. Medicines had been first discovered in that manner among the Greeks and Egyptians, and were tried out in that way during the high Middle Ages. As Sarton suggests: "Physicians were groping in the dark with no other guide than their own wisdom."[3] The only other resource for a man who was conscious of his responsibility in trying to cure the bodies of his fellows was to question men with whom he came in contact as to the success of the experiments they themselves had carried on. Now Albert did this consistently over a long period of time and a wide area of land. It appears clearly from many passages in his voluminous writings that he was never too preoccupied with other interests to take the time to learn medical lore from others, those especially who could give guarantee that they had tried out their remedies.

The second method to which Albert had necessarily to resort was the consultation of the medical works of the Ancients. He had absorbed whatever he deemed good in the works of Aristotle and Ibn Sina and Maimonides. If he showed a preference for Avicenna over Averroes it was because the former was a far better guide than the latter to the vast medical riches of the Muslim physicians on the Iberian peninsula. He was not a stranger to the medical school of Bologna which just at this time was applying the scholastic method to medicine. He caught

---

1 *Leon Moule, La Médecine vétérinaire en Europe au Moyen Age (Paris: 1900), 56-59.*

2 *George Sarton, A Comprehensive History of Experimental Science (Washington: 1931), 790.*

3 *Op. cit.,* 790.

the general enthusiasm for surgery which was in great part due to the epoch-making researches and clinical experiments of the Dominican bishop, Theodoric Borgognoni, whom Albert must have met at the court of Pope Innocent IV or at a Chapter of the Order.[4] From the lay brothers of the Order in practically every convent of northern Italy, especially Santa Maria Novella, Florence, he must have gathered precious data about dentistry.[5] It is a remarkable fact that, despite the prohibition of Frederick II, Albert dissected animals. Several centuries later Vesalius bore testimony to his having read with much pleasure these parts of the treatises of Albert. In dissecting small animals for the purpose of learning details of anatomy Vesalius professed that he was simply following the example of Albert.

It is plain, therefore, that by dint of study and observation Albert was as well informed as any so-called medic of his day. He possessed the scientific spirit which will not be satisfied until it has tested knowledge and found out conclusions for itself. "The aim of natural sciences," he said, "is not simply to accept the statements of others, that is, what is narrated by people, but to investigate the causes that are at work in nature for themselves," for "we must endeavor to find out what nature can naturally bring to pass." Like a true experimentalist he did not hesitate to make investigations of his own. Julius Pagel states in Puschmann's *History of Medicine* that Albert found out the uses of and experimented with salt, vitriol, alum, arsenic, marcasite, niter, tuchia, and amber. And he goes on to say: "Albert shared with the naturalists of the scholastic period the quality of entering deeply and thoroughly into the objects of nature, and was not content with bare, superficial details concerning them which many of the writers of the period penetrated no further than to provide a nomenclature. While Albert was a churchman and an ardent devotee of Aristotle in matters of natural phenomena, he was relatively unprejudiced and presented an open mind. He thought that he must follow Hippocrates and Galen rather than Aristotle and Augustine in medicine and the natural sciences. We must concede it as a special subject of praise for Albert, that he distinguished very strictly between

---

4 *Op. cit.*, 654-655.

5 *Fritz Jaeger, Zahnärztliches aus den Werken Alberts und seiner Schüler Thomas von Cantimpre und Vincenz von Beauvais (Leipzig: 1921), 61.*

natural and supernatural phenomena. The former he considered as entirely the object of the investigation of nature. The latter he handed over to the realm of metaphysics." And again he says: "Albert's efforts to set down the limits of natural science show already the seeds of a more scientific treatment of natural phenomena and a recognition of the necessity to know things in their causes—*rerum cognoscere causas*—and not to consider that everything must simply be attributed to the action of Providence." Albert was, indeed, a conscientious physician who tried to make his own all the medical knowledge available at the time. Did he flatter himself that he had mastered everything worth knowing in medicine? He answered categorically that "it is necessary to establish every experiment, not in one way only, but according to all the circumstances."[6] Was he fool enough to think that there was no such thing as a development of science? He answered with finality that "it must be said that not all scientific demonstrations have been made, but that many remain to be discovered."[7]

To Albert in a sovereign degree may be applied the words of George Sarton about the medical science of the time: "In our final appraisement of the medical achievement of this period, we must bear in mind, for the sake of fairness, that medical progress as we are able to register it today, year by year, was entirely impossible and unthinkable until relatively recent times. The outstanding medical advances have been due to the gradual invasion of the medical art by outside sciences—chemistry, physics, bacteriology, etc. With some pardonable exaggeration one might say that medicine progressed by ceasing to be what it was and surrendering its territory to other disciplines absolutely different from its own. Without the marvelous instruments which modern physicists have given to mankind, such as high-power microscopes, polarimeters, spectroscopes, sensitive manometers and galvanometers, X-ray and radium tubes, etc., the physician was essentially an artist, not a scientist, his main props were his experience and his common sense, his clinical intuition. To be sure, these have kept their full value to this day, and no manner of instruments will ever make up for the lack of wisdom. However,

---

[6] *Ethic. VI, tr. II, Chap. 25.*

[7] *Postr. Analy. I, tr. I, Chap. 1.*

during the Middle Ages, the physician had no help whatever but what he could find or hoped to find in books; no scientific guidance of any kind, except unfortunately a wrong one."[8]

And this brings us face to face with the charge of magic leveled at Albert from the time of his death, and even before it.

Albert's pupil, Thomas of Cantimpre, with the laudable intention of glorifying the master at whose feet he had sat, was responsible in great measure for the reputation for magic attached to the great professor's name. Knowing as no second man of his time the gossip of town and city, workshop and university hall, he gathered together the popular legends which had circulated among the people in Albert's lifetime and were extravagantly embellished after his death. This farrago of incredible tales[9] was seized upon by masses who had long looked upon Albert as the wonder of his age. As the authentic facts of Albert's life and achievements began to become dim through time, the legendary inventions became more striking and bizarre, based on the wide experimental knowledge possessed by him to which Peter of Prussia, writing about the end of the fifteenth century, thus alludes: "Moreover, this should be understood, that after Aristotle faith is to be put in Albert above all who have written in philosophy, because he has himself illuminated the writings of almost all philosophers, and has seen wherein they spoke truly or falsely, nay more, since he himself was experienced above all others in natural phenomena. It may be that some, relying on their metaphysics or logic, can impugn him by certain arguments, but I think that no matter of great concern since Albert himself says that faith is to be put in anyone who is expert in his art."[10] For three hundred years, therefore, the world was so much lost in wonderment over Albert's knowledge of natural phenomena that it had to resort to magic, as the only explanation of his intellectual proficiency. What can be answered to such an age-old tradition dating back to Albert's day?

First of all, it must be kept in mind that most of the books abounding in extravagant reports of experimentations and mysterious practices and cryptic and superstitious formulas are not the product of

---

[8] *Op. cit.*, 790.

[9] Thomas Cantimpranus, *Bonum Universale*, II, 57, *Pars* XXXV; *ibid.*, I.

[10] Petrus de Prussia, *Vita*, 288.

Albert's pen. For a long time books of a daring character in magic, for which the author was afraid to stand author, were ascribed to Albert. Lynn Thorndike has shown conclusively that by no possible chance could Albert have been the author of the *Liber Aggregationis*, or *Book of Secrets or Virtues*, attaching to certain herbs, stones, and animals. This monumental and widely circulated work was made up of the treatises entitled: *Experimenta Alberti*, or *The Experiments of Albert*; the treatise *De Mirabilibus Mundi* or *The Secrets of the World*; and the *De Secretis Mulierum*, or *The Secrets of Women*, sometimes also called *The Secrets of Albert.*[11] The *Speculum Astronomiae*, or *The Mirror of Astronomy*, is sometimes ascribed to Roger Bacon and again to Albert. It is generàlly admitted now that the *Philosophia Pauperum*, a kind of popular encyclopedia of natural sciences, comes from the hand of Albert of Orlamund. While some ascribe to the same author the *De Potentiis Animae* and *De Passionibus Aeris*, there are other historians who will not admit this ascription, though they do not suggest or indicate the author or possible author. The *Secretorum*, sometimes called the *De Regimine Dominorum*, is a pseudo-Aristotelian work known in Europe before Albert's time. Special treatises or tracts from this work, and from the others we have mentioned before, were excerpted and passed around under various names as works, genuine and authentic, of Albert.

This method of splitting up the spurious works of Albert on magic, accounts for the extremely large number of Albertinian works to be found in all the larger libraries of Europe dating back a few hundred years. One has but to look over the list of spurious works of Albert dressed by Weiss, Scheeben, Thorndike, and Meersemann, to be convinced that those ages were much given over to magic, or else were very gullible. This is especially true in the matter of fathering works on Albert which, from interior criticism alone, would have shown, unmistakably, another paternity. There can be no doubt, therefore, that justly or unjustly, Albert was looked upon as a magician. If there were need to prove that he was deemed a magician, the best argument would be to keep in mind the magic he must needs have exercised constantly in producing as many books on magic as have been ascribed to him. But even at that his magic would have been of a very inferior sort, lacking in freshness, resourcefulness, and inventiveness. For a

[11] Lynn Thorndike, *A History of Magic and Experimental Science* (Oxford: 1923), 720-750.

study of many of these works on magic show them to be not only intolerably dry and tame, flat and puerile, but painfully repetitious and dependent upon a parent book and upon a set of iron formulas. Albert himself would not have taken the time to write a big corpus of books that are slavishly imitative. If Albert must be made out to be a magician, it will be necessary to produce more original works somehow to guarantee the false ascription.

What grounds, then, are there for calling Albert, as Peter of Prussia does, *magnus in magia* and, as the other writers would have it, *expertus in magia*? Magic was frequently mentioned and always condemned by Albert in his Aristotelian and Biblical commentaries. In these works he is speaking as a theologian and takes magic in the theological sense and meaning. He distinguished a good and bad magic. It was the former which the Magi made use of in following the star to Bethlehem. The latter kind was always ascribed to the demons. Demoniacal marvels of magic cannot be compared with miracles, he says, for the former although more rapid in their operations than the normal operations of nature are not as instantaneous as miracles, nor are they as utterly independent of material agencies and instruments. It is plain that there was, in Albert's mind, a third kind of magic—natural magic he called it—which resembled very much that spoken of by William of Auvergne. It is like evil magic, inasmuch as it employs the forces of nature and the influence of the stars and other creatures, which while hard to describe cannot be said not to play a part in transformations of one kind or other. This natural magic is unlike bad magic, inasmuch as it does not resort to demons, or to the use of incantations and superstitious devices by which the diviners and necromancers set so much store. As can be seen, Albert settled the question of magic where every educated Catholic and religious-minded man expected it to be settled, and where, if religion had been abused and prostituted by having been called into play, it alone can be settled in a competent and definitive way—in theology. In defining theology Albert made it abundantly explicit that it is not the business of theology to interfere in matters pertaining purely, solely, and exclusively to the natural sciences. But as soon as the natural sciences venture into the domain of religion theology has the right and duty—a right which it cannot sign away and a duty which it cannot disregard—to defend not only itself but also religion and truth which it is supposed to explain and guard. It will be to the point in this connection to quote what the non-Catholic historian of magic, Lynn Thorndike, says on this point: "He nowhere in his commentaries on Aristotle or the works of natural science stops and discusses magic at any length. But there are a number of brief and incidental allusions to it, which imply that it is a distant and definite branch of knowledge of which, although he himself does not treat, he gives no sign of approval."[12] Albert was a good enough theologian in his own estimation to know what to say when he found magic impinging on religious territory. He was a good enough scientist in his own estimation to be willing to adduce any natural explanation of strange phenomena about which he was in the dark. He displayed a real scientific spirit and temper in conceding that there was a realm, vast and unexplored, about which he knew and surmised nothing or next to nothing. It was but honest to quote the words and opinions of those who professed that they did know something. It was not necessary to have recourse to miracles to explain natural phenomena, nor again, to make room for the occult acts and superstitious practices which claimed that by virtue of their own native and inherent power they could penetrate the difficulty. If men of good and honest repute had anything to say on the subject, it was but fair to listen to their claims. Everyone had the right to accept or reject their statements.

It is well to insist here, that, in view of Albert's really scientific stand in this matter, a certain class of historians might do well to take pause before speaking again of the Middle Ages as dark, afraid of the light, loving the dark, trafficking with and upon the ignorance of the masses, withholding knowledge from the people, deliberately fooling them by word-jugglery, twisting texts, suppressing texts which do not fit in with a preconceived notion of theological truth or teaching. How do such charges square with Albert's persistence in quoting men and opinions with which he was not in sympathy? Did he not leave it to the reader to arrive at his own conclusions on very actual topics, satisfying himself in presenting the data? And Thorndike continues: "He also cites even enchanters and necromancers without offering an apology and *now seems* to regard as subdivisions of magic those occult

---

[12] *Op. cit.*, 555.

arts from which we have just heard him exculpate the Magi."[13] We have deliberately italicized two words in Thorndike's quotation to show that he is not so sure about Albert's attitude. Albert is absolutely orthodox in treating of magic from the theological standpoint. Seeing the distinctions he drew in the use of the generic sense of the word *magic*, we may safely leave it to him to treat in his philosophical works of the forces of nature, unexplained adequately up to that time by science, and indifferently spoken about as magic, astronomy, or astrology.

And this brings us to the third point that must be remembered when speaking about the magic of Albert. If Albert was a good enough theologian to insist upon a theological examination and judgment of the magic that encroached upon religion, then, forsooth, he must be allowed freedom of investigation in the natural sciences which remained in their own domain so long as he persisted in using, not theological, but scientific norms and criteria. "For ancient pagans like Pliny and Seneca," Thorndike continues, "the study of nature seems to have taken the place of religion in large measure, but the introduction of Christianity did not result in the discontinuance or estoppal of the study of nature, nor in its reduction to a state of servitude. Medieval science was somewhat under the wing of the Church, as were so many other activities now purely secular, but science even in the Middle Ages was learning to use its own wings... But many secrets of nature still remained undiscovered in our period and hence it is not surprising that the conception of occult virtue in nature, of occult influence exerted by animals, herbs and gems, or by stars and spirits, still prevailed to such an extent among men of the highest scientific attainments then possible."[14] And the same author, a little later, goes on to say that the word *magic* may be taken in the Middle Ages "as a generic term to include all superstitious arts and occult sciences, and to designate a great primary division or phase of human thought and activity... Magic appears, in our period at least, as a way of looking at the world which is reflected in a human art or group of arts employing varied materials in varied rites, often fantastic, to work a great variety of marvelous results, which offer a man release from his physical,

[13] *Ibid.*

[14] *Op. cit.*, II, 792.

social, and intellectual limitations, not by the imaginative and sentimental methods of music, melodrama, fiction and romance, or by religious experience or asceticism, but by operations supposed to be efficacious here in the world of external reality. Some writers, chiefly theologians, lay great stress or resort to spirits in magic, some upon the influence of the heavens, some on both these forces, which yet others almost identify; but, except as theological dogma insists upon the demoniacal character of magic, or as astrological doctrine insists on the rule of the stars, it cannot be said that spirits or stars are thought of as always necessary in magic."[15] And in this connection Sarton remarks: "Note that the words *astrologia* and *astronomia* were then almost interchangeable; an astrological treatise might be called *Liber astronomicus*, while another like this one bearing the word *Astrologia* in its title would be of special astronomical importance."[16] These undeniable facts go a great way in clearing up the malodorous name attaching to Albert because of his preoccupation with scientific problems.

Fourth, it is worth stressing that, while the average medieval man had a high regard for science and respect for scientists, he did not on that account possess or lay claim to much more than the most rudimentary knowledge of the natural sciences. In theology and the natural sciences he was a man of simple faith, even when a sharp metaphysician, and lived in an atmosphere of faith. He looked upon miracles as the work and operation of the Creator who hid just behind the outer crust of things and controlled them. Albert argued against the unnecessary multiplication of miracles in natural phenomena. But the medieval man was not so soon and easily schooled into a sane and legitimate rationalism regarding the workings of nature. For one thing it was easier for him to believe in miracles than by painful exploration to establish the orderly working of the laws of nature. When, then, one of the intellectually élite, as a medic, for example, used methods and contrivances and remedies which for obvious reasons he did not feel called upon to disclose or divulge to his patient, or his patient's friends, it was the most natural thing in the world to ascribe to magic (or miracles, according to the outlook of the patient) the success or failure

---

[15] *Ibid.*, 974.

[16] *Op. cit.*, 990.

of the methods employed. Scientific jargons and clinical procedures, however crude and embryonic, soon came to be looked upon as possessing secret powers of their own. If the mental attitude of the patient and the curative power of the medicines administered are taken into account by every successful physician, we must be prepared to allow to the medieval as to the modern medic the use not only of his science but also his art. To rely solely on the latter provides fat purses for the quack, the mind healer, and the naturopath; to depend solely on the former gathers endless swarms of willing victims for the bone setter and the surgical specialists of whatever stripe. The medieval medic with practically no scientific apparatus to fall back upon, but with a large hoard of clinical wisdom to guide him in ordinary cases and emergencies could not be blamed overmuch if he tried to strike a professional pose, to utilize whatever scientific methods or apparatus were within reach. And thus astrology came to be confounded and identified with the practises of medicine in the popular mind. Sarton says justly and shrewdly:

> "Belief in the principles of astrology was universal. It would not have occurred to any medieval physician to question these principles any more than to a modern one to doubt the indication of a good thermometer. The only difference of opinion concerned the application of these principles, which varied a great deal according to the degree of wisdom and honesty, and the scientific education of each practitioner. The majority of them were probably too ignorant to have a real understanding of astrology; the chances are they did not broadcast the fact, but applied blindly the astrological rules published in many textbooks. In this they were not worse than the modern physicians who use their instruments in a purely empirical way without any real grasp of the methods involved. The point to remember is that the most scientific physicians, those who were looked up to by their humbler colleagues, were the main defenders of astrological medicine. This was the great tragedy of medieval medicine: not that its scientific armature was small, but that it was awry."[17]

[17] *Op. cit.*, 790.

Any medieval medic who wished to rise in his profession was not content with what he found in books or what he learned in his ordinary practice. If he made experiments on his own account, it was only a question of time till he came to be looked upon as a magician, especially if his discoveries succeeded in restoring health. And, by the same token, the greater his professional success the wider his popular repute for magic. For as Thorndike wisely remarks:

> "The history of magic is bound up with the history of science as well as with folklore, primitive culture and the history of religion. Sometimes our authors have spoken of natural magic but I rather wonder whether there could well be any other kind since man must always reckon with his natural environment. It is not without reason that the Magi stand out in Pliny's pages not as mere sorcerers or enchanters but as those who have gone farthest and in most detail—too curiously in his opinion—into the study of nature... After all it is not surprising that magic which was both curious and tried to accomplish things should investigate nature and should experiment. It is even possible that magicians were the first to experiment or shared that province with the first inventors and the useful arts and that natural science originally philosophical and speculative took over experimental method in a crude form as well as the conception of occult virtue from magic... It is therefore not surprising that men like Galen, Apuleius Apollonius and Dunstan were accused of magic by their contemporaries: that men like Gerbert, Michal Scot, and Albertus Magnus were represented as magicians in later, if not contemporary legend... and that no one of our authors, try as he may, succeeds in keeping magic entirely out of science or science entirely out of magic."[18]

Fifth and lastly, even though we might be induced to admit that Albert was too tolerant in the theological corpus of his work to give the magicians—astrologers, alchemists, *et sic al*—a chance to speak for themselves, and in the purely philosophical or scientific parts of his work was unwilling to drive the long-haired, round-backed, and greasy-gowned occultists from the bar of a candid hearing, we must

---

[18] *Op. cit.*, 977-978.

admit and maintain in justice to Albert that in several instances he retracted, or else clarified, his statements and assumed a more decided stand one way or the other. It is difficult, but not impossible, to establish this because of the chronological confusion of his many works. No one can read very extensively into these works without being forced to the conviction that he did change his opinion and was not afraid or ashamed to admit it. As far as can be established at the present stage of investigation into the chronology of his writings it is safe to hold that the theological were written before the scientific treatises.[19] It has been pointed out that there is a noticeable intellectual development in his attitude toward the natural sciences in his later productions.[20] He modified in his later writings some of the statements he had made earlier; is more inclined to give the sciences an opportunity to speak for themselves; is less inclined to give ear to some of the more bizarre recipes and remedies of an earlier year; gets closer to the inscrutable heart of natural things—all this, be it observed, without the sacrifice of his orthodoxy. A less honest man than Albert would have hesitated before taking back, publicly and explicitly, things he had said so positively on former occasions, things, too, which were accepted without questioning and demur. And a theologian, especially a medieval one, when there were plenty of heresy hunters abroad, did exhibit superb courage in ceding an inch to science which was more or less suspected by men whose piety was greater than their intellectual competency. A retractation in favor of the sciences could easily and was easily and quickly made to look like criminal hedging. Albert's reputation for sound theology and loyalty to the Pope made him courageous to do what had brought sorrow to Roger Bacon and Raymond Lull. For "every philosopher and even every theologian was obliged to have some understanding of it, if only to be able to discuss the cosmological views of Genesis. On the other hand, medicine was tied up with astrology: thus every physician needed a modicum of astronomical knowledge."[21] Whether it was the true science of cosmology, very imperfect then because men were so little acquainted

---

[19] C. Bäumker, Die Stellung Alfred von Sareschal und seiner Schrift De Motu Cordis in der Wissenschaft des beginnenden 13. Jahrhunderts (München: 1912), 12.

[20] A. Schneider, *Die Psychologie Alberts des Grossen* (Münster: 1906), 293-308.

[21] George Sarton, *op. cit.*, 749.

with the world in which they lived, or whether it was the youthful science of astronomy which limped most noticeably because of the lack of any instruments except the astrolabe, and hence opened the door easily to astrology, the truth remains that "every physician was intuitively an experimentalist and at this age of mankind their intuitions were becoming more explicit."[22]

These few considerations should go far to absolve Albert from the charge of having been a magician in the vulgar sense. He was no more an adept in the black arts than any of the learned and progressive scientists who were becoming more numerous daily.[23] Indeed, he was less so than any man of his age, not only because of the maxims he laid down for the fruitful prosecution of scientific natural studies but also because of the scientific way in which he carried on his experimentations.[24] It is a pure legend that he had special permission from the Pope to carry on experiments in necromancy.[25] This legend, however, testifies to the fact that the people were ready to believe that he was a man of such holy life that he would not seek a foul end in whatever experiments he might see fit to conduct. If later ages laughed with glee when calling him a magician it was because they could not deny that he was a man of blameless life. If his contemporaries called him a magician it was because, knowing his holiness of life, they were sure they were not belittling him even when they said that he was "expert in magic." And with the fuller knowledge of the history of natural science in the Middle Ages, it may turn out that both schools of thought were more mistaken in their estimate of Albert than many persons are prepared to admit today. We shall give only two examples

---

[22] *Ibid.*, 744.

[23] "What is less realized is that the thirteenth century marks an important epoch in the history of the experimental sciences, that Roger Bacon is not an isolated apparition or exception. There was a whole school of alchemists who performed the experiments mentioned by ancient writers and devised new ones." (F. Picavet, *Esquisse d'une histoire générale et comparée des philosophies médiévales*, Paris: 1905), 224.

[24] "Indeed writers on Albertus Magnus have not failed to notice that his scientific writings are neither commentaries upon Aristotle, nor compilations from a variety of sources; but that he both recognizes experience as a criterion of truth and frequently states the result of his personal observations." (Lynn Thorndike: "Roger Bacon and Experimental Method," in *Philosophical Review*, 1914), 285. In his *De Vegetalibus* alone Albert describes no less than fifteen experiments with herbs for medicinal effects.

[25] G. Meerscmann, *Introductio*, 14.

why such a reversal of opinion may be nearer at our door than we anticipate.

Up to comparatively recent times Albert's devotion to "physiognomics," as it is called, was taken as a sure proof and indication of his having been an addict of magic. When Claude Bernard published at Paris in 1859 his *Leçons de physiologie experimentale appliqué à la medecine,* he was assailed as the very incarnation of a medieval magician. But our modern study of biology dates from that period and Bernard appears as not the least famous biologist. And in our own day H. S. Jennings can write: "The greatest questions of biology deal with the origin and nature of individuals, their characteristics, their likenesses and their differences. The diversity among living individuals is the most striking fact about them, the fact of most practical importance; and it is the matter on which biology has the most to say."[26] Albert would have written in the same strain; indeed, he said things seven hundred years ago which sound very much like the platitudes of the contemporary biologist. P. Rondomi, E. A. Starling, S. Distefano, C. Ceni, A. Fouilee, to take only a few and the best known, repeat in substance what Albert was once blamed for as teaching the "physiognomies." A comparative study of Albert and N. Pende, probably the greatest biologist today, has forced this frank and unbiased confession: "The almost perfect agreement between the description of Albert the Great and that given by one of the greatest authorities of Endrocrinology is a strong and clear proof that our modern researches relative to our subject do not produce anything substantially new to the traditional doctrine of our school of psychology. Names change but the ideas remain the same."[27]

And, secondly, what Albert, and less clearly and extensively Thomas Aquinas, wrote upon the subject of the human head and its sensitive faculties, upon the heart, the nerves, and the pneuma or vital fluid in the blood—anatomical and physiological questions for which both were ridiculed—is being considered with respectful and admiring attention by contemporary biologists not so much for any new

---

[26] H. S. Jennings, *The Biological Basis of Human Nature* (New York: 1930), XVII; H. Ehrhard, "*Albertus Magnus als Biolog,*" in *Natur* (1923), Heft 7.

[27] F. M. Barbado, "*La Physionomie, le tempérament et le caractère d'après Albert le Grand et la science moderne,*" in *Revue Thomiste (1931), 117 sq.*

contribution they made to the subject but for the faithful adaptation—progressive and forward-looking—of the knowledge of the Ancients, especially, Galen.[28]

Perhaps, as medical science progresses men will come to see in the works of Albert a large fund of valuable knowledge as yet undreamed of, a faithful restatement of the medical knowledge of the past adapted and perfected in such a way that it will go far to offset some of the many puerile things which he, as a child of his age, made room for in his conscientious studies and observations on the healing and curative properties of created things which we tramp upon and close our eyes to in our concern about our own petty and selfish interests. Albert asked questions of nature, even tried to force secrets from it, for the purpose of coming to the relief of his fellow men. And, for this compassion for his fellows, men called him a magician.

---

[28] H. D. Noble, "*Note pour L'étude de la psycho-physiologie d'Albert le Grand et de S. Thomas: Le Cerveau et les Faculties sensibles,*" in *Revue Thomiste* (1905), 91-101.

In Libr. Sententiarum
De laudib. B. Virg.
In Psalmos
Suma theologie
In Diuum Dionisium
In Quatuor Euangelia
In Libros Metaphisic.

CHAPTER XVI
PHILOSOPHER

TO HIS contemporaries Albert was first and foremost a great philosopher. Long before he was acclaimed "the great" because of his universal knowledge—nay even before his death—he had been referred to frequently as *magnus philosophus*, and even on occasion as *maximus in philosophia.*[1] Even despite the strident remonstrances of Roger Bacon teachers cited him by name in the schools during his lifetime[2]—a distinction accorded to only one or two medieval thinkers.

That Albert achieved such authority as a philosopher even before his death seems to have caused some surprise to his contemporaries. It is Roger Bacon once more who, apparently having taken umbrage at Albert's academic prestige, remarked that he had never taken his master's degrees at Padua. And when Bacon learned of Albert's plan and determination to make Aristotle the common intellectual inheritance of the Latin world,[3] he wrote in outspoken disparagement: "He has never studied philosophy; nor did he attend lectures on it in the schools; nor was he ever in a *studium solemne* before he became a theologian; he could not have been instructed in philosophy in his own Order because he was its first master of philosophy."[4] All of which, if true, only serves to accentuate Albert's native genius.

Subsequent ages, impressed mightily by the scientific attainments of Albert, have persistently minimized his important contributions to the study of philosophy and have belittled his influence upon the current of medieval thought. It is true that the reputation as a philosopher which Albert achieved during his lifetime did not survive him very long, except among the Albertinists at Cologne and Cracow.

---

[1] *M. Grabmann,* L'Influsso di Alberto Magno sulla Vita lntellettuale del Medio Evo (Roma: 1931), 29-30.

[2] "*Nam, sicut Aristoteles, Avicenna et Averroes allegantur in scholis sic et ipse, et adhuc vivit, et habuit in vita sua auctoritatem, quod numquam homo habuit in doctrina.*" Rogeri Bacon, *Opera quaedam hactenus Inedita (ed. Brewer. London: 1839),* Opus Minus, 30.

[3] *Physicorum,* I, tr. I, Chap. I; Opp. III, 2.

[4] Rogeri Bacon, *op. cit.*, 327.

This early eclipse of his importance in the domain of pure reasoning was brought about partly by the unfinished state in which he left his philosophic investigation at his death, but mainly by the success with which Thomas Aquinas knit together into a coherent system the elements which Albert had made available in his paraphrase of Aristotle. If modern historians seem inclined to detract from Albert's greatness as a philosopher because of the somewhat fragmentary shape of his investigations, it is in great measure due to their leaving out of sight what he set out to do; what obstacles he perforce had to surmount in order to present the medieval world with a true and genuine Aristotle purged of Jewish interpolations and Muslim interpretations; what a profound influence he exerted in making the knowledge of Greek pagan antiquity acceptable and available for Christian uses. Slowly the modern world is beginning to vindicate for Albert something of the importance he enjoyed among his contemporaries as a philosopher of the first rank, greater far than Alexander of Hales and second only to Thomas Aquinas. And the world has learned during the past three quarters of a century how necessary and profitable it is to look to Albert for easily tangible stages in the history of the development of the experimental sciences and for suggestive hints and astounding discoveries in the records of the natural sciences. The impartial truth is that he was undeniably a great authority in the natural sciences, which even Roger Bacon was willing to concede and admit,[5] and that he was at the same time a great philosopher and theologian, as his fellows frankly recognized and confessed and as modern scholars are fast beginning to discover and establish.

Albert's importance in the history of philosophy has suffered because modern historians complain that he did not broach any new theory or set of theories, much less a new and independent system of thought. They argue, therefore, that he was a mere compiler and encyclopedist, a peddler of other men's thought with few if any additions of his own in the form of original criticism, observation, and suggestion. By deliberately choosing to do such secondary work as

5 "*Sapientes famosiores inter Christianos quorum unus est frater Albertus de Ordine Praedicatorum.*" Rogeri Bacon, *op. cit.*, 14; "*Vere laudo eum plus quam omnes de vulgo studentium quia homo studiossissimus est, et vidit infinita, et habuit expensum; et ideo multa potuit colligere in pelago auctorum infinito.*" *Ibid.*, 327.

revamping Aristotle, a task which offered no opportunity of displaying originality, he knowingly outlawed himself from the ranks of those who open new avenues of intellectual speculation, investigation, and research.

Now the truth is that Albert did not aspire to be the first man to enunciate any new philosophic theories. He was shrewd and experienced enough to know that there is always a goodly brood of men panting to be original, even at the cost of truth; men who refuse to go over any path, however direct and satisfactory, just because it had been discovered and traveled in the past. The medieval schools were afflicted with a swarm of theorists whose novel and undigested opinions, put forth with a show of learning and bolstered up with subtle sophistries, constituted the real menace of the hour.

Albert essayed a humbler but far more saving task. His claim and title to greatness rest on the sagacity he showed in selecting an old system, as correct and satisfying as any which had so far been put forward, and by bringing it into line with what had been discovered since it had first been broached hundreds of years before. In doing so he was compelled to bend it, work it over, breathe into it a new spirit and content, and adapt it thus to the purposes of a Christianized and Christian philosophy.[6] This determination to resurrect and re-create a system which had long been forgotten, subsequently misunderstood in all its native metaphysical robustness and virility and, finally, perverted by oblique commentators, now truly called for a colossal fund of shrewdness, sagacity, and common sense; for a nice discrimination, a broad vision, and a fine eye for the relative value of divergent and diverging systems of thought, considered in their essential and integral departments respectively; for a careful measuring of the inherent possibilities of a system which was to be put to new uses of which the originator had had no inkling nor any dream; for a reverence of whatever truth might still remain underneath a mass of data where much was false and more suspect; for a penetration into the very heart

---

[6] M. Grabmann, L'lnflusso, 41-50; A. Schneider says (*Die Psychologie Alberts des Grossen, Breslau, 1900), 16: "Er hat als erster mittelalterlicher Denker von Ansehen nicht nur den Eigenwert der aristotelischen Wissenschaft erfasst, sondern war sich auch darüber klar, von wie grosser Bedeutung die aristotelische Philosophie für den Ausbau des christlichen Lehrsystems ist*"; G. M. Manser, "*Albert der Grosse als Neuerer auf philosophischem Gebiet,*" in *Divus Thomas (Freiburg: 1932), 19-41.*

of problems which had arisen with the advent of the fuller light of revelation; for a sympathy of mind which was not afraid to recognize and credit truth, whether it was in the master himself or in his Arabian commentators, such as Avicenna, Averroes, Costa-ben-Luca, Algazel, Alfarabi, Abubaker, and Alkendi, or in his Jewish interpreters such as Isaak Israeli, Avencebrol, or Moses Maimonedes. Surely, only a man of stupendous intellectual courage, nay audacity, only a man who was sure about his own ground, only a man who had an unerring instinct for the truth, an overpowering sense of loyalty to the Church, and a keen mind to distinguish the valuable from much that was specious and sophistic could have looked upon it as his life's mission and business to despoil the pagan and the paynim of their riches in order to rear an impregnable fortress of Catholic thought. To be able to create an entirely new synthesis of thought, without a study and comparison of past errors and without reference to the faded aberrations of the human mind, is one of those idle and dangerous delusions with which modern academicians seek to beguile the intellectually immature. Albert escaped the snare. He realized that there were inherent merits and excellencies in Aristotle which entitled him to a sympathetic treatment at the hands of those Christian scholars who were anxious to satisfy the intellectual hunger of the medieval world, minded as it was, in its newly found economic independence and self-importance, to put on the trappings of the thinker and philosopher.

Now, Albert's importance as a medieval thinker is based squarely upon the fourfold purpose he had in mind in espousing Aristotle's philosophy.

First, he was the only medieval man up to his day who recognized the worth, not only of Aristotle's logical treatises, but of the entire body of his doctrine. None of his predecessors had taken over, part and parcel, the entire Aristotle. When Roger Bacon first heard of Albert's determination to utilize the system of the Greek, he boldly proclaimed that such an adaptation was futile and impossible. Albert achieved it.[7]

---

[7] B. Geyer, "*De Aristotelismo B. Alberti Magni,*" in *Alberto Magno. Atti della Settimana Albertina* (Roma: 1932), 63-80; E. Michael (*Geschichte des deutschen Volkes*, Freiburg: 1903, III, 68) says: "*Albert war es, welcher der christlichen Welt zum ersten Mal das ganze philosophische System des Aristoteles erschloss und dessen Wissensschatz in die Scholastik hineingeleitet hat.*"

For decades of years scholars were satisfied with Albert's reproduction of Aristotle's thought.[8]

Second, Albert made Aristotle available by a paraphrase after the manner of Avicenna.[9] Thus he enabled his contemporaries to arrive at a just and comprehensive appreciation of the entire body of the Greek's thought. With a fine historic sense he evaluated and criticized the Greek, Arabian, and Jewish literature which had merely grown up around Aristotle, while professing to have grown upon it and directly out of it. This impersonal attitude toward Aristotle brought Albert much opprobrium and suspicion. He was forced to remark that, as he was nowhere giving his own ideas, he had a right to expect that men would not do him the injustice of saying that he was standing sponsor for every opinion appearing in his paraphrase.[10] By such a truly honest and scholarly presentation of the genuine thought of the Stagirite he gave his age the first opportunity of getting in direct touch with a corpus of speculation which had been defaced and deformed. Michael assures us that nothing similar was to be attempted for centuries to come.[11]

Third, Albert gave his age a demonstration of his own native powers of reasoning in the *digressiones*, or monographs on important philosophical questions and problems, which he scattered throughout his paraphrase but always distinct from it. Only one who has made a careful comparative study of these dissertations is prepared to judge, not only of Albert's keen powers of criticism and nice sense of selection, but also of his own independence and originality of thought. He is not afraid to differ and dissent from Aristotle, and whenever he

---

[8] H. Wilms (Albert der Grosse, München, 1931, 99), says: "*Durch diese Erklärung, die Albert als erster zu den gesamten Schriften des Aristoteles gab, wurde das 13. Jahrhundert in die Lage versetzt, sich ein solch gründliches Verständnis des Stagiriten anzueignen, wie es weder vorher noch in den ersten Jahrhunderten nachher zu finden.*"

[9] Arthur Schneider (Die Psychologie Alberts des Grossen, 16), says: "*Seine philosophische Bedeutung besteht darin, dass er die genannten Schriften des Aristoteles nach der Methode des Avicenna paraphrasierte, dabei seine Leser nicht nur mit den Anschauungen des Aristoteles genau bekannt gemacht, sondern, historisch weit ausholend, auch die einschlägigen Lehren der neu bekannt gewordenen griechischen, arabischen and jüdischen Schriftsteller angab und kritisierte. In das ausgedehnte wissenschaftliche Material und die vielgestaltigen Gedankenmassen hat er sich mit ausserordentlichem Scharfsinn eingearbeitet und zurecht gefunden.*"

[10] *Politicorum*, LVII, Chap. VI, *in fine*; Opp. VIII, 803.

[11] E. Michael, Geschichte des deutschen Volkes (Freiburg: 1903), III, 117.

does so he does not fail to give abundant reasons for his attitude.[12] No doubt he does adhere in the big and large to his initial determination of following Aristotle whenever this does not imply or entail an abandonment, even in the smallest degree, of those positions preconized by the Church in her accredited and authoritative teachers, the Fathers of the Church, especially St. Augustine whom to belittle Albert puts down as little short of sacrilege and whom to question unduly he considers tantamount to blasphemy. For Albert in all his speculation was not aiming at making an academic name for himself, at any cost or risk, but always at buttressing truth, or at least, at making its acceptance easier and more reasonable for men. This instinctive reverence for the philosophic tradition of the Church induced Albert to leave large quarters for the Neo-Platonism which, deriving mainly from the introspective Doctor of Hippo, had been utilized for centuries by Christian thinkers with such good effect in solving the question of the relationship of faith and knowledge.[13]

It does not follow, however, that while professing great respect for the reasoning of Augustine, Albert accepted or approved in their totality the explanations put forth by the triple school into which the Augustinian doctrine had split up in that day.[14] Augustinianism had received a new life and impetus in that age from the speculation of St. Bonaventure, whom Albert esteemed highly for Thomas's sake, and to whose fiery words he had thrilled at the Council of Lyons. Bonaventure's charm of personality and seductiveness of sanctity did not disturb Albert's admirable impartiality of outlook. Thus we find him frankly differing from the Seraphic Doctor, and his chief exponents, Matthew of Aquasparta and John of Peckham, on the questions having to do with the illumination required by man to know the necessary truths, as also the composition of the angelic nature out of matter and form. On the other hand, he ranged himself with

---

[12] *"Dicet autem fortasse aliquis nos Aristotelem non intellixisse, et ideo non consentire verbis ejus, vel quod forte ex certa scientia contradicamus ei quantum ad rei veritatem. Et ad illum dicimus quod qui credit Aristotelem fuisse Deum, ille debet credere quod numquam erravit, si auten credit ipsum esse hominem, tunc procul dubio errare potuit sicut et nos." VIII Physicorum*, tr. I, Chap. 14. See also Albert's *IV Metaph.*, tr. III, Chap. 2.

[13] G. Manser, "*Das Wesen des Thomismus*," in *Divus Thomas* (Freiburg: 1926), 16 sq.

[14] B. Geyer, "*De Aristotelismo B. Alberti Magni,*" in *Alberto Magno. Atti della Settimana Albettina (Roma: 1932), 69-73.*

Bonaventure against William of Paris and Roger Bacon in rejecting a false theory about the active intellect and the soul.[15]

Forsooth, Albert was in search of the truth wherever he thought it could be found. He did not disguise the fact that he looked to Aristotle as the best human guide in the forest of questions that had grown up around the theory of knowledge. And this has led Leopold Gaul,[16] who has studied the question exhaustively, to say that Albert better than any other medieval man pointed out the divergent starting point of Platonism and Aristotelianism. He preferred the latter but did not on that account remain blind to the advantages of the former.[17] He sought to make a combination of the two systems, or better still, to effect a kind of amalgamation or absorption in favor of Aristotle.[18] Hence it comes that Albert's attitude toward Plato vacillates notably in his various works and is conditioned by the topic he is discussing.[19] Thus, for instance, in his paraphrase of Aristotle he is much more relentless toward Plato than in other works, especially the *Summa de Creaturis* where, if occasion seems to demand that he differ from Plato, he does so in a more benign way, often essaying to interpret him in an orthodox sense. This appears clearly in his treatment of Plato's doctrine on the nature and existence of the soul, as on the nature of the intellect.[20] Albert was intellectually sensitive enough to feel that the

---

[15] B. Luijcks, *Die Erkenntnislehre Bonaventuras* (München: 1924), 242 sq.

[16] *L. Gaul,* Alberts des Grossen Verhältnis zu Plato (München: 1913), 27.

[17] The open-mindedness of Albert appears clearly from his words: "*Nec est differentia inter Platonem et Aristotelem in re aliqua sed tantum in modo,*" *De Natura et Origine Animae,* tr. I, Chap. 2. How Albert depends and borrows from both Greek philosophers can be seen from his words: "*Non perficitur homo in philosophia nisi ex scientia duorum philosophorum Aristotelis et Platonis.*" *I Metaph.*, tr. 5, Chap. 15. He does not hesitate to correct Aristotle by Plato: "*Et quod dicit Aristoteles quod omnes philosophantes hoc posuerunt, falsum dicit, quia Plato, qui inter philosophantes fuit praecipuus, oppositum dicit.*" *Summa Theologica.*, tr. I, *quaest. 4, art. 5.*

[18] *B. Geyer, op. cit.*, 72.

[19] Leopold Gaul (*op. cit.*, 144) says: "*Wo Albert in Abhängigkeit von Aristoteles spricht, wird ein abfälliges Urteil über Plato gefällt. Wo er aber, dieser Fessel frei, seiner Meinung Ausdruck verleiht, da konnten wir eine viel grössere Nachgiebigkeit konstatieren.*"

[20] M. Browne, "*Circa Intellectum et ejus Illuminationem apud S. Albertum Magnum,*" in *Angelicum* (1932), 168-187; C. Bäumker (*Zeitschrift für Psychologie,* 1908, 440 sq.) insists that Albert is important for the study of the history of philosophy since he reproduces in his works the opinions of philosophers as these were received and worked over by the medieval schoolmen.

very spirituality of Plato's outlook made him congenitally more adaptable to Christian uses. With dexterity and ingenuity Albert tried to save Platonic elements whenever possible. Sometimes his efforts at working over Plato miscarried, as when in his *De Intellectu et Intelligibile* he evolved a theory of knowledge out of the data supplied by the Arabian commentators of Aristotle which resolved itself into a kind of mystical contemplation palatable to the deepest-dyed Platonist.

From such instances of conciliation we can gather a fair idea of Albert's universality of mind. He was no fanatical, blinded Aristotelian for all his whole-hearted devotion to the Stagirite. He was undeniably an intellectualist as only a profound absorption of Aristotelian principles, spirit, outlook and methods could have engendered and produced. But at the same time he did not banish from the synthesis of truth which he tried to elaborate, that Platonism which had been worked over by the pseudo-Dionysius, Augustine, and the Christian Neo-Platonists.[21] He was temperamentally loath to do this for, having a deep mystical strain in him, Albert would not rule out of court entirely elements which gave play to the heart and emotions. Hence it came that Albert could beget, through his encouragement and guidance, an Aquinas, in whose philosophic speculation there is scarcely any room for the scholasticism of the heart. But at the same time, by his tolerance toward Platonism and his serious attempt to work it into Aristotelian grooves, he made possible an Ulrich of Strasburg, whose exposition and summation of Christian Neo-Platonism in his *Summa de Bono* is, perhaps, the best medieval achievement of its kind in that age. Had Albert espoused exclusively the scholasticism of the head, as represented by a rigid Aristotelianism, he would never have merited the right to be looked upon as the legitimate father of the German mysticism of the *Gottesfreunde* of the Rhine. And, incidentally, it may be suggested that Albert's pupil, Meister Ekkehard, never would have entangled himself in his suspect doctrines had he exercised a little more of his master's intellectual

[21] A. Puccetti (*Sant' Alberto Magno, Profilo Biografico, Roma, 1932, 239)* says: "*Uno spirito eminentemente scientifico come quello di Alberto non potè che sentire la piu grande simpatia per un pensatore, che ammette l'esperienza naturale come fonte di conoscenza, e nella dimostrazione scientifica non parte che da dati di esperienza, da verità già dimostrate o evidenti. Se Platone suscita le emozioni più nobile del cuore umano, Aristotile ha la forza di piegare il pensiero ai diritti della verità. Nell' epoca moderna soltanto Kant puo paragonarsi a lui nella forza estensiva del suo sistema a tutti i campi della cultura.*"

charity.[22]

Finally, Albert did gather together with incredible industry[23] most of the elements which made for the elaboration of the *philosophia perennis* which the Church has favored so signally. If he did not succeed like Thomas Aquinas in building a cohesive, coherent, and consistent system, it was largely due to the rapidity with which he worked, a rapidity which did not allow him the time to weld his enormous materials together. Besides, his quenchless eagerness to drag together from every imaginable quarter the most disparate elements of knowledge deprived him of the time or desire to polish them in such a way as to make them easily and normally available. Without detracting one iota from Albert's powers of reasoning, it is true to say that he was chiefly bent on putting within reach of future scholars material which their patience, insight, and application would enable them to fashion into sharp blades of truth against error. With his ebullient and prodigal nature he, like a good husbandman, was supremely concerned about filling the granaries which we call his voluminous works. By temperament and the circumstances of his active life he was not the man to put every grain of knowledge he had garnered in the most outlying fields under the microscope of speculation. His intellectual eyes were uncommonly sharp and he relied mainly upon a hurried study and examination of the separate grains, as they came before him one by one, for his decision to store them up for further exploration and exploitation by his pupils. Theirs would be the task to scrutinize them individually and minutely before grinding them up into the doctrinal flour out of which they could bake the loaves of truth in the hot ovens of serious thought for the mentally underfed. Mandonnet[24] is correct in saying that Albert is the perfect incarnation of a pedagogue and professor; one who possessed the art of firing the ambitions of young men to know everything that was knowable; one who exercised the greatest skill in initiating them into sensible and safe methods of work and investigation; one who by ransacking the world for data upon which they could exercise their wits and faculties purchased for them, at great cost of time and labor

---

[22] G. Dorns, Die Gnadenlehre des sel. Albertus Magnus (Breslau: 1929), 64, 96, passim.

[23] "*Quae diligenter quaesivi per diversas mundi regiones.*" *Mineral. III, tr. 1, Chap. 1.*

[24] *P. Mandonnet, "Albert le Grand,"* in *Dictionnaire de Théologie Catholique*, I, 674.

to himself, some of the leisure required to think deeply and well. He dampened no man's intellectual ardor for any kind of work nor curiosity in any out-of-the-way lane of research; he crippled no man's manner or method of working toward a fuller possession of the truth; he clipped no man's intellectual wings in his own ambitious flight toward a better understanding of God's existence and nature and divinely fecund life and God's tender manifestation of Himself to men and His dealings with the least of them.

God and man—these are the two pivotal points which Christian philosophy must ever seek to explain and clarify. Due allowance being made for the shortcomings inevitable in any pagan philosophy, these two basic facts are precisely the ones which Aristotle had envisaged better and more fully than any of his compeers and predecessors. Though Christian philosophy does not contemn or disown the full light of revelation, but seeks to arrive at truth without calling it into play for the moment, it is easy to understand why a thorough Christian like Albert should have been attracted by the intellectual open-mindedness of the Stagirite. Albert, therefore, is a faithful reproducer of Aristotle's thought[25]—some scholars have gone so far as to maintain that from Albert's paraphrase it would be possible to reconstruct the essentials of Aristotle's system. But where the Greek halted and fell short the German pushed on and rounded out. Thus, for instance, in the core doctrine of metaphysics—the universals,[26] a question hotly debated in the schools of the eleventh and twelfth centuries—Albert does not rely upon Plato for an explanation, even though in some places of his works he does seem to betray a latent sympathy for certain aspects of his teaching. With Aristotle he holds the trine existence of universal—*ante rem*, or before the thing itself, as an archetype in the divine mind; *in re*, or in the thing, determining the very nature of the object; *post rem*, or after the thing, existing in the human mind by which it is abstracted to become the object of knowledge. Albert follows his master also in maintaining that the universal is produced in many and from many things.[27]

---

[25] G. von Herding (*Albertus Magnus*, München, 1880, 86), shows how Albert utilized the metaphysics of Aristotle wisely and with discrimination.

[26] G. Sestile, "*L'Universale nella dottrina di S. Alberto Magno,*" in *Angelicum (1932), 168-187.*

[27] *I. Sent.*, dist. 19, art. 15; Opp. XXV, 536.

The existence of God—the second pivotal point—had been established by Aristotle with arguments from natural reason. The medieval Schools of thought were hotly discussing the worth and validity of the metaphysical proofs of the Stagirite. Albert took over these proofs totally and reenforced them by arguments from the Fathers. Von Hertling points out[28] that Albert with consummate art succeeded in making it appear that the Aristotelian proofs were in accord with the argumentation of the Fathers. This is only one of several instances when Albert bolstered up Aristotle with orthodox reasonings from the Christian Fathers.

God's relation to the world, especially creation, Albert reduces to the question of causes: the efficient cause or agent; the final cause or purpose for the sake of which an object was produced, and the formal cause or idea according to which an object was made. Though Aristotle did most probably not teach creation explicitly, he did lay down principles which, if carried to their logical conclusion, would lead to the doctrine that the world was made out of nothing. Hence, Aristotle's reasoning was of comparatively small help to Albert. But by collecting numerous passages from his works and by placing them side by side with arguments drawn from the Fathers of the Church Albert succeeded in a truly classic and masterful way in enlarging and expanding the original Aristotelian metaphysics.[29] This is seen to good advantage in his persistence in trying to arrive at a fuller and completer comprehension of the nature of created things—a curiosity which in him amounted almost to a passion or mania. To do this he was convinced, after much study and searching of the works of preceding philosophers, that he could do no better than adopt the doctrine of matter and form, put forward by Aristotle.[30] According to him this primal matter, while found as a kind of tangible substratum in all created things, must needs be determined by some particular form in order that the individual and individualized thing may take a definite place in the gallery of created and knowable beings. Unlike most of his contemporaries, however, Albert speaks of a "twofold

---

[28] "*Um so interessanter ist es zu sehen, wie Albert es versteht diesen vollen Inhalt mit den aristotelischen Bestimmungen derart in Zusammenhang zu bringen, dass es scheint, als sei derselbe mit Notwendigkeit aus letzteren abgeleitet.*" G. von Herding, *Albertus Magnus*, 92.

[29] *I Summa Theologica*, tr. 3, q. 18, m. i.; Opp. XXXI, 119, 120, 167, 169.

[30] *II Summa Theologica*, tr. 1, q. 4, m. 2, a. 4; Opp. XXX, 11, 90.

form" in elements which mingle their "substances" quantitatively, without excluding prime matter. As in the resultant compound the primary *esse* becomes a fused or blended, an alloyed (*alteralum*) or divided element, he seems to be arguing in favor of the actual permanence of the elements in the chemical compound as against a virtual permanence which St. Thomas and many of the scholastics maintained. This sagacious explanation shows that Albert anticipated, at least in a confused way, the modern understanding of how the elements survive in the compound. And leaving Aristotle once more far behind, he leaped forward to the ranks of the moderns by boldly teaching the part which the causal form plays in the determination of individualized objects.

These courageous adaptations and elaborations of Aristotle's metaphysics were suggested in a general way and in many instances by the investigations of the Jews and Muslims in Spain who, to do them justice, were far in advance of the Christian thinkers of Europe in explaining and applying the Stagirite's principles. Grabmann declares[31] that Albert knew better than any of his contemporaries the vast riches of these investigators. That he laid them heavily under contribution is indisputable, but never to the extent which the authors of the *Realenziklopädie für Protestantische Theologie* would have it.[32] For Albert did not borrow slavishly or annex verbatim. He followed the rule of St. Augustine,[33] that in the defense of truth it is perfectly legitimate to pilfer the books of pagans. Albert utilized the true without qualm or question because truth like fresh air and sunshine is common property. The false he rejected resolutely, definitively, for reasons which he deemed sufficient but did not always allege. This universality brings Albert in active touch with our own age. But it can never be forgotten that the acquisition of learning was a far more difficult business in medieval times than in our day of rapid communication and easy international exchange of the findings of research and speculation.

In psychology the two fundamental questions of Christian

---

[31] M. Grabmann, *L'Inftusso*, 46.

[32] F. Nitzsch, in Realenzyklopädie für protestantische Theologie (I, 292), is simply venting his spleen when he says that Albert "*wie nachweislich, fast jeden philosophischen Satz entlehnt hat.*"

[33] *De Doctrina Christiana*, XL.

philosophy must ever remain the existence and nature of the soul, and the existence of the human mind with all its delicate and complex functioning processes. Arthur Schneider,[34] who has treated exhaustively of Albert's psychology, points out, first, that he never dealt with the subject in a systematic way; second, that in touching on the basic questions in various places in his many works he always showed such a fine sense of discrimination in what he adopts and what he rejects or adapts that he justly merits a high place among those who have helped the development of this department of philosophy and, third, that he displays such a wide acquaintance with the theories which were broached before and during his day that he deserves to be looked upon as a polyhistorian of psychology, even as Tschirch[35] maintains that he has deserved this title for his medical knowledge. It is beginning to be recognized today that Albert is probably the most important medieval figure in what has come to be called experimental psychology.[36]

Albert speaks about the soul in both his philosophical and theological works. In the former series he passes in review the definition of the soul given by Thales and all his successors. He judges these in the light of what Aristotle said. But he does not accept the Stagirite without very notable reservations. He criticizes Isaak Israeli, who tried to bolster up the doctrine of Aristotle by having recourse to Neo-Platonic theories.[37] By eliminating the many definitions on the subject he establishes that the rational soul is the form of the human body. He is not so clear and explicit as to whether there are in man many substantial forms or only one, immediately informing prime matter without any form of corporeity. From what he says in his

---

[34] Arthur Schneider, *Die Psychologie Alberts des Grossen* (Breslau: 1900), 364.

[35] *"Ein Polyhistor in des Wortes bester Bedeutung begnügt er sich nicht mit oberflächlichen Angaben oder Namen und ihren Synonymie, sondern geht überall tiefer auf den Gegenstand ein."* T. Tschirch, *Handbuch des Pharmakognosie (Leipzig: 1908), I, 127.*

[36] F. M. Barbado, *"La Physionomie d'après Albert le Grand et la Science Moderne,"* in *Revue Thomiste (1931), 90-128;* Id., *Introduccion a Psicologia experimental (Madrid: 1928), 147;* Id., *"Doctrina aristotelica thomistica de sensu tactus cum modernis doctrinis comparata,"* in *Xenia Thomistica (Roma: 1924).*

[37] *A. Schneider,* op. cit., 17, 201, 368; M. Browne, *"Circa Intellectum,"* etc., in *Angelicum (1932); J. Bach,* Des Albertus Magnus Verhältnis zu der Erkenntnislehre der Griechen, Lateiner, Araber und Juden (Wien: 1881), 180-183.

Summa de Creaturis[38] it is evident that his concept of matter and form is more strictly Aristotelian than was the case in the doctrine of the Augustinian teachers. He holds that the soul confers *esse* on the body; that in the organic body there is no specific form prior to the soul and that an inanimate body is only equivocally one with an animate body.

In his theological works Albert again investigates the definitions of the soul and the lucubrations about its nature put forth by Augustine, John Damascene (whom he literally reintroduced to the Middle Ages), Bernard, Alcuin, Remigius of Auxerre, Alexander Neckham, Cassiodorus, and Seneca, whom he mistook, as did all his contemporaries, for a Christian author. Albert seemed not to be completely satisfied with what these Christian writers had to say on the subject. He did not vouchsafe a definition of his own. He sought to combine what seemed to him to be true in these many authors. He did refute, rather than did Thomas Aquinas and William of Auxerre, the dangerous monopsychism of Averroes, that there is but one rational soul for all men.[39] He did brusquely reject the pantheism of Abelard, made popular by Almaric, that practically every created being, and not only men, had a rational soul. He tried to save Augustine, who seems to waver between creationism and traducianism in speaking of the soul, by interpreting his words in a benign and orthodox sense.[40] He rejected Plato's theory of the preexistence of the soul and also his teaching on the transmigration of the soul. He was positive in opposing the vagaries of Avicenna and Alfarabi and Avencebrol, though none of these, for all their exaggerations, could arouse the ire of Albert quite so much as Averroes who seems to have been his intellectual *bête noire.*[41] It appears more manifestly clear every day that it is not a purely fortuitous thing that Albert should have received the aureola of the doctorate in the Church in our own day when the Freudians are trying

[38] *Pars. II, tr. II, Chap. 29.*

[39] A. Masnovo, "*Alberto Magno e la Polemica Averoistica,*" in *Alberto Magno. Atti della Settimana Albertina (Roma: 1932), 44-62; M. Grabmann* ("*Die wissenschaftliche Mission Alberts des Grossen,*" in *Angelicum*, 1929, 348) says: "*Albert der Grosse scheint unter den Theologen des 13. Jahrhunderts der erste gewesen zu sein, der in eindringendster Einzeluntersuchung und in philosophischer Beweisführung diesen averroistischen Monopsychismus widerlegt hat.*"

[40] *Summa de Creaturis*, q. XVII, art. 3; Opp. XXXV, 148; A. Schneider, *op. cit.*, 434; H. Doms, *Die Gnadenlehre des sel. Albertus Magnus* (Breslau: 1929), **55**.

[41] A. Masnovo, *op. cit.*, 44-47.

to resurrect the Averroistic theory that in our subconscious self there are several coexisting personalities. By opposing Averroes so vehemently—an opposition which seemed unjustified to many modern scholars and exaggerated in the minds of others—Albert was building for our own day without knowing it. By teaching so consistently that the intellect was not numerically one for the whole human race he anticipated the objections of the professors of our machine age, with its mechanistic preferences, when individual men are not allowed to claim an individual and immortal soul and are, therefore, not responsible ultimately. Thomas Aquinas had a *bête noire* which could ruffle his spirits as much as it was possible for him to lose control over himself—it was not Averroes but Avicenna. By challenging the monopsychism of Averroes always and everywhere Albert comes in very close touch with our modern times. He is the sworn enemy of our modern mystagogic Averroists—the Vedantists, the Cosmists, the Theosophists, the Anthroposophists —who, pretending to enrich and glorify man by their theories of the multiple soul, only succeed in disintegrating him psychologically and dethroning him spiritually.[42]

In dealing with the second basic subject of Christian psychology, namely, the existence and powers of the human intellect, Albert had occasion to take in turn the theories which had been put forth before his time. No question was more bitterly and universally agitated in the medieval schools, catering as they did to men who were vividly conscious of the mental processes going on within them. Albert went directly to the heart of the dispute by taking a decided stand on the question of the *intellectus possibilis*,[43] or mind which actually understands and can give a reason for the successive stages in the act of understanding. His teaching on the subject has been accepted ever since. But in order to establish it he was compelled to beat off Arabian and Platonic teachers such as Aphrodisias, who made the intellect to consist of the perfect mixture or blending of the material and immaterial elements in man; Averroes, who made it a cosmic transcendental and universal potency; Abubaker and Avempace, who identified it with the imagination; Avicenna, who, while admitting the spiritual nature of the mind, utterly debased its activity by making the

[42] B. Alio, Plaies d'Europe et Baumes du Gange (Paris: 1932), 133, 147, passim.

[43] M. Browne, *op. cit.*, in *Angelicum* (1932), 196 sq.

act of knowing something passive; Avencebrol, who wished to reduce it to something like prime matter. By vindicating the supremacy and autonomy of the intellect, which obtains its knowledge through the senses, Albert warded off those later prophets of pantheism, immanentism, and transcendentalism who are playing such havoc with psychology in our day. He presented the world with a moderate realism which is not out of joint with the nature of the intellect nor too haughty to utilize the data supplied by the senses.

Albert is unique among the doctors of his age in that he did not coin any new philosophical terms. He was rather weak in forming definitions, not because he did not see clearly but rather because seeing too much, he did not see distinctly. He is a past master in analyzing the definitions of others; in selecting the false and the sophistical for rejection, and the half true or equivocal for a complete transformation and transmutation into iron orthodoxy. He never blushed to pay gladsome tribute to any of his predecessors. He was not the signatory to any school of thought. Hence, he was always free to reject any individual theory of any individual thinker without on that account feeling bound to cast the entire system overboard. He was typically German in his preference for the historico-critical method. Names meant little to him; ideas, everything. For he wrote: "As for ourselves it is a question rather of the thing said than the person saying it."[44] Wherefore Professor Bernard Geyer says truly: "Blessed Albert the Great holds a unique place among the doctors and schools of the thirteenth century and he cannot be claimed by any school or philosophical or theological coterie. Hence, also, he was not the founder of any school though all schools drew from his fullness. But the doctrine of his disciple St. Thomas prevailed in such wise that even in the school of the Augustinianists the Aristotelico-Thomistic doctrine on the theory of human knowledge was gradually accepted. Thus, verily, St. Thomas became the Common Doctor although not all his doctrines were approved by all, thus giving rise to a new variety of schools of thought. But inasmuch as St. Albert the Great was, as it were, above and beyond and beside this variety of schools—all of which owe him much—he should be hailed and venerated by all doctors and

---

[44] *"Nobis de dicto potius quam de dicente est quaestio," De Animal.* 281.

Catholic schools as the Universal Doctor."[45]

He was the first medieval teacher to point out with anything like satisfying completeness the close relationship and dependence of speech on thought—an achievement which will make him no stranger among the most modern philosophizing humanists. He explained for the first time, much as a modern would do, the relation of private opinion and common sense—the theory of values. Arthur Schneider remarks: "As regards this problem of the *sensus communis* one must admit that Albert operates with great dexterity and vouchsafes a really satisfying solution of those questions which have caused the greatest difficulties in Aristotelian exegesis."[46] By writing purely philosophical treatises and tractates Albert laid the foundations for a Christian philosophy as an independent science. He separated Christian philosophy from theology without hurt to the science of God. He made Christian philosophy see that it was the handmaid of theology, all the more serviceable because able to walk on its own feet; all the more confident because it had its face turned toward the sun shining in the empyrean of theology. He was the father and founder of Christian Aristotelianism which from the approval it has received from the Church bids fair to last as long as man wishes to know himself and is desirous of achieving the destiny he can carve out for himself under the eyes of God.

[45] B. Geyer, *op. cit.*, 79-80.

[46] A. Schneider, *Die Psychologie*, 137.

Chapter XVII
THEOLOGIAN

IN PROPOSING to himself to assimilate the wisdom of pagan antiquity to the wisdom of the Christian world and in leaving no stone unturned to achieve this colossal task, Albert was following the only course open to him as an honest thinker, a conscientious educator, and a loyal Christian. As an honest thinker he was obliged to select a system of philosophy which seemed to him best suited to satisfy the curiosity of his mind; as a conscientious educator he was bound to instruct in the best ways of thinking those disciples who would be called upon in the future to solve the difficulties which were agitating the world; as a loyal Christian he could not forswear his faith. Deliberately he chose Aristotle as his guide in the labyrinthine ways of thought. But in adopting the Stagirite Albert was painfully conscious of his false and truncated teaching on the question of the creation of the world, the origin and immortality of the soul, the creation of particular objects from no preexisting matter, and the ordination of man to a supernatural destiny.

Would he follow the Averroistic school of Aristotelian interpreters by adhering to Aristotle despite the Church's positive teaching on these fundamental truths? Would he like them, pervert the minds of his students, and through their teaching subsequently muddy the stream of Catholic tradition, by advocating the eternity of the world; by denying the immortality of the soul, the providence of God, human liberty and responsibility; by championing a crude pantheistic monopsychism according to which there was a world-soul of which the souls of individual men were but parts or emanations? There were goodly numbers of Christian professors—and their ranks were growing apace every day—who in their exaggerated loyalty to what they considered genuine Aristotelianism, and in their desire to avoid breaking with the Church, elaborated the monstrous theory of a double category of truths, self-identical and independent, but in an open and irreconcilable opposition to one another. The conclusions of philosophy and theology could be true in their respective domains and a man owed loyalty to the body of truth he was investigating at the moment. Reason and faith, they held, were in conflict and their respective findings might be and frequently were in opposition, because both envisaged different objects, proceeded from different starting points, employed divergent principles, and operated by different methods. The academic world was threatened with intellectual anarchy, and there were many who, ensnared by the slippery sophisms of the Averroists, espoused a system which did violence not only to the psychological laws of man's being but entailed forfeiture of the Catholic tradition. As a keen philosopher Albert felt outraged to be called upon to subscribe to such an awkward system; as an educator he recoiled from polluting the minds of the intellectual leaders growing up around him; as a Christian he abhorred such a subtle assault upon and chronic injustice to the teaching prerogative of the Church and the educative value of her dogmas. He could not remain oblivious of the fact that though Aristotle stretched the reasoning powers of man further than any other philosopher he, without any fault of his own, had not been able to make them answer questions which pure reason alone, even at its best, could not supply. But he knew that as a Christian he had at his disposition unerring helps which solved the difficulties Aristotle could not explain, helps whose use and exercise would not invalidate Aristotle's arguments or processes of reasoning. To be a philosopher man needed not disregard theology or take refuge in the dishonest subterfuges of the doctrine of the dual truth.

Now Albert taught that philosophy and theology did really differ by reason of the different objects they were respectively minded to explore: philosophy was concerned about the problem of *ens*, or being, whereas theology focussed all its attention on God. They differed, too, by reason of the principles upon which they respectively proceeded: philosophy depended upon metaphysical or self-evident truths whereas theology relied upon the dogmas of the faith which, because they came into the possession of man by revelation, could obviously not be discovered by man's unaided reason alone. Both sciences had truth for their object, and inasmuch as they discovered truth they afforded revelations of the author of truth, the Primal Truth, God, though in different spheres. Hence, there could not be an irreconciliable opposition or contradiction between the two sciences, as there could not be ultimately any question about truth which must essentially be one and immutable. Each science in its own sphere vouchsafed man a revelation of God. But it did not follow that there was a harmony of identity or coordination between both sciences. The only possible union must necessarily be one of subordination since the higher presupposes the existence of a lower. Theology was undoubtedly the higher by reason of its object and the light of revelation in which it walked. Philosophy operating freely and in its own right needed not blush to take a secondary or subsidiary station, since it was not called upon to investigate problems which did not belong to its sphere of investigation. Hence, theology was not arrogant in claiming the right to utilize the findings of philosophy. Philosophy itself was really scientific only when it confined its operations to its own problems. It might rightfully look to theology for an answer to questions which only a science endowed with a superior light and assistance could presume and dare to resolve with anything like finality. In this wise Albert describes the nature, rights and functions of Christian philosophy, which walked arm in arm with theology without the blush of degradation or the suspicion of complete absorption. He vindicated for the *philosophia perennis* which he created the privilege of using the arguments excogitated and employed by the Fathers of the Church in their efforts to make faith a reasonable service. The philosophical uses to which the Fathers of the Church might be put in Christian philosophy were clearly demonstrated by Albert in his *Commentary on the Sentences of Peter Lombard*, in his *Summa de Creaturis*, and in his *Summa Theologica*.[1]

In Albert's delimitation of the respective provinces of these two sciences theology utilized philosophy without being called upon to make excuses or apologies, while philosophy looked to theology without blush or fear. It was the first really successful wedlock of the

[1] M. D. Chenu, "*La Théologie comme science au XIII siècle*," in *Archives d'Histoire doctrinale et littéraire du Moyen Age (1927), 31-71; C. Freekes, "Glauben und Glaubenswissenschaft nach Albert dem Grossen,"* in *Zeitschrift für katholische Theologie (1930), 200 sq., (1931), 314 sq.; A. Gardeil, "Crédibilité,"* in *Dictionnaire de Théologie Catholique*, III, 2268-2269; T. Heitz, *Essai historique sur les Rapports de la philosophie et de la foi de Bérenger de Tours à S. Thomas d'Aquin (Paris: 1909), 132-144.*

two sciences. Since the days of the great Archbishop of Canterbury, St. Anselm of Aosta, thinkers had been trying to elaborate a verification of the definition of theology as *fides quaerens intellectum*: faith invoking reason in order to save reason from running amuck in regions where the light of revelation was needed to find the way. The many skeletons of heresies along the Roman Road of Dogma proved conclusively that men of the best intentions and the greatest intellectual powers were doomed if they forgot or disregarded the postulates and imperatives of each of the two sciences. In theology, man walked on dizzy heights, using the light of faith all the time, without on that account spurning the light of reason. Albert's success in assigning both sciences their respective fields, without allowing them to sink into the bogs of misunderstanding as to their proper functions and mutual helpfulness, was the most remarkable conciliation between the two sciences which had so far been effected. Thomas Aquinas would soon seal the pact definitively.[2]

Now, Albert with his deeply mystic nature had a teleological preoccupation before his mind in all his diversified intellectual labor. He admitted it in the preface of practically every work he wrote. He was seeking the footprints of God's passage in nature as in the invisible fields of the mind. It is this search for God everywhere which made William Arendt write complainingly that in all his scientific researches "Albert always speaks as a theologian."[3] Balss and the *Realenziklopädie für Protestantische Theologie* concur in the same criticism.[4] That Albert, however, did not permit his theological bias to run away with him is plain from the complaint of Henry of Ghent who said that Albert obfuscated theology by giving too much prominence in his work to philosophy and by Gerson who, in revamping the theology of St. Bonaventure, remarked that Albert's preferences for philosophy brought hurt to theological science.[5] The genius of Albert was so all-inclusive that it is true to say that knowledge of all and every kind was precious in his sight. It has been said that by temperament he was a

[2] M. Grabmann, "*De Quaestione: Utrum theologia sit scientia speculativa an practica, a B. Alberto Magno et S. Thoma Aquinate pertractata,*" in *Alberto Magno. Alto della Settimana Albertina (Roma: 1932), 107-128.*

[3] *W. Arendt,* Die Staats- und Gesellschaftslehre Alberts des Grossen (Jena: 1929), 86.

[4] H. Balss, Albertus Magnus von Cöln als Zoologe (München: 1928), 140.

[5] M. Grabmann, *op. cit.*, 108.

naturalist and scientist, by deliberate choice a philosopher, by mood a theologian. He seemed to verify in himself the full significance and implication of the Anselmian axiom: *Credo ut intelligam.* His piety and native theological bent or sense made him look upon the faith not as an imposing dumb sphinx but as a living voice giving luminous explanations of the manifold mysteries around him on all sides which, given his intellectual curiosity, aroused his passion for knowledge. In the light of dogma the mysteries of nature resolved themselves into concrete exhibitions of God's loving kindness which men were meant to explore for the purpose of extracting thence a deeper appreciation of God's goodness and beauty. The mysterious nature and processes of thought served but to allure him to a deeper investigation of the Primal Truth which cannot ever be fully grasped here below. Hence it came that Albert made a greater effort to understand St. Anselm's doctrine than most scholars of that epoch, that he treated him with more consideration and utilized him with greater finesse than any of his contemporaries.[6] It is this intellectual sympathy for and affinity with the spirit of St. Anselm which prompted Joseph Schwane to write[7] that "Albert rather than Anselm is the father of scholasticism if by that name we understand theological science impregnated with Aristotelianism."

We are prepared therefore, to find Albert interchanging arguments from philosophers and theologians in order to elucidate the dogmas of the faith. He does so consciously and consistently. Consciously: because he was always aware of the nature of the argumentation he was invoking at the moment and never in any doubt as to what was its validity and its compelling force; hence, he tried conscientiously to observe the distinction he had drawn between philosophical and theological reasoning. Consistently: because he never tried to make one set of arguments do service for the other—thus, for instance, when in philosophy he quoted the Fathers of the Church, it was not because of the authority their names carried in the eyes of believers but because of the validity of their arguments. Realizing that theology had run perilously near stereotyping into a cold formalism, by reason of the

---

[6] G. Sestile, "*Alberto Magno e S. Tommaso d'Aquino nei loro diversi atteggiamenti psicologici riguardanti la dottrina della Teodicca Anselmiana,*" in *Memorie Domenicane (1931), 400-406.*

[7] *J. Schwane, Dogmengeschichte (Freiburg:1882),III, 46-54, 103-109, passim.*

overobtrusion of the argument drawn from authority, he was at pains to introduce into the study of the sacred sciences the reasoning methods of Aristotle and the Peripatetics. Finding that Aristotle's natural theology was substantially conformable to the propositions of the faith on the nature and existence of God and the ways by which man could arrive at a knowledge of the First Cause, he did not hesitate to say that it would be possible to construct a true natural theology from the doctrines of the Stagirite without recourse to revelation but not in conflict with it. Yet he did not hesitate to reject Aristotle when he found him out of step with Catholic dogma, insisting that in such a case Augustine was to be preferred.[8] And he made his position clear by maintaining that, though the soul had an impress of the Trinity, Aristotle could never help man to arrive at a knowledge of that august mystery.[9] And it is worthy of note that precisely on the doctrine of the Most Blessed Trinity Albert wrote better than any man before him and was not surpassed subsequently even by St. Thomas. To forget this fact might lead scholars into looking upon Albert as a lop-sided theologian deserving the criticisms of Henry of Ghent and John Gerson.

Had Albert not been dowered with a markedly sharp theological sense he would never have succeeded so well in distinguishing between faith and reason, between theology and philosophy; he would never have formulated so clearly their separate domains; hence, he would never have been the first to consider theology a separate and distinct science. And it does not militate against this claim to find that Albert differed from Aquinas in describing the nature of theology and its end. However, his treatment and concept of theology as a sacred and supernatural science, using argumentation in the Aristotelian way, coincided with Thomas.[10] Had Albert been less a philosopher, it is safe to assume that he would not have excelled in theology. If he cultivated philosophy so assiduously it was in the shrewd conviction that it would sharpen his theological sense. Certainly he did not Christianize Aristotle for mere intellectual pleasure or pastime. It was meant to develop his own appreciation of theology about whose superior claims and rights he discourses so lucidly and eloquently in the first part of

---

[8] *II Sent. dist. 13, art. 3, ad 1.*

[9] *Ibid.*, tr. III, q. 1, ad 2.

[10] M. Grabmann, *op. cit.*, 119.

the third treatise of his *Summa Theologica.*[11] But in that same eulogy on the eminent rôle of theology he does not forget to write a bill of guarantees for philosophy, saying: "Whatever is known by two ways instead of one, is better grasped; hence what is known by faith and reason is better understood than that which is known only by faith."[12] For all his love of the faith and its dogmas Albert could not be induced to prove traitor to reason.

Now Albert's merits as also his shortcomings as a philosopher determine to a greater degree than has generally been admitted his standing as a theologian. If he excelled in explaining so well the dogmas of religion it was because, aside from his erudition, he employed more generously and expertly than his predecessors every bit of philosophical data which would make faith a reasonable service.

The chief merits of Albert's philosophical labors are his critical evaluation of various past systems of thought, his astounding erudition, his critical utilization of the most disparate elements of knowledge, and his originality and geniality of outlook on many occasions. These characteristics of his philosophical contributions to the sum of knowledge in his day appear strikingly in what he added to the study and advancement of theological science.

It must be borne in mind, first, that theology in the Middle Ages was not as clearly divided up as in our own day. Hence, we cannot expect to find in Albert's works a systematic presentation and treatment of dogmatic, moral, pastoral, and ascetical theology in separate tracts, treatises, or courses. Since the medieval man looked upon the salvation of his own soul as his chief business in life, moral reflections were attached not only to dogmatic disquisitions but practically to every form of mental productivity whether in philosophy or the sciences. Knowledge in those ages of faith was looked upon as

---

11 *"Intellectus noster perficitur variis luminibus et elevatur; ex lumine suo connaturali non elevatur ad scientiam Trinitatis et Incarnationis et Resurrectionis; ex lumine autem influente a superiore natura ad supermundana elevatur, quae potentia sola divina et voluntate sunt. Et his lumine desuper fluente assentit, et certius ea scit, quem ea quae ex naturali sibi connaturali scit." Summa Theologica, P. I., tr. I, cap. I, ad 2. Again he says: "Duo sunt modi Revelationis: unus quidem modus est per lumen generale in nobis et hoc modo revelatum est philosophis: hoc enim lumen non potest esse nisi a primo lumine Dei. Aliud lumen est ad supermundana constituenda, et hoc est elevatum super nos. Et hoc lumine revelata est haec scientia." Summa Theologica,* P. I., tr. I, q. 4, ad 3.

12 *Summa Theologica,* P. T., tr. III, q. 15, n. 3, art. 2.

a rule of right living and not as an intellectual plaything, curio, or treasure. Secondly, since theology was rightfully considered the queen of all the sciences the remaining branches of learning were glad to recognize their dependence on it and, in case of a recalcitrant mood, were violently whipped into line. Modern science, without the logical justification of medieval theology, asserts as great a hegemony and dictatorship for itself without such favorable immediate results. Hence, we must be prepared to find a great deal of straining in the arguments of medieval theologians, especially when there is question of adducing reasons for their arguments and positions, or of compelling other branches of learning to do service for their peculiar form of argumentation. Hence, too, there is in most medieval theologians on occasion a sharpness of tone amounting sometimes to invective, a directness of dialectical argument which argues at least for the honesty of their convictions and their love of truth. In several instances Albert was a match for the most vitriolic of his contemporaries.

With these two preliminary observations constantly in mind it will appear from a study of Albert's theological labors that he was more critical in his attitude toward, and treatment and utilization of, the corpus of theological literature at his command than any of his predecessors. First, as regards the texts, whether of Aristotle and his commentators or the theologians whom he quoted, Albert displayed an unwonted and keenly incisive spirit and attitude of reserve. We know from his own words that he compared variant texts of the Stagirite in order to get at a correct reading; that he revealed in the commentators false ascriptions of authorities; that he rejected parts of Aristotle's text because of internal criticism of the text itself.[13] In his *Commentary on the Divine Names* he used the translation of John Saracenus, abandoning it on occasion for one by John Scotus whom he went out of his way to compliment for his fine rendering of the original.[14] It is true to say that, with the possible exception of Robert Grosseteste, no medieval scholar manipulated textual criticism so largely, easily, and with such amazing and happy results. If he did not always succeed in discovering the true author of a text, as in the case of the pseudo-Dionysius, it is well to remember the condition of criticism in that uncritical age.

---

[13] G. Meersemann, *Introductio*, 104.

[14] *Ibid.*, 99-100.

In the next place, Albert discovered a really fine critical sense in evaluating the authentic thought of the authors he read and quoted. It is safe to say that with his sharp powers of perception he understood without much difficulty or long application everything he read. It is well known how benignly he interpreted St. Augustine when he seemed out of tune with the theological thought of the medieval world. On occasion he gave very ingenious reasons for his emendation of another's thought. Hence it comes that in recapitulating the thoughts of writers he is very fresh and concise. He selects with sure instinct the skeleton thought and cuts away ruthlessly the literary flesh. Hence, too, it follows that his books are not a mosaic of quotations which do not touch intimately the truth he is trying to establish. Albert quoted an unusually large number of authorities but he did not quote one authority profusely or exclusively. His quotations are always as brief as the thought demanded. And in this respect he was unique among medieval scholars.

Finally, he did not quote the disassociated thought of an author, separated from the context, but evaluated his entire process of argumentation or even his system. One feels in reading Albert that he knows the authors he is utilizing. He dissects systems mercilessly but fairly. He worked so rapidly that he did not always take the time or pains to give a minute criticism. But one feels that there was never any doubt in his mind as to what judgment should be passed eventually on a body of thought. One or two decisive blows sufficed him to dispatch a theory or point of view. In this summary adjudication—pointed, direct, sometimes violent—Albert differed from Thomas Aquinas, who worked more slowly and systematically. Albert overturned, Thomas demolished; Albert smothered, Thomas strangled; Albert tore up false theories by the root, Thomas tore the ground from the root so that there was no chance of life for the suspect doctrine. This, perhaps, is one reason why Albert's theology soon became outmoded, was soon superseded.

The second characteristic of Albert's philosophical spirit reflected in his theological work is the large part played by erudition. Albert was more widely conversant with theological literature than any of his contemporaries. He knew intimately the Fathers of the Church, ecclesiastical writers, pagan and recent authors as no other scholar of the epoch. He was not so much concerned about names but solely about ideas, as he himself avows. Hence it comes that he has more than one title to be looked upon as the first historian of dogma in the modern sense. He knew the heresiarchs, who seem to come to life in his pages. The errors they made in treating of the dogmas of the faith were a matter of such vital and personal concern to Albert that he writes as if they were still in the flesh, going about their unholy and nefarious business of poisoning the minds of the unwary and ignorant. This tone of actuality and immediacy saves his writings from becoming a dusty gallery of dead men's dead opinions. He often traces an error to its last lair and frequently establishes a hoary paternity for opinions which were looked upon in his day as up-to-date. This is particularly the case with the false Trinitarian doctrines he refuted and those, also, having reference to the existence of God. The historico-critical temper is highly developed in all of Albert's theological writings and, as heresy has a way of coming to life in successive ages under new names, his treatment of suspect doctrines gives a note of continuity to his discussions. In his *Commentary on the Divine Names* he returns no less than seventy times to the pantheism of Scotus Erigena which, from the consideration it received from a coterie of newfangled professors, he looked upon as highly insidious and menacing. He even grapples with anonymous authors, as when in his *Mystical Theology* he combats the semiagnosticism of a writer who has been identified as Thomas Gallus († 1246).

It is not to be wondered at, therefore, that in his Scripturistic works Albert gathered together elements and laid down norms for what centuries later came to be spoken of as the history of dogma or the evolution of belief. He makes it plain in scores of passages how the ages witnessed a fuller and more explicit uncovering of the meaning, content, significance, and beauty of individual points of faith. A treatise on ecclesiology has been pieced together from scattered passages in Albert's works and it has a distinctly modern ring. His *Valiant Woman*, which would have been impossible without a wide and intimate acquaintance with the theological thought of the past, presents astounding and highly suggestive elements of the new apologetic which deals with Catholicism as a whole and not as a loosely joined assemblage of parts, as a living thing and not as a system. Because the difficulties urged against the Church in the past were looked upon by Albert as a whole body of teaching he is not forced, by the very manner of his dealing with them, to take the roundabout way of dealing with individual doctrines. Because the Church is a living entity in Albert's conception he sees more in her wonderful life than can be said by logic-choppers about her orderly operation in the world. This kind of apologetic, so much in accord with the universalist temper of Albert, was entirely new in that age. If the hint he dropped in his manner of approach to his conception of the vital life of the Church as a living organism was not taken up by defenders of the Church for ages to come, it was due in great measure to the fact that Albert was inexplicably indifferent to ecclesiastical history—an indifference all the more strange in a man who lived at a time when the papacy was at its apogee of secular power and influence, when the inner life of the Church was not cribbed and confined by her exterior and secular activity, and when the successors upon the Fisherman's Throne seemed endowed with prophetic vision in laying down norms for the Church's dealings with the newly born democratic spirit which was testy and cocksure, if it was anything at all.

Had Albert kept history more consciously and consistently in the foreground in drawing up his map of the theological background of his apologetic, he undoubtedly would have achieved modernity in the best sense of the word. This does not mean that he was out of touch with his times or indifferent about the currents of thought which, filtering down from the professors, affected mightily the unthinking masses. He did give extended consideration to the lucubrations of recently deceased thinkers—thus from his elaborate refutation of David of Dinant's *De Tomis.* Father Thery[15] has been able to reconstruct the essential body of this pernicious teaching. He did flay the social abuses of his age in many places, but especially in his *Commentary on St. Luke*, and from what he says we can gather how the secular affluence of the Church was planting stumbling stones for the feet of the simple faithful. But in the big and large Albert did not call into requisition the historical data with which he must have been familiar from his wide reading of the records of the past. And it is worthy of note that, of the large body of writers who have essayed to treat of various aspects of his universal interests, not a single scholar so far has deemed it worth his while to envisage this phase of his work. The reason for this may

[15] G. Thery, Autour du decret de 1210: David de Dinant (Le Saulchoir: 1925), 84-133.

probably be that there is so little positive data to show that he exercised in historical erudition practically the same sound and sharp critical sense and instinct which he showed in dealing with the historical aspect of philosophical and theological doctrines.

The third merit of Albert's philosophical work, reappearing on the surface of his theological productiveness, is his successful utilization of elements of learning which no preceding theologian had dreamed of laying under contribution. First, it need not be insisted upon that Albert pilfered the pagan teachers freely. He performed the miracle of almost making a Father of the Church out of Aristotle. He knew and utilized Jewish and Muslim learning better than any medieval scholar.[16] He did not forget or overlook his findings in the natural sciences when writing theology or preaching to the people. Thus when analyzing the act of contemplation he has an open eye to the effects of physical health, the condition of the blood, the state of digestion upon the mental processes. He is familiar with the idea and effects of what are called today dreads and tacks. He anticipates the moderns by insisting upon the need of taking into account the physical and psychical conditions of a man when trying to banish scruples or when seeking to get at the root cause of crime and repeated acts of abnormal practices, or when setting out to resolve cases of conscience. This is a very attractive side of his intellectual activity and one deserving of the fullest study. He was not the man to multiply sins by utterly disregarding the influence of the body on the soul, in many cases lessening the real gravity of delinquency. He was one of the first, if not the very first, to introduce medical and physical considerations in dealing with questions of moral theology. As a consequence of this sane and measured utilization of data of a scientific kind, which he had come by through personal experimentation or the conscientious reports of trustworthy witnesses, he gave an entirely new tone to the discussion of many moral problems—a direction which was to blossom forth in a most genial way in the *Summa Confessorum* of his pupil John of Freiburg. This aspect of his theological thought opens up a wide field for the most fascinating and fruitful investigation, especially if the

[16] M. Grabmann, "*Die wissenschaftliche Mission Alberts des Grossen und die Entstehung des christlichen Aristotelismus,*" in *Angelicum (1929), 340; L. Newmann,* Jewish Influence on Christian Reform Movements (New York: 1925), 110-114; I. Hulick, A History of Medieval Jewish Philosophy (New York: 1918), 304 sq.

study be pursued in the light of his teaching on phrenology in which he was a forerunner of Gall, on physiognomy in which he anticipated Lavater, and on the *amore quodam voluntatis*, "the certain love in the will," which is nothing else than a metaphysical adumbration of the modern superconscious.

Finally, Albert's exhibitions of originality in philosophical speculation are duplicated in the domain of theological research. For it appears from Albert's general tone of enthusiasm in lecturing on theological questions that he felt himself engaged on thoroughly congenial and supremely delightful work. Even in his declining years, when he was hopelessly broken in body, he was thrilled so deeply in speaking of the things of God that he undertook the composition of an elaborate *Summa Theologica*, intended for professors and experts, in which he gathered, as in a choice nosegay, what he considered best in the theological investigations and speculations of a lifetime. In all his formal theological writings his language is uncommonly rich and elastic, colorful, pulsing with life and feeling, bulging with figures of speech and comparisons drawn from all domains of knowledge and experience. He seems to have set himself the aim of divesting speculation of its coldness, remoteness, formalism. Herbert Doms[17] has pointed out that in some passages, where the sublimity of the subject swept him off his feet he seems to be thinking aloud, in German modes of thought, which surrendered themselves only haltingly and awkwardly to the fixed and precise literary forms of Latin. One needs little imagination to picture what an electrical effect such impassioned and inspired outbursts must have had upon the German, if not the foreign, youths gathered around his chair. This exuberance, this virtuosity, this immediacy of language, combined with his adept use of

---

[17] Herbert Doms (*Der sel. Albertus Magnus*, Breslau, 1930, 18) says: "*Aus solchen und ähnlichen Stellen der lateinischen Albertus-Texte mit ihren reinem Pathos, mit ihrer ganz unlateinischen Wort- und Satzstellung klingt nun meinem inneren Ohr die deutsche Sprache eines mittelalterlichen Predigers entgegen, die erst gleichsam secundär ins Lateinische umgedacht ist, und wenn wir auch heine Zeile von Albert in deutscher Sprache sicker verbürgt besitzen, so scheinen mir doch gerade in Stellen mystischer Versunkjenheit in Alberts Schriften die zur Muttersprache nach Alberts Tode auftretende Mystik eines Meisters Ekkehart vorzuliegen, ähnlich wie ja auch die ersten deutschen Dichter des Mittelalters sich noch der lateinischen Sprache bedienten: denken wir an die Dramen der Hroswitha oder an der Ysengrinus, den Vorläufern des Reinecke Fuchs. Es würde sich lohnen diese Dinge einmal mit behutsamen Händen zu untersuchen.*"

Aristotelian methods, helped to make Albert the idol of his pupils.

To his credit it must be said that this literary finesse was never employed by him for mere display or empty effect. It was but the vibration of a mind and heart stretching themselves consciously Godwards. This perfervid tone came naturally to Albert, for he was by bent a mystic and the mystical element was never far removed from his most rigid and coldest speculation. He was not only a professor of mystical theology, being the only man of the medieval period to write a commentary on the entire pseudo-Dionysian corpus, but he was a mystical professor of theology who did not hesitate to add the fire of divine charity to his most formal lectures, as anyone would be inclined to expect from a man who defined theology as the science which serves the purposes of piety: *scientia quae secundum pietatem est.* Without the least trace of egotism Albert introduced the recital of personal experiences in his theological writings in order to elucidate a point. And even where he does not directly speak of himself the sharp eye can discover in countless passages veiled references to what had transpired in his inner life or in his secret dealings with men.

He is original above all medieval authors in the literary form he gave his thoughts, in the personal touches and turns of thought, in the frankly direct, almost brusque, method of his approach to the core question of the subject he treated of. He was a poet, though we have scarcely anything in rime or meter from his pen. He sang because he loved and he loved because he insisted that theology helped man to a fuller vision of God, and the fuller the knowledge the deeper the love. Hence arose his unique power of giving fresh and suggestive outlooks, intimations, explanations, descriptions, and interpretations of theological questions and moods of which other theologians seemed not to have had an inkling. It explains why he marks a distinct advance and an almost unapproachable emixnence in treating of the Most Blessed Trinity and, especially, the procession of the Holy Ghost from the Father and Son through love;[18] why he treated of the gifts of the Holy Spirit, especially the gift of Wisdom, as none of his predecessors;[19]

[18] A. Stohr, "*Die Hauptrichtungen der spekulativen Trinitatslehre in der Theologie des 13. Jahrhunderts,*" in *Theologische Quartalschrift (1925), 113-135; M. J. Scheeben,* Die Mysterien des Christentums (Freiburg: 1865), 98.

[19] B. Lavaud, Les Dons du Saint Esprit d'après le Bx. Albert le Grand, in *Revue Thomiste (1931), 162-183.*

why his explanation of the progressive stages of union with God through contemplation made room for psychological data of which no theologian so far had stopped to take cognizance;[20] why he wrote at greater length and with more feeling of the Most Blessed Sacrament than any earlier writer;[21] why his treatment of all phases of Marian doctrine impelled Rudolf of Nijmegen to call him "the secretary of Mary" and Peter Labbe, S.J., *Albertus Deiparae Philosophus*: Albert, the philosopher of the Mother of God. On occasion he paused to draw pictures of inner experiences which are counted among the finest which a Christian pen has ever achieved, as, for instance, when he describes the banquet of the soul with the Godhead in the mansions of the blessed or when, again, he explains the powers of the Precious Blood to cleanse the human soul.[22]

Pope Pius XI, in his encyclical *Studiorum Ducem* (June 29, 1923), suggested that by providential disposition Thomas Aquinas was carefully shielded and screened from contact with the world so that, in the company of his own pure thoughts, he might be formed to become the Angelic Doctor with a sharp eye for an understanding of the mysteries of faith and the secrets of the soul united to God. Perhaps the same Providence was at work when Albert's ways were cast in the busy marts of men. For being by nature so strongly inclined to mysticism he was hindered, by the very circumstances of his life, from devoting himself exclusively to mystical subjects. As a professor Albert was called upon to discourse on the various questions of dogmatic theology without having an opportunity, ordinarily, to convert this knowledge to the uses of devotion. How difficult he must have felt this academic inhibition can be seen from his conduct in turning the propositions of Peter Lombard's *Sentences* into fervent prayers. As a citizen of the world, a prince of the Empire, and a bishop of souls, he

---

20 H. Doms, Die Gnadenlehre des sel. Albertus Magnus (Breslau: 1929), passim; G. Meersemann, "*La Contemplation mystique d'après le Bx. Albert est-elle immédiate*," in *Revue Thomiste (1931), 184-198.*

21 *G. Esser, "Die Gnadenfülle der allerseligsten Jungfrau Maria nach der Lehre Alberts des Grossen,"* in *Theologisch-Praktische Quartalschrift (1882), 273-288; J. M. Bover, "La Mediacion universal de la Santisima Virgen en las obras del Bo. Alberto Magno,"* in *Gregorianum (1926), 511-548; J. Kramp, "Albert der Grosse und die Sermones de S S. Eucharistiae Sacramento,"* in *Gregorianum (1922), 239-253; A. Franz,* Die Messe im deutschen Mittelalter (Freiburg: 1902), 469 sq.

22 H. Doms, Die Gnadenlehre, 137.

was brought into active touch with the everyday life of men and communities of men. Now the ordinary life of the average man is frayed and seamy. Hence, this eager listener to the subdued whispers of the Divine Lover on the mountain peak of meditation must, perforce, attune his ear to the sad stories of human failure, frailty, and frustration. The mystic theologian is almost bested by the moral theologian; the moral theologian almost outstrips the dogmatic theologian. It is one more instance of that paradox in the history of mystical thought when we find the seer forced to turn sewer of the robes of conscience which sin had torn apart; when the dreamer becomes the doer; when the contemplative must needs act as chaplain of souls in crowded centers and adviser of the commercial-minded and practical man of affairs. With the exception of St. Theresa of Avila, Albert best exemplifies the practicality of the professional student and mystic.

He may justly be looked upon as an innovator in the method of teaching moral theology, not indeed as an independent ecclesiastical science, but as a department of clerical knowledge which could give a rational account of its own measures and prescriptions. For the space of forty years he touched upon most of the aspects, implications, and applications of three fundamental questions of moral theology: the reason and psychology of the human act; reason and the norms of morality; reason and the acquired moral virtues.[23] These questions had scarcely been touched upon before Albert's day with the fullness, consistency, and consecutiveness which they deserved and demanded. The primary reason for the neglect and oversight of these basic problems in moral theology was due to the very nature of the method of teaching sacred science at the time. The Lombard's pupil, Peter of Poitiers, had provided a casuistic textbook which satisfied the professional needs of the clergy during a period when the theological schools were languishing and when learning was difficult to acquire except in university centers. Robert de Courcon, Stephen Langton, and Godefroid of Poitiers, following the lead of Peter the Chanter and Master Martin, produced casuistic works in which the canonical

[23] Odon Lottin, "*Le Rôle de la Raison dans l'Ethique d'Albert le Grand,*" in *Alberto Magno. Atti della Settimana Albertina (Rome: 1932), 153-177;* Id., "*Notes sur les premiers ouvrages théologiques d'Albert le Grand,*" in *Recherches Théologie ancienne et médiévale (1932), 73 sq.*

element was given a preponderating rôle and importance, largely as a result of the revival of interest in Canon Law at the University of Bologna, following upon the work of Gratian, a revival which reached its apogee in the codification of Canon Law by St. Raymond Penyafort at the command of Pope Gregory X. In the second place Albert's immediate predecessors, almost to a man, were in a high state of reaction against the philosophical element introduced into the study of moral questions by Abelard and his school, especially Gilbert de la Poirree. Thus the fundamental questions of natural ethics were scarcely ever touched upon in the schools when Albert appeared on the scene. With the exception of William of Auxerre, who wrote the first treatise on natural law, about 1220, no professor discussed the moral but only the theological virtues. Albert began in good earnest to treat of these neglected questions of moral theology in his *Tractatus de Natura Boni* (1235-1240), prosecuted his study with a clarification of his doctrine in the second part of his *Summa de Creaturis*, in the *Summa de Homine*, in the third part of his still unedited *Summa de Bono*, in his *Commentary on the Sentences* (1245-1248), in his unedited course on the *Nicomachaean Ethics* written down and edited by Thomas Aquinas, in the printed course on the *Nicomachaean Ethics*, and, finally, in his *Summa Theologica*, written after 1275.

In espousing Aristotle as a guide in the study of theology Albert was necessarily obliged from the very beginning of his scholastic career to treat of the basic questions of natural ethics which theologians had not treated of, with the exception of that metaphysical professor who hid his identity (was it in fear or shame?) under the name of Philip. Aristotle helped Albert in no small measure in analyzing the questions on the faculties of the soul, liberty and the analysis of the human act under the impulsion of the will as the efficient cause, and under the dictation of the reason as the formal cause. He almost created the idea of synderesis in moral theology, but not so completely or clearly that the finishing touches of Aquinas could be dispensed with. He was far in advance of his predecessors in his treatment of conscience, habits, the virtues (especially prudence), the distinction between mortal and venial sins. Though his fellow religious and friends, Roland of Cremona and Hugh of St. Cher, had essayed to place the study of moral theology on a rational basis, the chief merit for having done so belongs to Albert. That he did not neglect the tedious task of descending to particular and specific cases is clear from the fact that the great medieval Franciscan preacher, Berthold of Ratisbon, submitted cases of conscience to him for solution, especially in the matter of money lending;[24] that he was called upon to quiet the fears or scruples of persons in high and low station; that he flayed the evils of the time in his sermons and commentaries on Scripture, especially on the Gospels of St. Luke and St. John, not as a professional reformer or chronic critic but as an adviser who had a definite program of social reform and an unfailing method for the betterment of individuals. Arendt has shown[25] that Albert's political doctrine was not divorced from his moral teaching. No man wrote more sanely on scandal and the sins of the flesh, and in dealing with the latter he betrayed an instinctive modesty, reserve, and restraint which were remarkable in that age of plain, often uncouth, speaking. His frequent dealings with nuns enabled him to treat of simple and solemn vows of religion in an epoch-making way.[26] His development of the Church's teaching on the duty and blessedness of almsgiving is a genial presentation of a subject which in all ages lends itself easily to exaggeration. His important and clean-cut teaching on usury, or interest taking, should prove especially illuminating in an age of economic problems like our own. It is abundantly plain that Albert not only opened the way but cleared it notably for the superb treatment of most of the questions of moral theology by Thomas Aquinas. It is not without significance that we possess Thomas's autograph of Albert's notes on Aristotle's Ethics[27]—a sure proof of the eagerness with which the young Neapolitan gathered up the wisdom of his Suabian master. And the concern of Albert to have his thought accurately preserved is evidenced by the fact that he looked through the notes carefully—a trial to his eyes if not his patience on account of Thomas's miserable scrawl and intricate system of shorthand, second only to the craziness of Albert's own

---

24 K. Rieder, *Das Leben Bertholds von Regensburg (Freiburg: 1901), 46 sq.; F. M. Wagner, "Bruder Bert hold und Albertus Magnus,"* in *Germania* (1863), 105 sq.; also other answers of Albert: in *Zeitschrift für deutsches Albertthum* (1844), 575 sq.

25 W. Arendt, Die Staats- und Gesellschaftslehre Alberts des Grossen (Jena: 1929), passim.

26 H. Laurer, Die Moraltheologie Alberts des Grossen (Freiburg: 1891), 63.

27 A. Pelzer, "*Le Cours inédit d'Albert le Grand sur la Morale à Nicomaque,*" *in* Revue Scolastique (1922), 333-361, 479-520; M. Grabmann, "*Die Stuttgart Handschrift des ungedruckten Ethikkommentars Alberts des Grossen,*" in *Aus Ethik und Leben (1931), 55-65.*

handwriting.

There are many other merits and excellencies in Albert's enormous mass of theological writing waiting to be discovered and brought out in all their brilliance by careful and conscientious scholars. Students of our own and coming ages, if only to refute the silly charges that the Church has been the implacable foe of intellectual and scientific progress, have the obligation—which is none the less a privilege—of making ever clearer Albert's prodigious industry, unrivaled erudition, adept utilization of the most disparate elements of learning. They can let in a breath of fresh air on the critical study of the sources of medieval theological tradition by accentuating Albert's personal note in many of his most abstract reasoning processes, his original method of approach to difficult problems and his expert handling of them, his frequent fresh outlook, his deep psychological insight into the workings of the human mind and heart, and his sage understanding of the variability of the social consciousness, of the half articulate masses of his age. They must show, often in contrast with other writers of that period, Albert's consistent sweet sanity and persistent reasonableness, his keen appreciation of the kind of teaching needed by his age and desiderated by its most farseeing educators. We are agreed today—though past ages have long since admitted it—that no single medieval theologian, with the exception of Thomas Aquinas, soared higher and nearer to God on the strong winds of scholastic philosophy and theology than Albert the Great, that none in his upward sweep remembered so lovingly the poor struggling thinkers on this planet who were trying painfully and laboriously but as best they could to fit together the wondrous patterns of God's oceanic love for humankind.

Lest students of Albert's theological labors be charged with blind enthusiasm when insisting upon his eminent gifts and achievements, they have been among the first to admit that, as in everything human, so, too, in Albert's work there are discoverable its own imperfections, such as the lack of a perfectly operating architectonic spirit, which might have succeeded in welding a bewildering mass of data into a tightly knit system and synthesis; that there is in him at times a bit of confusion when assigning things to their proper places and in their right proportions; that there is a sudden inexplicable hesitation to grasp the first implications and draw the last conclusions of an elaborate body of argumentation; that sometimes his divisions are not clear; that on occasion he divides up his matter too nicely thus losing sight of the central theme, the core question, the main contention; that at infrequent intervals his arguments get in another's way thus producing vagueness and confusion; that he does not always reject outright theories which fit ill into the general synthesis he was aiming at; that occasionally he fails to press out of a proposition all its rich savor. But these are the defects of a great man conscious every waking moment of his life that in the short span of a lifetime he had a gigantic task to perform in the face of great odds. For his tireless energy in collecting data he has been compared to Origen, and his stupendous work shows the minor blemishes of the great Alexandrine doctor without his major shortcomings. For having subjugated to Christian uses the proud, stubborn, and vagrant wisdom of the Greek and Jew and Moslem he has been compared to Godfrey de Bouillon—and like Godfrey's Kingdom of Jerusalem, Albert's hegemony in the schools did not long survive.

Had Albert been an isolated student or research worker, a selfish bookworm, shielded from the distractions of a busy and beneficent life in the mad swirl of the medieval world, perhaps he would have found time to eliminate these small blemishes from his written works. For these shortcomings are the inevitable result of the rapidity with which he perforce had to work in order to dispatch the many tasks which somehow found their way to his cell's door. They arise naturally out of the eagerness with which he followed up any new avenue of knowledge, made known to him by the discovery of a new manuscript, or by the appearance on the scene of a new teacher, that so, in his apostolic zeal, he might shield his students or the academic world against the danger of infection or pollution; out of the multiplicity of interests which solicited his mighty brain, that saw in every manifestation of life or activity a theater for the conquest of souls or an arena to maintain their possession; out of distractions incidental to the offices of trust he filled and the importunities of his friends and pupils which he in his big-heartedness always tried to satisfy in a regal fashion; and lastly out of the mystical bent of his heart which induced him often to stop in the very midst of an argument to paint engaging pictures of a devotional kind for the spiritual edification and benefit of his auditors. If our experience proves the truth of the poet's words that we love our friends mostly for their faults and foibles, then the very slight blemishes in Albert's theological writings, which show him to have been the willing victim of his own magnificent, magnanimous, and munificent nature, cannot but increase our admiration for a man who, despite his undeniable greatness, did not seek to disguise his inherited trends nor cover over his acquired outlooks; who did not blush to reveal his moods and methods, his prejudices and preferences; who did not disown his native loyalties, nor deny his congenital antipathies. His consistent striving to be a saint without ceasing on that account to be a man makes him one of those lovable men from whom we do not shrink to take advice because we sense that he has the understanding heart of charity. As the twenty-eighth Doctor of the Church he has been deemed big enough in heart and mind to take his place in that select and resplendent gallery of heaven where he stands with Augustine, from whom he was not afraid to differ for all his love of him, with Ambrose, from whom he borrowed his own understanding Romano-legal spirit; with Anselm, from whom he learned the utilities of psychology in explaining the mysteries going on within a human heart that is keeping high festival with its Guest and Lord. In a word, Albert the theologian has well merited the words which Dante, the theological master poet, has put into the mouth of the prince of theologians:

> *Questi che m'è a destro più vicino*
> *frate e maestro fumni, ed esso Alberto*
> *fu di Colonia, ed io Thomas d'Aquino.*
> (*Paradiso*, X, viv. 97-99.)

CHAPTER XVIII

THE FIRST THOMIST

AFTER the close of the Council on July 17, 1274, Albert remained at Lyons for a short time. For on the last day of that month he received a commission from Pope Gregory X to preside at the election of an abbot at Fulda, or in case he could not be present in person, to see to it that the selection be made in accordance with the established norms of the Church's law. Probably on his way to Cologne Albert remained over in Fulda, long enough to propose Bertheus, whom the monks forthwith proceeded to elect unanimously.[1] Shortly afterwards King Rudolf of Hapsburg empowered Albert to hand over to Eberhard von Dienst, the newly elected Bishop of Münster, his regalia as lord of the Empire and receive from him in writing a promise to appear in person in the royal presence within a twelvemonth.[2] In April, he consecrated the main altar of the Abbey Church at Maria Gladbach. In September, Countess Mathilda of Sayn, anxious to redeem a landed estate which had been handed over in 1250 to Archbishop Conrad of Hochstaden and the diocese of Cologne in default of the payment of a debt, came to Albert for the purpose of making a new agreement with the Archbishop, Siegfried of Engelberg. Together with the Minorite Friar, Gerad von Andernach, he acted as judge in the transaction and determined the coinage for the liquidation of the obligation. At the same time Albert was named as arbiter for any further misunderstandings or transactions of any kind whatever between the Countess and the Archbishop. Two years later the financial litigation was definitively settled.[3]

In January of the next year he executed a privilege of Gregory X, dating from July of the preceding year, in favor of the Knights of St. John. He signed the agreement of the Provost and Chapter of Mechtern to dissolve a conventual corporation in Cologne in favor of the

[1] *J. Guiraud, Les Registres de Grégoire X (Paris: 1901), 148, n. 390.*

[2] *R. Wilmans, Westphälisches Urkundenbuck, III,* 497, n. 965; H. Scheeben, *Chronologie,* 108.

[3] H. Cardauns, *Konrad von Hockstaden* (Köln: 1880), 65 sq.; H. Scheeben, *Chronologie,* 107.

Archbishop, who was to give guarantee that he would attend to the bodily support of the monks of the suppressed convent. In September he pushed on to Antwerp for the purpose of dedicating the Dominican Church of St. Paul. The Friars, on their arrival in 1243, had taken up their residence outside the city, and in 1262 had begun the erection of a Church and convent within the city walls. With that undisguised love of the northern peoples for beautiful churches, the faithful had prevailed upon the Friars to erect an edifice large enough to hold the crowds that flocked to their sermons. The capitular fathers who had come to Antwerp that year for the legislative work of the province were present for the dedication, and among them were men whom Albert had initiated into sacred science and who, therefore, held him in high esteem not only as an old master but also as a tried friend. On his homeward journey he tarried at Louvain, on September 13, to consecrate an altar in honor of St. John the Baptist and St. John the Evangelist, and another in honor of St. Catherine of Alexandria, the martyred virgin philosopher who had been held in high veneration in the Order because of her having appeared several times to its holy founder. It was, probably, on this occasion that Albert used the wooden, carved pulpit still shown in Louvain as the rostrum from which he had announced to the people the tender condescensions of the Christ. On this same journey he laid the foundation stone of the Dominican Church of St. Paul at Maastricht.

It was, probably, during this brief stay in the Low Countries that the truth was borne in upon the mind of Albert that threatening storm clouds had been gathering in Paris against the Christian Aristotelianism which he had been so instrumental in introducing into the Christian schools. Albert, no doubt, was conscious that his pedagogical innovation had not proved entirely pleasing to all Christian scholars. The opposition in Germany was not rabid, not only because the German peoples had not sufficient surcease from war to prosecute purely intellectual pursuits, but also because any timid show of a recalcitrant spirit had been overshadowed and beaten down by the name and prestige of Albert after his consecration as a bishop. Whatever criticism of the new ways existed in Germany was confined to backstairs to which Albert never went for his opinions on current movements and among the half-baked students with whose strictures he never bothered. This secure entrenchment of Christian

Aristotelianism in Germany accounts for the rather disdainful way in which Albert had answered in 1270 the questions of John of St. Giles, who was in the very midst of the intellectual storms in the French schools.[4] Albert in his reply to John of St. Giles had expressed a mild surprise that such questions as the unity of the intellect should be discussed at all.[5] Relying upon his own academic prestige at home he had dismissed the objections raised abroad with a dictatorial finality which was not only not accepted in good part in France but was not sufficiently impressive to snuff out the false lights which the Averroistic Aristotelians had succeeded in lighting in advantageous places. The French have ever been more interested in speculative problems than in practical questions. No wonder, then, that the Averroistic wing of the Aristotelian army, which clung to everything the Stagirite had said or was supposed to have said, was hatching a determined opposition against those who, like Albert, took cautiously the texts of Aristotle which, coming by way of the Iberian peninsula, had been tampered with and doctored by Maimonides and Averroes. For without formulating any elaborate system of textual criticism Albert was by nature a critic of undoubted and astounding sharpness and incision. And this is precisely what the French Averroistic wing of the movement was not. Its leading spirits were captivated by the sight of an Aristotelian manuscript almost as much as by its content. At least, they were not very critical in their attitude toward the actual text of Aristotle. They were too eager to be termed "modern" to take the pains to ascertain for themselves whether it was worth while to be modern with the forms of learning put within their reach. Hence, the caution of Albert toward the texts of Aristotle seemed to their ebullient spirits to be but a congenital lack of enthusiasm. The German would not be swept off his feet by the sight of any text that happened to come from the copyists' schools established all over Spain by the Mohammedans. This did not mean that, once having accepted Aristotle, the German would not go as far, if not farther, than the scholars from France and Spain. It merely signified that Albert wanted to be sure that he was getting what he bargained for, what he

---

[4] P. Mandonnet, *Siger de Brabant et l'Averroisme Latin* (Louvain: 1908-1911), II, 29 sq.

[5] *"Hic error habet tres partes, et nimis periculosus est, habetque multos defensores; et quia defensores hujus haeresis dicunt quod est secundum philosophiam, licet fides aliud ponat, ideo oportet quod secundum philosophiam destruantur." Albertus M.,* Summa Theologica, P. II.

espoused.

Siger de Brabant who appeared at the University of Paris during these years of intellectual ferment did not have this instinctive caution of Albert. He had done yeomen work in his younger days in procuring Aristotelian texts and propagating their content. Besides, he was endowed with great powers of assimilating another's thought and possessed a facile gift of restating what he had gathered from others with a certain greasy unction that appealed mightily to the young.[6] This enthusiastic treatment of Aristotle by Siger accounted in great measure for his large following. For in any large school there must always be a large fringe of students who do not care to summon up or cannot put forth the intellectual effort required to examine every inch of ground they have had an opportunity of covering. Such men can easily be swept off their feet by one who speaks in glowing terms about abstract principles. And it must be borne in mind, too, that with all his powers of a popular tribune, Siger was a man to be reckoned with. His mind was nimble and resourceful. He could give an ostensible reason for nearly everything he taught, though just as often as not his reasons proved, on closer examination, to be only glaring sophisms or unproved assumptions. He was especially cunning in what he did not say, for he left unsaid what it was not to his purpose to insist upon. He was just the kind of leader the intellectually rash needed and wanted.

While the storm was thus gathering, Robert Kilwardby, one of the leading protagonists of the Platonico-Augustinian current in the Order, was removed from his chair at Oxford University to the archiepiscopal seat of Canterbury. In his place of authority he could afford to marshal his undoubted learning against the Christian Aristotelianism propounded by Albert and Thomas. Certainly it would not have been seemly for an English bishop to come to close grips with a German bishop, for there is such a thing as professional courtesy and ecclesiastical etiquette. But to take Thomas to task for teaching in the new manner would not be against the unwritten rules of the episcopacy. And to cross swords with a man like Thomas would not be demeaning, at any time, even for an English primate within a few weeks after his episcopal consecration. Applauded by sympathizers in

---

[6] Thus Siger referred unctuously to Thomas and Albert as the *praecipui viri in philosophia* ("*De Anima Intellectiva*," in Mandonnet, *Siger, II*, 152).

his own Order and by the Franciscans—especially by Roger Bacon, who resented the rising popularity of Thomas more than the scientific preeminence of Albert,[7] and by Robert Peckham who still smarted at the remembrance of his inability to get Thomas flustered in a public dispute at Paris[8]—Robert, unfortunately for his high office, entered into secret communication with Stephen Tempier, Archbishop of Paris. Together they would do something notable.[9]

Now, Tempier was not a dyed-in-the-wool schoolman. He had grown up in a university atmosphere of secret antipathy to the Friars and, though he had never openly challenged their right to teach in the schools, he never had displayed any very great eagerness to see that they received fair play. As chancellor of the university it was his business to examine every professor's teaching to see whether it squared with orthodoxy. Whether he was partially blinded by his dislike of the Friars; whether he did not quite see the drift and implications of the Averroistic Aristotelianism that was being introduced subtly by Siger de Brabant and the handful of disgruntled professors left over from the days of William of St. Amour; whether he did not take the time to see how the Christian Aristotelianism was quite a different thing from the new importation; whether he was swayed by the fears of John of St. Giles and Giles of Lessines who, as Dominicans, should have known the difference, the fact remains that Tempier, in April, 1271, in the church of St. Genevieve, did decree that only theologians, not philosophers or masters in the arts, should

---

[7] Roger Bacon says (*Opera Quaedam, ed. Brewer, 30*): *"Jam aestimatur a vulgo studentium, et a multis qui valde sapientes aestimantur, et a multis viris bonis, licet sint decepti, quod philosophia jam data sit Latinis, et composita in lingua latina, et est facta in tempore mea et vulgata Parisius, et pro auctore allegatur compositor ejus. Nam sicut Aristoteles, Avicenna, Averroes allegantur in scholis, sic et ipse; et adhuc vivit, et habuit in vita sua auctoritatem, quam numquam homo habuit in doctrina."* E. Gilson, *La Philosophie au Moyen Age (Paris: 1931), 165-166.*

[8] *F. Ehrle, "Johann Peckham über den Kampf des Augustinismus und Aristotelismus,"* in *Zeitschrift für katholische Theologie (1889), 172 sq. From the Process of Thomas's Canonization:* Dixit (Bartholomaeus a Capua) se audivisse a pluribus fratribus Praedicatoribus fide dignis, quod quando idem frater Thomas una vice disputabat Parisiis, ubi erat frater Joannes de Pizano Ordinis Fratrum Minorum, qui postea fuit Episcopus Cantuarensis, quantumcumque dictus frater Joannes exasperaret fratrem Thomam verbis ampullosis et tumidis, numquam tamen ipse frater Thomas restrinxit verbum humilitatis, sed semper cum dulcedine et humanitate respondit. (*Acta Sanctorum*, Martii I, 736.)

[9] H. Scheeben, *Chronologie*, 120.

engage in disputes on theological points.[10] Siger had brought theology in the purview of the arts' faculty and had arrogated for the masters the right to teach it with purely philosophical helps. A repercussion of this attitude is evident in the legislative action of the Order, for the Chapter at Montpellier, in 1271, suggested that the brethren should not devote too much time to the natural sciences. And the next Chapter at Buda ordained that the brethren give up all books on alchemy—which then was synonymous with the natural sciences.[11]

Now in the Low Countries Albert had an opportunity of placing his ear to the sounding board to hear what had long been preparing. Rumors about what was going on in England reached there before they were seized upon at Paris or even before they were delivered to the ears of Tempier. In the Low Countries Albert heard that Kilwardby, a few days after his consecration on October 11, 1272, had selected a few propositions which he looked on with disfavor. Also that he abused his episcopal privileges by granting an indulgence of forty days to all who would condemn the propositions he had stigmatized.[12] And Kilwardby's sympathetic agents, returning from Paris to Canterbury, would tell with glee along the way that some similar step was being contemplated by the Archbishop of Paris. All this was welcome news in the Low Countries where Siger had made his academic bow to the hearty applause of those who were charmed by his confident manner and beguiled by his independent methods. He had recruited many of his followers in his own homeland, who were easily transformed into wild enthusiasts because champions of a challenged cause.[13] And perhaps Kilwardby's couriers were indiscreet enough to divulge the information that Tempier was willing to try to make out that Thomas

---

[10] Denifle-Chatelain, *Chartularium Universitatis Parisiensis* (Paris: 1889), I, **473, 543;** P. Mandonnet, *Siger, II*, 176.

[11] *Acta Cap. Gen. O. P.*, I, 178-230.

[12] Denifle-Chatelain, *Chartularium I*, 556.

[13] How high feeling ran at the time can be seen from the sarcastic references of the schoolmen to one another: "*Quidam sophistice de scientia Dei sicut de scientia hominis disputantes, non intelligunt dicta philosophorum.*" ... "*Omnino ergo ridiculosum est quod dicunt.*" ... "*Absurdum est omnino quod dixerunt in secunda fictione.*" ... "*Non ergo tantum secundum theologos sed etiam secundum philosophiam, cujus causa dicta est ignorantia, quia multi parisienses non philosophiam, sed sophismata, sunt secuti.*"

and Siger were common bed-fellows in Aristotle's house.[14] Both the Frenchman and the Englishman were convinced that the new system must be scotched at any cost. If the condemnation, or better, prohibition of the English and French Archbishops miscarried, then their joint condemnation of propositions taken from the two Aristotelian currents would tend to confuse the two schools of Aristotelianism in the popular mind. In any event Thomas would be struck. If the episcopal bolt of lightning was not enough to break the Aristotelian school into shivering pieces, then the sworn opposition and discomfiture of Siger de Brabant and his followers would surely effect it.

Such were the rumors circulating in the schools. No better place, outside of Paris and Canterbury, to gather up the threads of the dispute, could be imagined than the country whither Albert had gone in 1276. Albert was not the kind of man to keep aloof from his own brethren or scholars belonging to any grade of society. He was not averse to listening to the informal talk of the common people. Hence, though the information he may have gathered in Louvain and Maastricht may have been fragmentary and contradictory, there was sufficient of it of a trustworthy character to wake him from his indifference or false sense of security regarding the oncoming storm and to call forth his fighting spirit. If, as he tells us somewhere, he was interested enough to watch the men and women of the Low Countries weaving together threads of wool into a finished piece of cloth and unravel it if necessary, we may be sure that he, in the long, silent hours of his journey back to Cologne, worked out to his own satisfaction the complicated case of how disaffected men had woven a straight-jacket in which they were minded to hold fast the wondrously resilient mind of his pupil Thomas. He had enough common sense to know that in striking Thomas they were striking him who had made Thomas what he was. He would think out a way of unraveling the machinations of Thomas's enemies.

And as he drew near Cologne he heard how the very anniversary of Thomas's death had been selected—could it have been without malice?—as the day of his condemnation. Now Albert may have fallen

---

[14] Tempier forbade the professors of the Arts Faculty to discuss theological questions in April, 1276. D'Argentre, *Collectio Judiciorum*, I, 175-178.

behind a little in his devotion to the work of Christianizing Aristotle which Thomas had carried through so successfully; he may have lost interest in the new movement in the schools because of the random episcopal duties which he was glad to perform for bishops who had been kind to him, or friends to whom he wished to show himself grateful and appreciative; he may have exhausted his strength in finishing the works in which he stored up much learning about which Thomas did not bother but which on that account were not utterly despicable nor negligible; he may have sighed for the rest that should come with the evening of life—but he would not, could not brook an insult that dishonored an old friend and pupil, an insult made all the more despicable because it ridiculed the death and violated the tomb of Thomas. Good men may know the uses, utilities, and sanctities of patience and may try with all their might to translate them into everyday practice. But there is a thing which the best men cannot and will not tolerate and that is to see partisans conspire together to besmirch maliciously the memory of a dead warrior. There is such a thing as honor and courtesy among combatants, and the real fighter is the man who keeps inviolate the unwritten rules. This Tempier and Kilwardby evidently had not done. To gain their point they were willing to go the lengths of pairing Thomas with Siger in a common condemnation. There was a bad faith, dirty trickery here, however noble and justifiable they may have thought their collusion against Thomas. So a mighty wave of just wrath and anger—the *saeva indignatio*—surged up in the generous, sportsmanlike soul of the white-haired warrior, who had always observed the clean rules of fight. The lion in Albert was aroused over the injustice to one who had spoken out so that all the world had heard it—that "dumb Sicilian ox" of the long ago whom he had once given the first chance to bellow aloud so as to drown the tittering remarks of his fellow students; that incomparable teacher who, now that he was dead and mute, could not arise in the full vigor of his manhood to argue down with unassailable arguments, the invidious, unjust, chronically uncharitable strictures of ecclesiastical politicians. Albert never appeared in a nobler light. Like Moses coming down from the mountain top with eyes glittering in holy anger, so Albert, resplendent with the sacred light of truth and justice flaming in his eyes, will take the road to Paris once more, forgetful of everything but the manly task he had to discharge in vindication of his dead pupil's orthodoxy.

Hugh of Lucca, who was Albert's sole companion on the way, told the knight, Bartholomew of Capua, who related it at the canonization of Thomas Aquinas, that his religious brethren, fearing for Albert on account of his age and the fatigues of the journey, endeavored for a time to dissuade him from carrying out his plan of going to Paris. But he declared emphatically that he would go forthwith and uphold the works of his disciple. Arrived in Paris he assembled the university and ascended the Dominican chair; he addressed the assembled professors on the words: "What a glory it is for one who is living to be praised by the dead." He represented the undying glory of Thomas, compared with whose immortality all else, himself included, seemed shrouded in the shadows of death. He eulogized the great and extraordinary qualities of Thomas and declared that he was prepared to defend his writings before a jury of competent men. No heterodoxy could be ferreted out of his many works as no hidden stain could be tracked down in his life. And, Bartholomew continues, after many discourses and measures adopted for the defense and approval of Thomas's writings, Albert set out once more for Cologne.[15]

A close study of this statement of Bartholomew brings out in vivid light the high romance of Albert's journey to Paris in defense of Thomas. In the first place, we must say to his eternal credit that he did not give the date of Albert's departure. Bartholomew takes it for granted that as soon as Albert had ascertained with sufficient assurance that a storm was brewing and preparing to break he immediately started on the journey. He did not wait for the threat of the condemnation to impel him to go.

Next, Bartholomew did not make the sorry and egregious blunder of some modern historians, even the best, like de Loe and Michael, who, by carefully arranging the dates on hand, maintain that Albert reached Paris on the eve of the condemnation, March 7, 1277. The old chronicler gave his readers credit for sufficient perspicacity to see that such a tardy appearance on the scene would have been entirely too late. By that time the die would have been cast and no amount of

[15] Denifle-Chatelain, *Chartularium*, I, 543; *Acta Sanctorum*, Martii, I, 722 sq.; P. Mandonnet, *Siger, II*, 176 sq.; T. Masetti, *Monumenta et antiquae et veteris disciplinae O.P.* (Roma: 1864), I, 246.

discussion would likely have induced Tempier to retract his words or go back on his plans. As a bishop he could hardly have been asked to confess in public a change of mind or temper. Bartholomew assumes that Albert would forestall the carrying out of what appeared all too evident from the general trend of things. He would call the professors to a meeting in which he would let loose the sluice gates of his eloquence; would stand guarantee in public for the orthodoxy of Thomas; would stake his reputation for learning and his prestige as bishop on his commitment to Thomas's cause. He would throw the magic of his name, age, prestige, and station into the scale. He would see how many faithful men there were in Israel willing to rally in his call: "To thy tents, O Israel!"

If Albert were to wait until the Archbishop of Paris should pass judgment what could he hope to effect? Would the Archbishop, after the verdict had been delivered, permit a strange bishop to come to the Paris diocese to challenge him in his own territory? If there was to be any hope of success, it could only be by an early departure for Paris. We cannot be mistaken about what Bartholomew means to convey. He gave no date for the departure because he would not have men do Albert the injustice of thinking that he dallied at such a critical juncture, that he deliberately postponed getting into the trenches before it was too late, that he allowed the enemies of Thomas to get an advantage over the friends of Thomas in an affair where every minute counted and where one minute late would have been as bad as a year. So we are safe in assuming that late in the year 1276 Albert was on the way to Paris.[16]

It is impossible to say what kind of an impression Albert's impassioned plea made upon the university professors. If they had a smallest dash of good sportsmanship in them they could not have helped admiring the old man whose fighting spirit had not been dampened with the years or crippled by the infirmities which were beginning to make themselves manifest. That Albert's championship of Thomas did not go without effect is plain from the fact that the proposition on the unity of the substantial form, which had first been included among the two hundred and nineteen theses selected for

---

[16] H. Scheeben, *Chronologie*, 120; F. Pelster, *Kritische Studien*, 92; de Loe in *Analecta Bollandiana* (1900), 307.

condemnation, did not appear. Kilwardby, on March 26, 1277, had not had time to hear from Paris that this particular proposition had been withdrawn in the sweeping censure.[17] And so Kilwardby, with that dictatorial tone which peeps out in his works, that attitude of finality so common among men who do not wish to argue out a point for fear of being worsted in the argument, proscribed Thomas's teaching on the unity of the substantial form without a qualm of conscience or a blush at the ignoble part he had played in the whole sorry business. If Albert did not triumph completely at Paris he did at least achieve something, and in his heart he was content—for the time being.

But on his way back to Cologne he must have discussed the whole affair with Hugh. He must have grieved that he had not been able to save Thomas's fair name from indignity in a place where it had every reason to be revered. Paris did enjoy the theological hegemony of the world. Hence, men would look with narrowed eyes at Thomas for what Paris had done to him so unjustly. Men inimical to the new method of teaching might create a hostile attitude against Thomas by falling back upon the Paris prohibition of some of his theses as argument enough to shun his works. Men might start, as had been done in certain quarters of the Order, a whispering campaign against Thomas. Albert grew suddenly quiet as was his wont when he was forming a plan. He knew that his own name was not without honor at home. He knew, too, that no one could impugn his reputation as the most learned living man. Did not high and low come to him when in doubt? Now he resolved that he would let no one sit in the shadows or stray into the shadows of a blind opposition to Thomas because of the Paris prohibition. If Paris suspected Thomas, Cologne would not. He would see to that. For that he would sacrifice everything. He would enlighten the minds of his own people, so averse to political chicanery, about the collusion between Paris and Oxford which had made possible the regrettable prohibition. He would not peddle scandal nor stoop to broadcasting the backstairs gossip or dark-cellar parleys of those responsible for the condemnation. But he would, most certainly, put Thomas forward in his true light and would stake all on the championship of his orthodoxy. Whether he discussed these things

---

[17] Denifle-Chatelain, *op. cit.*, 558; F. Ehrle in *Archiv für Literatur und Kirchengeschichte* (Berlin: 1886), II, 236.

with Hugh we do not know. But we do know from the implied statement of Bartholomew that the very first thing Albert did on returning to Cologne was to go over Thomas's works carefully and defend the impugned theses in private and public. Albert never acted hastily. In his old age he was cautious and circumspect like every sensible man. He knew how much depended upon his attitude. For nothing in the world would he take it upon his conscience to set his own people on the wrong track in championing Thomas. He was sure enough on every score as to Thomas's presentation of the truths of the faith in the Aristotelian manner. But he would check up on his judgments. He would be doubly certain before counseling the people not to flinch or weaken in their allegiance to Christian Aristotelianism. He submitted himself to the task of studying Thomas. His assurance was transformed into a living certainty. There could be no mistake about commending Thomas as the savior of the Catholic head and heart. Albert was willing, after having been Thomas's precursor, to say like another precursor for the One whom both he and Thomas loved: "It is necessary for him to grow, for me to diminish." And with a gesture even nobler and more generous than the one he had made when he braved the winter blasts and the journey's fatigues to go to Paris, Albert now deliberately took a subsidiary place, effaced himself.

Albert was never so great as in his deliberate withdrawal of himself in favor of Thomas. One man in a thousand years can be magnanimous enough to efface himself for one he knows to be greater. One man in a thousand years has the honesty of mind and the sincerity of heart to admit to himself that he has been outrun, outstripped, outshone. So long as the name of Thomas will be heard the name of Albert must be mentioned, because he taught Thomas how to shine and, after the light of his intellect had been put out by death, made him shine at his own expense. Albert was the first champion of Thomism as well he might be, since he is in very truth its grandfather. Up to that time the Christian Aristotelian method, made possible by the colossal labors of Albert, was called by its right name. By his championship of Thomas at Paris and Cologne Albert changed the name of the movement he had inaugurated into Thomism and became its first defender and good genius. And if Thomism has had such an enduring life it is not only because of its own inherent excellencies but also because of the magnificent sacrifice of a great man. Albert understood and proved by his own effacement that Thomism was many things, but chiefly a life. To make it just an academic system was to denature it, to cramp its feet as the Chinese dwarf the feet of their women. And this was just what Albert did not do. He made the birth of Thomism possible by begetting Thomas's spirit. And when Paris would chain that spirit, Albert sent it on its way down the centuries.

The first consoling results of this heroic conduct of Albert, to let Thomism live and move and have its own being, came in 1278, when he saw the secret opposition toward it scotched once and for all in the General Chapter at Montpellier. Thomas had finally come into his own. He had been discovered and declared a prophet in his own country. With an ardent desire to recoup the past and save the good name of the Order, Blessed John of Vercelli sent Raymond de Meuillon and John Vigouroux to England to break the strong antipathy against Thomas.[18] Even before the Church intervened to the extent of making Paris retract what it had condemned in Thomas, the Order sent men to England to force a retractation (or in lieu of this, an expulsion from the Order) from those brethren who had treated Thomas more shabbily than Paris at its worst. The Order could not strike Richard Kilwardby who, in accepting the miter, had put himself outside its jurisdiction. Perhaps, had not Albert resigned his see and come back to the Order, he would have found himself in the same company with Kilwardby in this great crisis of thought. Who knows? Humility is often discovered to be good sense in the last analysis. Surely it had been in the case of Albert.

After this gallant campaign Albert, despite his years, did not allow himself to slip resignedly into a state of complete inactivity. He snatched every free hour either to retouch some of the completed works of his earlier life or to finish treatises which he had been forced to interrupt by reason of his many engagements and activities. This eagerness to set his house in order could not have been induced by anything but the thought of his oncoming end. Though he had enjoyed exceptionally good health all his life and displayed an energy which no multiplicity of works could diminish or exhaust, he could not help but

---

[18] *Acta Cap. Gen. O.P.*, I, 199, 204. Thomas's doctrine was made obligatory in the Order at the Chapter of Paris, 1286. *Ibid.*, 235; H. Felder, *Histoire des Études dans l'Ordre de S. François* (Paris: 1908), 480, 412, 433.

notice the first harbingers of the final collapse. The thought of death brooded over the impassioned plea he had made for Thomas at Paris. It hung like a mellow light over the last efforts to complete his written works, which were the pet products of his tireless activity. In full possession of all his mental faculties he passed in review the various ways by which he might dispose of those temporal possessions which, by a special dispensation of the Holy See, obtained at his own request, he had been able to retain after his cession of the episcopal throne of Ratisbon.

Now if one thing shows forth how typically a child of his own age Albert was, it was his resolution to use his possessions for the completion of a beautiful choir where his religious brethren might carry on their choral duties with becoming dignity and splendor. Germany at that time was outdoing all her past records in the erection of beautiful churches. Perhaps the fashion and standards were set for the country at large by the builders of the Cologne Cathedral. A wondrous generosity on the part of the people, who were greatly impoverished by the many wars of the period, enabled these builders to realize their most grandiose dreams in monuments which are eloquent of the tender love of the masses for the Eucharistic Christ. Albert had been entranced during the first years of his Cologne professorship with the marvel in stone which was taking shape before his eyes within a few rods of the Dominican convent in the Stolkgasse. Later he had seen in France and Italy those superb cathedrals which embodied the holiest aspirations of the people. As bishop he had been zealous for the beauty of the Lord's house. All during his life he had so consistently manifested an attraction for fine buildings and an appreciation for architecture which would show forth in stone something of the fine inspiration of Catholicism, that the people credited him with drawing up the plans of the Cologne Cathedral, the Freiburg minster, and the graceful *Schwabenbrücke* in the same fair city of the Black Forest. Modern historical research has established beyond the peradventure of a doubt that Albert did not participate so intimately in the erection of these and other matchless monuments. But the fact remains that by his frank and enthusiastic espousal of the Gothic form of architecture he did do as much as any man of his time to make it acceptable and popular in Germany.[19] One need not press the extant documents too much to see in the building ambitions of the Cologne Dominicans a direct response and reaction to the inspiration and encouragement of Albert. So lavish were they in their architectural dreams that the General Chapter of 1261 found it necessary to recall to their minds the regulations regarding the erection of churches and convents, which had been enacted three years before at a convocation of the Order. But even such stringent measures did not suffice to preserve the brethren from the general fever for rearing magnificent structures for the service of God.

It is plain from the words of Albert's last will and testament that he wished the brethren to dispose of his possessions after his death for the purpose of completing the choir which his generosity had set on foot as early as 1271. It was in this year that he laid the corner stone of a choir adjacent to the church, where the brethren dispensed the word of God with abundant fruit. For some undiscoverable reason building operations had been suspended—perhaps it was lack of funds or the strict insistence of the authorities of the Order on simplicity in architecture. After Albert's return from Lyons, in 1274, the walls were carried to a height of thirty feet, in accordance with the regulations of the constitutions, and covered over, until a better day, with a temporary roof. After Albert's death the choir was completed, towering in its graceful lines over the rather squatty apse of the adjoining church. In the stained-glass window in the choir, donated by Archbishop Siegfried of Westerburg, there can be read under the likeness of Albert the words: *Condidit iste Chorum.* There can be no doubt as to the fidelity with which Albert's confreres carried out his last wishes.[20] The old legend relates that the antique choir was demolished. Modern excavations, however, would seem to indicate that the walls of the new choir were superimposed upon the original foundations and parts of the old walls incorporated into the new. Albert's choir has always been looked upon as one of the first and finest gems of Gothic architecture in the Rhineland—a fit monument of dignity and beauty to one who loved every manifestation of beauty wherever found in God's superb nature. While it was in process of

---

[19] H. Finke, Die Freiburger Dominikaner und der Münsterbau (Freiburg: 1901), 33, passim.

[20] H. Scheeben, *Chronologie*, 96-98.

construction Albert looked forward to the day when it would stand a thing of surpassing beauty to challenge the attention of the passer-by in the very heart of the loveliest city of the Fatherland. Hence, he presented the choir with many beautiful appurtenances for the altar, and made provision in his will that his episcopal gems and belongings be used in the beautifying of the place. He presented a magnificent cross, filled with precious relics, which was suspended, midair, from the rood between the choir and the church.

In order to foster devotion to the Passion of our Lord among the people Albert gave to the church of the Friars a beautiful, heroic-sized crucifix, containing the relics of many saints and a particle of the true cross. Bishop Salvus of Recanati, Vicar General of Pope Nicholas, granted an indulgence of one hundred days to all who should venerate this relic of the cross. On another occasion he presented the church with a second notable relic of the cross and a thorn from the crown pressed upon Christ's Head during the Passion. He had received it as a gift from St. Louis IX on his return from the crusades in the Holy Land in 1256. The holy king had brought it with him for La Sainte Chapelle in Paris which serves so well as a reminder of his tender piety. The fact that he presented it to Albert is eloquent proof of the high regard in which he held the bishop. The relinquishment of such precious relics was considered so extraordinary by the people that some of the more skeptical-minded began circulating reports that they could not be genuine by any possible chance. To silence forever such scandalous rumors Albert proved the genuineness and authenticity of the relics by casting them into the fire within sight of the brethren. It was recourse to the Ordeal of Fire of which there are many records in medieval annals. According to contemporary chronicles the relics remained unharmed in the flames for a long period of time. The same test with the same results with regard to another particle of the cross occurred in the Church of St. Cunibert, belonging to the Canons Regular of Cologne. In such dramatic ways did Albert seek to promote devotion to the Passion of Christ which had ever been the burden of his preaching and one of the topics to which he always gladly returned in his writings.

CHAPTER XIX

THE END

BARTHOLOMEW OF LUCCA writes that "after resigning his bishopric Albert returned to his school of Cologne where he resumed his lectures until his death, which embraced a period of nearly eighteen years. He attracted to that city a vast number of students and there composed some of the aforementioned works. Finally, in the year of our Lord 1280, he slept the sleep of the just, being more than eighty years old. And although for nearly three years before his death he had lost the full use of his memory, so necessary for the development of his doctrine, he who before, by a special favor from above had surpassed all his brethren as a professor, did not slacken in his piety and his zeal for God in performing with scrupulous exactitude all his religious profession exacted from him."[1] This is the briefest, most direct and positive account of what transpired at the end. It was written by one who was always careful in his statements and, in the present case, was absolutely certain of what he was saying, since he had been on terms of close personal relationship with Albert during the closing years of his life.

It would seem, therefore, that there was noticeable for some time the oncoming disintegration of Albert's physical and mental powers due to old age. It was no sudden, unexpected, complete collapse. It was no dramatic exit from the stage of an active and rugged life. Seeing Albert's intense intellectual application to study, covering a long period of years, accompanied by the many duties and worries of responsible positions, and his many self-imposed and self-assumed tasks, it is the most natural thing in the world to assume that the human machine should eventually have given away. Albert, as far as we can gather, had never had a day's illness in his life, though from an examination of his relics, in their fourth official exhumation and recognition, in May, 1932,

[1] Tholomeus de Lucca, "*Historia Ecclesiastica*," in *Muratori; Scriptores Rerum Italicarum* (Mediolani: 1728), II, 1151 sq.; Echard et Quetif, *Scriptores Ord. Praed.*, I, 169.

Dr. J. Tillmann felt justified in claiming from certain excrescences and interlocking vertebrae that he had been a lifelong victim of chronic rheumatism. However that may be, we know from the documents and the achievements of the man that he never spared himself in his work. Thus he had used up every ounce of energy he possessed.

It may be, too, that Albert suffered from a slight stroke of apoplexy, from which he rallied sufficiently to be about his business in some fashion.[2] In his will, made in January, 1279, he wrote that he was well and in full possession of his powers: *sanus et incolumis.*[3] There is no record of anyone having contested his will. He was sufficiently responsible to participate in the exhumation of the body of St. Cordula, in February of the same year, and physically strong enough to carry out the ceremonies of translation. In May he ratified and executed for the Chapter of Kaiserswerth privileges granted by Pope Innocent IV. In August he did the same thing for the same Chapter in the case of privileges bestowed by Rudolf of Hapsburg, Henry VI, and Henry VII. Now, the parties concerned never doubted his sanity nor did any lynx-eyed lawyer or shyster ever challenge his rational fitness to transact business. From documents, therefore, it can be shown that up to fifteen months before his death Albert was a sufficiently responsible agent to transact legal affairs. Hence, it follows that his collapse was gradual, almost imperceptible.

Biographers in the fourteenth century have given a dramatic turn, or at least one that never appeared in the earliest biographies, or to the gradual weakening of Albert's mental faculties. These legends have taken a strong hold on the popular fancy. Thus Valosetanus writes in 1413:

> "The blessed Father Albert, now bent with age, was one day deliverying as usual his lecture to a numerous and illustrious audience in the convent of Cologne, and while he painfully sought for proofs to establish his thesis his memory suddenly forsook him, to the great surprise of everyone. After a brief silence he recovered from his embarrassment and expressed himself thus: 'My friends, I am desirous to disclose to you the past and the present. When in my youth I devoted myself to study and distinguished myself therein, I chose for my inheritance, under the impulse of the Holy

---

[2] H. Scheeben, *Chronologie*, 127; Echard et Quetif, *Scriptores*, I, 170.

[3] H. Scheeben, *Chronologie*, 123-127. Schmeller discovered Albert's will in 1850 (*Learned Notices*, London, 1850, 44, note 5;) *Münchener Gelehrte-Anzeigen*, 30, 45.

Spirit and the Blessed Mother of God, the Order of Friar Preachers, and the Divine Mother encouraged me to apply myself unceasingly to study. This I have done through persevering efforts and the help of prayers. What I could not gather from books I have ever obtained through prayer. But as I frequently with sighs and tears besought thsi sweet and compassionate Virgin, and on one occasion ardently importuned her to bestow upon me the light of eternal wisdom, and at the same time to strengthen my heart in faith that I might never be absorbed by the science of philosophy nor shaken in my belief, she appeared to me and comforted me with these words: 'Persevere, my son, in virtue and in works of study. God will guard thy knowledge and preserve it pure for the good of His Church. In order not to waver in thy faith, all thy knowledge and phiosophical distinctions shall vanish at the close of thy life. Thou shalt become like a child in the innocence and simplicity of thy belief: after this thou shalt depart to God. And when thy memory shall one day fail thee in a public lecture it will be a sign of the approaching visitation of thy Judge.' My friends, what was then foretold is about to be accomplished. I know and recognize now that my time is spent and that the term of my life is at hand. I confess, then, in presence of you all that I firmly believe every article of the Christian Faith, and I earnestly implore those whom it concerns to administer to me the Sacraments of the Church when it ashall be fitting. If I have spoken or written anything whatsoever, or if in future I shall give utterance to anything, which is not in harmony with Catholic belief, let it be destroyed.' Having thus spoken, he ended forever his teaching. He then descended from his chair bathed in tears, and, bidding an affectionate and tender farewell to his students, retired to the privacy of his humble cell."[4]

Not to be outdone, Rudolf of Mijmegen added a few particulars: "Every philosophical principle," he says, "then escaped his recollection; and he remembered no more the text of Holy Scripture nor that of Aristotle."[5] And Peter of Prussia, remembering bits of floating legend about Albert's entrance into the Order and trying to reconcile the mental collapse at the end, tells the following story. On entering the Order Albert soon discovered that he did not possess sufficiently strong intellectual powers to insure his retention. Rather than be dismissed, he determined to leave on his own account. Before putting aside the habit he prayed to the Blessed Mother of God who, appearing

---

[4] Echard et Quetif, *Scriptores*, I, 169.

[5] Rodolphus de Novimagio, *Legenda*, 68-71.

to him, consoled him, promised him such wisdom that he would astound the world. Lest he be puffed up by learning he would be deprived of his knowledge before his death. The loss of his memory should be the signal for the approaching end.[6]

If there be any truth, however infinitesimal, in these later stories, it is that Albert, like every good Christian, had common sense and humility enough to know that the breakdown of his mental faculties demanded more than ever that he must needs be on his guard against the final assaults of the devil who, in his utter meanness, takes no compassion on a man worn down by age and infirmity to such a degree that he may easily be taken at a disadvantage in the tempest of temptation.

Bartholomew assures us that despite his weakening powers Albert did not desist from his pious practices. Perhaps it would have been truer to say that, as far as he could, he increased them. He knew now, for a certainty, that the grim reaper was just around the corner. He withdrew into solitude to strain after the echoes of heavenly music which stole down to him over the vast stretches of eternity. He would not let in the jarring noise of the world.

Henry of Hereford remarks that Albert visited daily the site he had selected as his final resting place meditating there on death, calmly and unafraid.[7] He increased his prayers to the Blessed Mother of God in whose protection he placed all his hope. Like a homesick child he wept sweet tears of desire to be with her in the mansions of her Son. As if preparing himself to join in the songs of the angels and saints before the Lamb, he sung canticles in Our Lady's honor as he hobbled to and from his burying place, or up and down the chaste corridors of the convent. There was nothing melancholy about his preparations for the last journey. He groaned in spirit often, recalling, no doubt, that prayer which his former preaching companion, Berthold of Ratisbon, has preserved for us in all its musical untranslatable tenderness: *Herre, ich wolt daz ich wer ein Mensch nach deinem aller liebsten Willn*—"Lord, I would that I were a man after Thine all amiable will; would, Lord, that I were a man who had never offended or wounded Thee with his sins and who could never again afflict Thee; would, Lord, that I were a man

---

6 Petrus de Prussia, *Vita*, 234.

7 Henricus de Horvardo, *Chronicon*, 202; Rodolphus de Novimagio, *Legenda*, 72.

who could repair all the sins committed by all men so that, Lord, Thy Passion and Thy death would not have been suffered in vain."[8] This prayer had been the favorite outburst of his mature manhood, palpitating with the great love he bore in his heart for the King of the Five Wounds whom he had never tired of preaching. Here were the dreams of youth and the regrets of old age blended perfectly in a wistful cry of compassionating love of the good Lord, the answer to the meaning and riddle of life which he had discovered by years of virginal longing and prayerful thought. No wonder he was, even in his decreptitude, so kind and tender and compassionate with those who broke in upon the silence of those last years. If he must speak with men now that he was preparing in earnest to speak to God, he would speak to them about nothing but the love of the Lord Jesus.

But a tireless man like Albert could not content himself with prayers, however fervent. Hence, we are prepared to accept the statement which Peter of Prussia took over from the oldest known chronicle of Albert's life, that he continued teaching almost to the day of his death, despite the gradual dissolution of his powers.[9] Those who loved Albert from immediate association with him knew for a certainty that he would have been utterly unhappy without work of some engaging kind. These last lessons, for all his herculean efforts, might fall far behind the standards of excellence and brilliancy he had established in the first years of his professorship and had maintained ever since. But men were willing to miss the wonted enthusiasm and sparkle of his discipline, feeling assured that in his broken words and rambling explanations they would discover the spirit which had characterized all his teaching. It was a faint repetition of that scene at Ephesus when the aged Apostle was carried to the conventicle of the brethren, not to discourse upon the high speculations of the Fourth Gospel, but to insist upon the spirit and purport of the selfsame evangel. Outside the cloister, men who heard about the continuance of

---

[8] J. M. Wagner, "*Berthold und Albertus Magnus*," in *Germania: Vierteljahrsschrift für Alterthumskunde* (1863), 106 sq.; Petrus de Prussia, *Vita*, 326. In the prayer which Albert affixed to his sermon on the Gospel for the 25th Sunday after Trinity, there is not only a wistful longing for dissolution but also a typically medieval familiarity with the thought of death. These habitual thoughts must have asserted themselves frequently after his partial physical collapse.

[9] Petrus de Prussia, *Vita*, 324; H. Scheeben, *Chronologie*, 129.

Albert's teaching career during these dark days, little surmised that he had insisted upon being permitted to remain in the professor's chair. Perhaps, in their ignorance they did the brethren the injustice of thinking or saying that it was high time to take pity on the old professor and give him the rest he had so well merited.

In this spirit, no doubt, the Archbishop of Cologne, Siegfried of Falkenberg, who had always loved Albert, came to ask his advice and to exorcise the tragic loneliness of the last days. "Siegfried came to the Dominican Convent to visit, as usual, his dear Albert, the friend of God and man, and knocking at the door of his cell, called out: 'Albert, are you there?' The venerable Master did not open the door, but merely answered: 'Albert is no longer here: he was here once upon a time.' The Archbishop, hearing these words, heaved a deep sigh and burst into tears. 'It is true,' he exclaimed to those who accompanied him, 'Albert was once here, but he is here no longer.' He meant to say that this renowned man, after spending himself on earth in teaching and preaching the Gospel, in writing and in the practice of the greatest austerities, now detached himself from everything here below, and lived only as an inhabitant of heaven whose eyes are henceforth fixed on his everlasting home."

And Peter of Prussia, who utilized the old chronicle which gave the details of this visit, borrowed further particulars.[10] He tells how Albert, who had been a great pedestrian all his life, shuffled unsteadily up and down the cobbled paths of the cloister garth, lost in prayer and meditation. He saluted only with a friendly melancholy gesture those countless men and women of Cologne with whom he had been in touch during his more active years and who came to cheer him by their visits in the gathering gloom. He would not stop for the exchange of words nor busy himself longer with their worries. But his awed visitors, with the intuition of love, understood the old man's silence and passed on with a sigh.

And so on the fifth day after St. Martin's day, as he sat in the large wooden chair in his cell, fully dressed in his holy habit, with only a rug thrown over his knees, he saw the brethren gather around him. His strength was slipping fast away but he made not so much as a groan. Summoning all the strength that remained to him he made as if he

---

[10] H. Scheeben, *ibid.*

would speak; his eyes lit up for, surely, these were loving brethren. For did they not do the things he would have them do but had not the strength to tell them to do? The strains of the *Salve Regina*, which he had so often sung in procession when the work of the day was done, the dying song of every Dominican, surged up in his ears. It was good, he murmured half aloud, to be a Dominican after all, at death, saluting the Order's sweet Lady and fair Queen. It was the end. It was Friday, November 15, 1280, just at the twilight hour. Death had no marvels for Albert. The marvel for the brethren was the serenity with which he went away. Father Henry, the Prior, and Gottfried of Duisberg, Albert's companion and confessor, closed his eyes. The bereaved brethren all felt that the old master had gone to his reward; Gottfried, his ghostly father, knew it for a certainty.

Rudolf of Nijmegen, basing his words on the established custom of the day when the viscera of a deceased bishop were always sent to his episcopal church, regardless of where the body was to be buried, relates that this was done in Albert's case.[11] Henry of Hereford states that Archbishop Siegfried of Westerburg personally offered up the Mass and conducted the burial, surrounded by the Canons of the Cathedral, the Chapter, the monks of the city, the nobility high and low, the municipal officials, and a large outpouring of the faithful.[12] Only in his death, did men get an inkling of the number of Albert's friends and clients. A document of January 11, 1483, makes plain that the body had been inclosed in a wooden casket and covered with a slab protruding a few inches above the floor of the choir in Cologne which Albert's generosity had made possible. In death Albert faced the main altar, where in life he had found the center of all his thought and the mainspring of all his prodigious activity.

At an early date it was necessary to place a wrought-iron fence about the tomb. As there was question of Albert's canonization in the days of Pope John XXII, it was probably due to the press of the faithful that this precaution for guarding his tomb was taken. On this fence was placed an ornate Latin inscription of which the following is a free rendering:

---

11 Rodolphus de Novimagio, *Legenda*, 72.

12 Henricus de Horvardo, *Chronicon*, 204.

Prince of thought, in art, in science skilled,
Cask of Wisdom's waters, truth distilled,
Plato's better, master need he own
No mortal sage but Solomon alone;
Here in deathless fame, great Albert lies;
To Thee, O Christ, grant that his spirit rise.
Five days had passed since Martin's festal morn,
Twelve hundred eighty years since Christ was born,
When, seeking Thee, O God, with every breath,
He found and made a jubilee of death.
Turn back, all ye, that read this craven scroll,
And pray eternal rest unto his soul.

That Albert had passed at death into the mansions of light eternal was the universal belief of those who knew him best, especially Gottfried of Duisberg, his confessor for a dozen years. He was still alive when the following story was passed from mouth to mouth. Perhaps Gottfried first related it. Certainly he never denied or contradicted it. One night shortly after Albert's death Gottfried remained behind in church after the chanting of Matins. Suddenly Albert appeared in a cloud of light, clad in pontifical robes. His head was surmounted by a miter on which a large diamond sparkled. Gottfried, recognizing his old master, asked him what he desired. "My son," said he, "the mind of man cannot comprehend the light and splendor with which the Lord in His mercy has been pleased to encompass me. This corporeal beauty gives but a faint and imperfect idea of it. The luminous rays which stream from this miter on my brow, signify the ineffable glory which I possess. The precious stones which cover my robes are the books on Holy Scripture which I published, with God's grace, in defense of the Faith and to make the Divine Wisdom known. And because in my lifetime I drew many persons out of the darkness of ignorance to lead them to the light of truth and the knowledge of God, the Lord has accorded to my prayers the deliverance of six thousand souls from the flames of purgatory."[13]

There is recorded another apparition of Albert to a certain master Dietrich who was teaching in Treves. Historians have identified this man as Dietrich of Freiburg with whom Albert had dealings during his life. The date of the apparition can be assigned to any time after the

---

[13] Rodolphus de Novimagio, *Legenda*, 76-77.

year 1297, for it was in this year that Dietrich received the master's cap. This legend had no parallel with any of its predecessors. As it was well attested, during the lifetime of Dietrich, it has been generally accepted as authentic and true. It is to the effect that one night a woman, recently deceased, appeared to him saying: "Father, in sight of the Blessed Trinity I peaceably enjoy eternal happiness." And Dietrich asked: "And what about Master Albert?" To which she replied: "He enjoys unspeakable bliss even beyond our own."[14]

Another contemporary undisputed story is concerned with a Cistercian Abbess who, with her sisters, prayed for Albert after his death in grateful memory of the many kindnesses he had shown the community during his life. Falling asleep for a brief space one morning she beheld Albert standing, without however touching the ground, before the people in church ready to address them. "Great God," she exclaimed with alarm, "Brother Albert will fall." But a person who stood near, observed: "Brother Albert need not fear, it is impossible that he should henceforth fall." Thus comforted, the pious Abbess heard his sermon, which opened with these words: "Full of grace and truth," to which he added this reflection: "Such are the marvels which my eyes now behold."[15]

Peter of Prussia adds a fourth apparition taken from the *Little Treatise on Spiritual Graces* which Henry of Halle constructed out of the *Revelations* of St. Mechtilde of Helpode. This saint died November 19, 1299, and her revelations were written down by her confessor between 1291 and 1303. Peter evidently saw an unexpurgated edition, for he gives the precise quotation which does not entirely agree with the text of the Solesmes edition. We read how St. Mechtilde "beheld the souls of Albert, of revered memory, and of Brother Thomas of Aquin, of the Order of St. Dominic, enter heaven. She saw a throne on which was seated the King of the mansion of the saints, and two venerable personages who advanced toward the King. On their robes were written in letters of gold words of marvelous brightness, and which exhaled a fragrant smell. Before them walked two angels bearing candlesticks of ravishing beauty, and who tarried before Him who sat upon the throne of majesty. It was then revealed to her that these two

[14] *Ibid.*

[15] *Ibid.*

personages were no other than Albert and Thomas of Aquin. Being illumined here below by divine knowledge and inflamed with the force of spiritual love, both were presented by two angels to the King as participators of the gifts of the Cherubim and Seraphim. The bright letters of gold written on their garments represent their knowledge of the Divinity and Humanity of Jesus Christ, which they taught in their numerous works; therefore their souls are now in possession of happiness that has no equal. They are now become like saints, because they sought during their passing life to resemble them in everything by their virtues and knowledge."[16]

After the first translation of the body, which took place about three or more years after Albert's death, it was left untouched till January 11, 1482, when, on the urgent exhortation of Pope Sixtus IV, Herman, the Archbishop of Cologne, opened the tomb in the presence of the Master General of the Order, Salvius Casetta, and the German Provincial, James Sturbach. Only with great difficulty was the door of the stone vault opened and in it the wooden casket was found, the lid eaten away by age and dampness. On removing the earth the body was found in a remarkable state of preservation, the head intact, the eyes still in their sockets, the chin covered with flesh and part of the beard. One ear could still be seen. The shoulders were entire, the members were covered with dry flesh and the feet joined to the legs. The right arm was detached from the body and sent to Pope Sixtus who, in turn, gave it to the Dominican Master General. The remaining relics, inclosed in a glass case or chest, remained visible to the people.

On June 2, 1693, the tomb was opened again and a notable relic was severed from the body for the Bishop of Ratisbon.

There was another opening of the shrine in 1804 when the relics were transferred from the old Dominican church of the Holy Cross, where they had so far remained, to the parish church of St. Andrew where they were suspended in a carved wooden case over the north door of the church. This hurried translation was made necessary by the invasion of the Rhenish provinces by Napoleon's troops. The Dominican church was despoiled and eventually torn down to make room for the post office of the city. There is a lingering souvenir of a

---

[16] *Petrus de Prussia, Vita,* Chap. 56; *Revelationes Sanctae Mechtildae* (Solesmes: 1910), II, 332.

site once glorious in the plaza on the Stolkgasse, which is called today *An den Dominikanern*. A superb chapel in St. Andrew's Church was erected after the beatification of Albert in 1856 through the generosity of the faithful. The relics were transferred to the marble altar in November, 1856. The chasuble preserved on the wall of this chapel under a glass case is not the vestment Albert wore during his life or immediately after his death. It is the silk cloth in which the relics were wrapped in 1482.[17]

Miracles were reported at the first translation, among others the instantaneous cure of a poor girl of Cologne born blind; of a woman who had been confined to bed a hopeless cripple for years; of a man who having lost his sense of smell for years was able to perceive the sweet fragrance exhaling from the tomb. A Friar who suffered from chronic pains in the head was instantly cured. The visible and indisputable cures wrought through the intercession of Albert fired the faith of the people who from the day of his death had not hesitated or desisted from looking upon him and invoking him as a saint of God.[18]

Ratisbon had every reason to glory in the name of Albert. She boasted of the magnificent memorial Gothic hall where he had lectured and where the pulpit he used is still shown. Formerly the hall was attached to the Dominican Convent, which has long since disappeared, and was thronged with pupils for one hundred and forty-nine years. Then the students migrated to the University of Cologne, which had been founded in the meantime and continued without interruption till the time of the Reformation. In the course of time the hall has undergone many changes, due to vandalism. But it was always restored, especially in 1693, by the Bishop of Ratisbon, Albert Ernest, Count of Würtemburg. He transformed it into a chapel, and on the altar of pyramidical design, on the right side of the entrance, he placed a large silver bust of Albert, holding in his hand a book and a serpent, the ancient symbol of logic. Under the bust, in an aperture covered with glass, a large relic of Albert could be seen. Destroyed at the revolution, this chapel rose more splendid from its ruins. Today

---

[17] M. Weiss, *Reliquiengeschichte Alberts des Grossen* (München: 1930), *passim*. The many minute studies on the discovery and authenticity of Albert's relics are listed in *Revue Thomiste* (1931), 211, n. 176-184.

[18] Rodolphus de Novimagio, *Legenda*, 73-76.

students receive religious instructions in this hall, sacred with memories of the past. The pious people of the town still tell the curious-eyed tourist that when the first Protestant minister ascended the pulpit in this hall to preach the new gospel he immediately lost the power of speech. Which, whether true or not, would have been the most decent and graceful thing for him to do in such a sacrosanct training school of athletes of Christ, reared according to the ideals of Albert. Much restored and altered, the old Dominican church at Ratisbon still stands a mute witness to a glory that has departed.

Lauingen, Albert's birthplace and cradle, still exhibits in a corner of the market place the supposed house of his birth. There, too, can be seen the fine square octagonal tower, built between 1457 and 1478 to defend the citizens from marauders. It does duty as an observatory today. At the base is an original painted figure of Albert, in full pontificals, with this inscription below: "Albert the Great, illustrious by his science, was born at Lauingen in the year 1193. He was bishop and lived eighty-seven years."

Above is a figure of the *White Horse of Lauingen* which, the legend tells us, lived in the town in Albert's time. The horse would not be led by anyone but the little lad Albert, who even in his tenderest years seemed to possess magic powers over nature. The country swarms with a whole cycle of naïve legends which, whatever their historical worth or significance, are worthy of study for their originality and utter independence of the legendary relics of medieval times. Rarely do we find specimens of folklore and legend so fresh, poetical, ethereal, and symbolical. The *White Horse of Lauingen*, in the popular mind, is a graceful symbol of the town's great son, who alone, at the cost of much labor and in the face of much opposition, had dragged a vast mass of learning from the four corners of the world to the Christian schools of Europe. There is a small Museum of Albertiniana at Lauingen and the second altar in the new church was dedicated to Albert. Several relics of the saint are preserved there.

Many other cities of the Fatherland glory in the possession of priceless relics of Albert and their history has been traced and their authenticity established by the lifelong studies of Melchior Weiss, in his *Die Reliquiengeschichte Alberts des Grossen* (Munich: 1930), who has added materially to the precious information gathered by such tireless research workers as J. J. Merlo, H. Goflet, J. Kirch, and F. Peters.

These earliest manifestations of belief in Albert's holiness of life—nay even in the prodigies which occurred at his tomb—seem never to have inspired his religious brethren with the idea of taking steps for his ultimate canonization. Now this must not be interpreted as meaning that they had formed a low estimate of Albert's sanctity or doubted his enjoyment of the bliss of heaven. It was but another instance of the traditional indifference of the Order about the posthumous glory of its sainted children, an attitude for which Pope Honorius III had bitterly chided the first generations of the brethren in the case of St. Dominic himself. Hence, it need not appear strange that the first inspiration and impetus for Albert's canonization should have come from John XXII, for as Rudolf of Nijmegen says: "When there was question of inserting the name of Thomas Aquinas, his pupil, in the catalog of the saints the question of Albert's canonization was mooted as some assure us; but owing to the negligence of the brethren who did not promote the cause it was never carried through."[19] We know from an early biographer that they did not even keep a record of the miracles which occurred with such frequency at his tomb. This same spirit persevered for centuries. For in a Dominican martyrology of 1616, which is a reprint of another published in 1604, these words occur at the end of the customary sketch of the life of the saint of the day—in this case, the life of Albert on November 15—"It has happened through the indifference and negligence of the brethren that such a great man has not as yet been numbered among the saints by the authority of the Roman Pontiff."[20] And long after Pope Benedict XIV, in his classic work, *On the Beatification and Canonization of the Servants of God*, remarked: "St. Albert the Great budded forth such virtues that he is entitled to canonization."[21]

Popular devotion to Albert did not die out despite the indifference of the brethren.[22] Hence, in 1487, Peter of Prussia, after having written

---

[19] *Ibid.*, 81.

[20] *Analecta Ord. Praed. (1932), 550.*

[21] *Ibid.*; Benedictus XIV, *De Servorum Dei Beatificatione et Beatorum Canonizatione*, I, Chap. 31, no 12; III, Chap. 31, no 9; IV, P. 1, Chap. I, no 13, p. II, Chap. 5, no 3-5.

[22] A. M. Walz, "*Zur Heiligsprechung des sel. Albertus Magnus*," in *Katholische Gedanken* (1929), 366-389; A. M. Walz, "*Le Culte du B. Albert le Grand*," in *Revue Thomiste* (1931), 302-313. The large literature on the cult of Albert is cataloged in *Revue Thomiste* (1931), 211-214, n. 185-229. The documents for the cult can be

his famous life of Albert, composed a liturgical Office which was sanctioned by Innocent VIII for use in the Dominican convents of Cologne and Ratisbon. In 1662 Gregory XV permitted the celebration of the feast for the city of Ratisbon. This was the occasion of great rejoicing in the city which had always remained faithful to his memory. To celebrate the event fittingly the students of the Jesuit College produced in Latin a sacred drama which had to do with the colorful life of Albert. Perhaps a memory of this histrionic glorification of Albert served as an inspiration to Edmond Rostand, who in the last years of his life, when the shadows of death were beginning to chasten his outlook on things, drew an outline for a drama which he proposed calling *L'Automaton* and which was to depict, with applications sorely needed for our mechanistic age, the incident when Thomas Aquinas in fear and trembling broke into pieces the speaking statue which Albert had fashioned in his cell.[23] In 1670 Clement X prescribed the feast of Albert for the entire Dominican Order. Before this day several German cities, identified in some way with the life of Albert, had obtained permission from the Holy See to keep the anniversary of his death, and these annual celebrations were marked with a great outpouring of piety. But a sudden and drastic end was put to these manifestations of popular devotion by the Napoleonic troops which, in June, 1799, invaded the Rhenish provinces, drove out the Cologne Dominicans in the short space of two hours, destroyed their church and the choir which had been erected through Albert's munificence, and necessitated the translation of his relics in 1804 to the church of St. Andrew where they still remain. With the coming of peace many sporadic attempts were made to obtain full honors of the altar for Albert, especially after Pius IX, in 1856, had extended the feast to the diocese of Cologne and

found in the *Positio* for the canonization. (Roma: 1931), 55-168.

[23] Raymond Lerouge, Edmond Rostand Intime (Revue des Deux Mondes, 15 Avril, 1930), 774-789, says: "*La pensée de la mort était pour lui l'âme de notre âme, la parcelle qui, introduite dans le tumulte effervescent des états de conscience animaux, les fait cristalliser selon un système nouveau et irréductible. Il rêva de reconstituer expérimentalement la mécanisme de cette transformation et, comme toute conception chez lui prenant la forme dramatique, il imagina le drame suivant... Cette pièce, lorsque j'en eus connaissance n'existait qu'a l'état de projet le poète n'avait point trouvé l'intrigue qui lui eût permis d' articuler les phases de son action. Je ne sais si par la suite, il lui découvrit les développements nécessaires*" (*ibid.*, 784-786).

other German dioceses as also to Paris. At the Vatican Council the German bishops urged the canonization, and since that time practically the entire German Catholic body, backed by petitions from all over the Catholic world, have asked the Holy See for the final apotheosis of Albert. After a careful examination of the cause Pope Pius XI, on December 16, 1931, decreed to Albert the honors of equipollent canonization, adding at the same time the ardently desired glory of a Doctor of the Church.

This crowning aureola had been considered for nearly three hundred years as eminently befitting Albert, whose writings in the entire domain of sacred learning have exercised such a wide and beneficent influence. As far back as 1648 Albert had been enumerated among the accredited Doctors of the Church by Joseph Zucchi in his learned *Metaphysica.* A Dominican breviary, printed in 1672, expressly called him a doctor. In that and subsequent ages this honorific title was frequently applied to him, without, however, any liturgical or ecclesiastical approval. The Dominican Order on various occasions petitioned for this honor, but was always put off with the reply by the Roman Congregations that no Order of the Church, with the exception of the Benedictine by reason of its great antiquity, could entertain the hope for more than one doctor from its ranks. But Pius XI, having set aside the precedent in favor of the Society of Jesus with its twin doctors, St. Peter Canisius and St. Robert Bellarmine, deigned to listen to the united petition of the Catholic world—its bishops, universities, savants, and even secular assemblies, such as the German Reichstag—by according Albert the aureola of the doctorate, not only because of his eminent talents and services to Catholic science, but also because of his intellectual formation and guidance of Thomas Aquinas and his espousal of Thomism when it was first assailed and challenged.[24]

[24] The documents for Albert's doctorate can be found in the *Positio* (Roma: 1931), 1-78

EPILOGUE

REPEATING the Scriptural word that "no one is a prophet in his own country" (Marc. vi. 4) the popular adage has it that no one is a hero to his own valet. In the case of Albert there was an exception, if we may take the words of Blessed Humbert de Romans, fifth Dominican Master General, in their plain sense and obvious meaning. Now it must be borne in mind that Humbert was one of the most acute ecclesiastical figures of his age. He displayed uncommon sagacity in his *Opus Tripartitum*, in which he drew up a schedule of the affairs which he deemed should come up for discussion and dispatch at the Council of Lyons in 1274. That he was none the less a keen observer of men and of the most diverse classes of men appears clearly from the shrewd and incisive historical hints which he prefixed to the skeleton sermons he published in his vast homiletic repertoire: *De Modo prompte Cudendi Sermones*. The affectionate tone he assumed in trying to dissuade Albert from accepting the episcopacy and the high appreciation he entertained of Albert's intellectual hegemony, as manifested in that unique document, is matched by the almost lyrical admiration for his character and sanctity in the following words which date from a little earlier period:

"This celebrated man, Brother Albert, seems like the tree of life planted in the center of the terrestrial paradise, bearing incessantly the fruits of honor and grace. In outward appearance he was of noble stature, and endowed with great physical strength. His body was well proportioned, and perfectly fitted for all the fatigues of God's service. From the day when he entered the Order he walked courageously in the path of justice, by the observance of its Rule and the mortification of his flesh, seeking thus by a long martyrdom to triumph over the solicitations of the enemy. He frequently passed the nights in prayer, and in his sublime contemplation offered himself a holocaust on the altar of the heart. In the morning he celebrated the Divine Mysteries with the greatest purity of soul and the most ardent love. He was incessantly occupied either in reading, writing, dictating, preaching, or hearing confessions. He never allowed his mind to repose where there was question of divine works. And as wisdom cannot enter into an evil soul, nor dwell in a body that is enslaved to sin, he ever preserved the purity of his conscience, that he might read with fruit the Holy Scriptures, which he passionately loved. Consumed with the fire of charity, he labored for the salvation of his neighbor with untold success. The example of his life, his angelic piety, his stupendous learning, and his indefatigable zeal in uprooting error procured him an incredible influence, not only in Germany, but in almost every part of the earth. Although most amiable in his exhortations, he was severe in his reproofs, and the mortal enemy of vice. He was also a model of greatness of soul; for, in his care of his brethren in Jesus Christ, he knew neither kings nor the powerful ones of the earth. As a preacher, he weighed all in the balance of justice, and distributed to each one according to his needs, whether he preached to the rich or the poor. He struck everyone with the arrow of truth. He edified wherever he abode. He ever showed himself truly evangelical by the observance of humility and poverty which the Rule of the Order exacts. When on his visitations of the convents, he excited the brethren to the practise of holy zeal, all heard with extreme pleasure the Word of God, which fell from his lips as from a source of paradise. His ordinances, which are still to be found in many convents, prove the solicitude with which he watched over his Religious. When, sometimes by order of the Holy See, or at the instance of the bishops, he visited the houses of monks, canons regular, or nuns in their dioceses, in order to discover what was practised therein contrary to the rules of perfection, he, with admirable zeal, brought back into the path of observance all those who had unhappily departed therefrom. He even adopted the severest measures when these were needed. But as he was a spotless mirror of every virtue, and as it might be said of him that he had no equal, that no one observed the commandments of the Most High in the same degree, he was loaded with God's favors, and was the object of the good will and love of all. Far from glorifying himself in this, he referred all to grace; filled with deep humility, he perceived the spirit of pride which sought to rise within him on such occasions. He ever strenuously avoided the thrusts of the enemy, in order not to fall, dazzled by the glare of human flattery, into the abyss of pride. As he beheld everything in the light of God, he walked in His presence, ever ready to go whithersoever the inspirations of the Holy Spirit called him. He despised earthly honors, and esteemed not the tiara or the episcopal crosier more than the wallet and staff of the monk. He loved nothing here below except Christ and His justice."

Since those colorful days of the thirteenth century, when Albert appeared to his contemporaries as the very incarnation of a real schoolman and ideal savant, much has been said and written about him in each subsequent century. Some have deliberately set out to blacken his fair name for holiness of life or integrity of teaching; some with the best will in the world have failed to see his colossal proportions of moral grandeur or intellectual eminence; some have separated the saint from the savant only to give us a miserable caricature; some have sacrificed the saint to the scholastic only to afford us an awkward cartoon. Few scholars who aspire to the good name of genuine scholarship have dared to pass over his name and achievements in dealing with that vivid age or in searching for the first manifestations of many intellectual and scientific truths which we fondly look upon as modern or contemporaneous products.

Pope Pius XI, guided by the unfailing light of the Holy Spirit, has drawn a picture of Albert, the man, as he was in his native greatness of heart, richness of intellectual endowment, and radiance of moral heroism; he has allocated him his true position in the story of the development of the mind and in the history of Christian sentiment and Catholic thought; he has laid bare his powerful influence for good upon the ages and has pointed out his lofty place in the shining galleries of those who have died in the Lord. If for no other reason than that of showing the care and caution of the Church in selecting and measuring her heroes and in describing their bewitching beauty and irresistible impressiveness the Decretal Letter, *In thesauris sapientiae,* deserves a thoughtful pondering.

and esteemed not the gold or the episcopal crozier more than the wallet and staff of the monk. He loved nothing here below except Christ and His justice."

Since those colorful days of the thirteenth century, when Albert appeared to his contemporaries as the very incarnation of a real Schoolman and ideal savant, much has been said and written about him in each subsequent century. Some have deliberately set out to blacken his fair name; the pioneers of the age of scientific research, some with the best will in the world, have failed to see his colossal proportions of moral grandeur or intellectual eminence; some have separated the saint from the savant only to give us a miserable caricature; some have sacrificed the saint to the scholastic only to afford us an awkward cartoon. Few scholars who aspire to the good name of genuine scholarship have dared to pass over his name and achievements in dealing with that vivid age of its searching for the first manifestations of many intellectual and scientific truths which we fondly look upon as modern or contemporaneous products.

Pope Pius XI, guided by the unfailing light of the Holy Spirit, has drawn a picture of Albert the man, as he was in his native greatness of heart, clearness of intellectual endowment and radiance of moral heroism; he has allocated him his true position in the story of the development of the mind and in the history of Christian sentiment and Catholic thought; he has indicated his powerful influence for good upon the ages and has pointed out his lofty place in the shining galleries of those who have died in the Lord, if for no other reason than that of showing the care and caution of the Church in selecting and presenting her heroes and in describing their new dignity, beauty and ineffable impressiveness. The Decretal Letter, in masterly sentences, deserves a thoughtful pondering.

DECRETAL LETTER

OF OUR MOST HOLY LORD, PIUS XI, BY DIVINE PROVIDENCE POPE, REGARDING ST. ALBERT THE GREAT, OF THE ORDER OF PREACHERS, BISHOP, CONFESSOR, AND DOCTOR OF THE CHURCH.

Pius, Bishop, Servant of the Servants of God, for an everlasting memory:

"In the treasures of wisdom is understanding and religiousness of knowledge."[1] In the book of Wisdom,[2] too, Solomon shows us in inspired words the reason why he sought from God the possession of wisdom—because it is wisdom that links the soul intimately with God and far excels every other good. A life which combines religious perfection with the study of wisdom has a marvelous power of arousing and lifting up the hearts of the faithful—"that their hearts may be comforted, being instructed in charity, and unto all riches of fullness of understanding, unto the knowledge of the mystery of God the Father and of Christ Jesus; in whom are hid all the treasures of wisdom and knowledge."[3] Indeed the more nearly a man approaches God by wisdom, the more the spiritual dominates his life; for "wisdom is the teacher of the knowledge of God, and the chooser of His works."[4] A man attains the divine wisdom in proportion as he imitates the life and deeds of our Savior, who said: "He that shall do and teach, he shall be called great in the kingdom of heaven."[5] Gloriously eminent as a follower of our Lord Jesus Christ was Albert the Great, Friar Preacher, master in theology, and at one time Bishop of Ratisbon; marvelously combining the contemplative and active lives, he was a conspicuously great man in his own age and is still great in our day; by his preeminent qualities as a teacher and his surpassing skill in so many departments of knowledge, he has won the special title of "the Great."

Albert the Great was born at the end of the twelfth century of a distinguished military family, at Lauingen, in Suabia, in the diocese of

[1] Ecclus. i. 6.

[2] Wisd. vii. 2.

[3] Coloss. ii. 2-3.

[4] Matt. v. 19.

[5] *Ibid.*

Augsburg. He left his native land in pursuit of learning and went to Padua, where he studied the liberal arts, medicine, and science. There he came to know and love the newly founded Order of Friar-Preachers, and fell under the spell of the eloquence of Blessed Jordan of Saxony, Master General of the Order, and, when he had overcome his uncle's objections, was enrolled among the sons of St. Dominic. He was in all things wholly devoted to God, and he was especially remarkable for his tender devotion to Our Lady. Early in his career he was sent to Cologne to complete his theological studies. During this time he assiduously trained both his mind and his heart with a holy eagerness, and, mounting from strength to strength, "he resolved as a giant to run the way."[6] Mingling and seasoning study with prayer, he fashioned his mind and shaped his whole manner of life so as to fit himself for preaching and the salvation of souls, and to make himself a useful and capable Friar Preacher. He was so keenly alert for the attainment of wisdom that he soon outstripped his fellows and took the heights of all the secular sciences with a masterly ease, and, as our predecessor, Alexander IV, said of him, "he drank so deeply and assiduously of the fountain of divine lore, that its fullness might be said to be stored up in his breast."[7]

He was ordained priest; and in order that he might give to others the treasures of his contemplation and knowledge, he was appointed to teach at Hildesheim, Freiburg (Breisgau), Ratisbon, and Strasburg. His fame soon spread, and more widely still when he was made master in theology and professor in the renowned University of Paris. Later on, Albert was sent to teach at Cologne, where, at the bidding of his superiors, he founded and subsequently governed a *studium generale* of his Order. There, among many other famous disciples, his most illustrious pupil was Thomas Aquinas, whose genius he perceived and proclaimed; and all his life Albert held Thomas in a close friendship of holiness and learning; he stoutly defended his teaching when Thomas was dead, and always paid tribute to his greatness.

A model of prudence and justice to all, it is not to be wondered at that again and again Albert was called upon as an arbiter in public and private disputes: these he always settled with a strict sense of fair play

---

[6] *Ps. xviii. 6.*

[7] *Bull of election of Albert as Bishop of Ratisbon.*

and with rare skill and strength of purpose. His marvelous mastery of affairs, coupled with his zeal for religious observance and his love of Christian perfection, led the Friars of Germany, assembled in chapter at Worms, to elect him as their Prior-Provincial. The capitular Fathers were well aware of their need: they knew the times in which they lived. They knew how the vanity of the world can sometimes creep into the cloister; they knew, therefore, that their ruler must be a man of holy life, of strong will, and conspicuous for prudence and every kind of virtue. Their hopes were not disappointed in Albert, who threw himself with indefatigable zeal into the work of ruling his province, which extended from the shores of Flanders, through Germany, to Poland and the very confines of Hungary. It was his custom to traverse the whole province, visiting convents, holding chapters, and, by example and word, urging his subjects to follow the way of regular observance, after the sublime example of his Master, who "began to do and to teach."[8]

His prudence in management, his skill in civil business, and the fame of his learning and holiness, reached the ears of the supreme Pontiffs, who therefore specially chose him out to deal with important and difficult undertakings. It is specially worthy of mention that he was commissioned by Pope Alexander IV to organize, with the help of his Friars, the defense and propagation of the Catholic Faith among the heathens of Livonia and Prussia; Alexander also confided similar duties to him in the kingdom of Brandenburg.

Albert was chosen by his Order to vindicate the rights of the Mendicant Orders and plead their cause with the Holy See. For this purpose he appeared before the Papal Court then at Anagni, and so successfully refuted his opponents and so impressed his hearers that the Pope chose him to undertake a public disputation against the errors of the Averroists, and also appointed him to expound the Gospel of St. John in the school of the Papal Court. So deep was the impression of learning and virtue that he left behind him in Rome, that the same Alexander IV appointed Albert Bishop of Ratisbon, a see at that time ill-favored both spiritually and temporally; and the task fell to him not only of tending the flock committed to him but also of relieving the see of its heavy burden of debt. Notwithstanding his episcopal dignity,

---

[8] *Acts i. 1.*

Albert observed religious poverty, and this proved an efficacious means of reforming morals and restoring ecclesiastical discipline. He in no way relaxed his love of study and contemplation. Ever zealous in rooting out vice and in reviving collapsed morals, discreet in settling quarrels, diligent in the administration of the sacraments, yet he continued perseveringly in the task of writing, and ever worked to promote sound doctrine while watching over his flock.

With the permission of Urban IV, he resigned the see of Ratisbon; and then, at the bidding of the same Pope, and armed with the authority of the Apostolic See, he preached a crusade through Upper Germany and Bohemia. When he had completed this mission, he returned of his own accord to the regular life of his Order, and spent the remaining years of his life preaching, teaching, and writing. In many dioceses, too, he was always ready to perform pontifical and episcopal functions, to undertake long and difficult journeys in the interests of religion. He visited Antwerp, Basel, and Strasburg, whence, after some stay, he returned to Cologne, which was to be his last resting place.

He interested himself in the religious Orders of both men and women, made visitations under episcopal command, and worked with energy to stimulate communities to greater fervor by his own spirit of wisdom and holiness. Willingly and generously he gave his good services to all the faithful in the cause of religion, and he was never known to refuse anyone his counsel and help. And it is well known that he lived in terms of friendship with St. Louis, King of France.

Although his office and dignity entitled him to deep respect, it was not his way to overawe but to show himself a father, always inspiring confidence, never fear, after the example of St. Paul, who spent himself and was spent for the souls of his fellows.[9] Although worn out with age, he attended the second Council of Lyons, in which the Greeks made their profession of faith and happily returned to the unity of the Church. In that same council it was at Albert's instance that our predecessor, Blessed Gregory X, sanctioned the election of Rudolph of Hapsburg as King of the Romans, a matter in which it can be confidently affirmed that Albert was acting for the good of both ecclesiastical and civil society.

---

[9] *II Cor. xii. 15.*

But all this life of business and activity was as nothing compared to the immense labor of his studies and his many learned written works, in which are gloriously displayed the force and acuteness of his genius, the fullness and depth of his mind, the overflowing wealth of his erudition, and his indefatigable zeal in defending the faith. Hence, historians and those who have written about him have rightly singled out for special praise the extraordinary universality of his mind; for he was occupied not only with divine things and the truths of philosophy, but also with all the other human sciences. Bartholomew of Lucca, a contemporary, declared that, in his knowledge of all the sciences and in his method of teaching, he excelled all the learned doctors of his day. Indeed an examination of the mere titles of his innumerable works will show that no single science escaped his attention: astronomy, cosmography, meteorology, climatology, physics, mechanics, architecture, chemistry, mineralogy, anthropology, zoology, and botany were some of the subjects he wrote about; and to these he added works on such practical arts as weaving, navigation, and agriculture.

As became a true Catholic teacher, Albert the Great did not let his mind dwell merely upon the consideration of the external world, as is so often the case nowadays with those who devote themselves to scientific research; but observing due order in all things, he passed from the natural things to the spiritual, and coordinating and subordinating the various spheres of knowledge, he proceeded by a real progression from things inanimate to things living, from living to spiritual creatures, and from the spiritual he mounted to God, the Author of all. And indeed God, the generous Giver of all good things, had endowed him with the abilities needful for the accomplishment of his great work. Albert had an insatiable thirst for truth, a patient, tireless energy of inquiring into natural phenomena, a vivid imagination joined to a tenacious memory, a sane esteem for the established wisdom of the past. Above all, his was a religious mind, ready to perceive the matchless wisdom of God shining out through all creation. His was the spirit of the psalmist who invites all the elements of the world to sound forth the praises of the Creator, the spirit of which we read in the books of Job, Wisdom, and Ecclesiasticus, the spirit by which the Holy Ghost moves men to praise and bless God as the lavish Giver of every gift.

It is especially noteworthy that he gathered together with

painstaking industry every grain of the ancient wisdom and gladly accepted whatever truth had been discovered by the innate power and ingenuity of the human mind, and, once he had separated it and purged it from all error, he made use of it to illustrate or defend the truths of faith. In particular he extracted such help from the works of Aristotle, which at that time were beginning to be disseminated throughout Europe. Putting aside all false interpretations of Aristotle, he not only warded off an impending peril to Catholic teaching, but, so to say, snatching a weapon from the enemy's hands, he used the ancient philosophy to support and defend revealed truth. Thus Scholasticism, enriched with the treasures of Aristotelian philosophy, entered upon a more excellent way and showed forth more clearly the wonderful accord that exists between right reason and faith. Albert was the forerunner; and it was given to Thomas, his chosen disciple, to take up the work and with happy daring plumb the depths of philosophy and scale the highest peaks of theology.

By Albert's efforts the whole of philosophy and in particular the Aristotelian philosophy was adopted to serve—under the light of revelation—as a sound and fit implement for the Christian theologian. All his intellectual activities were inspired by one high, steadfast purpose, namely, to seek whatever of truth, goodness, or beauty was to be found in pagan wisdom, and to offer, nay, consecrate it to Him who is the First Truth, Supreme Beauty, and Essential Perfection. Albert it was who broke the shackles that held the natural sciences in bondage to the pagans, Mahometans, and Jews. At that time, owing to the prevailing misuse of the natural sciences, God-fearing men were inclined to look upon them with a certain suspicion, for they thought them a danger and a snare to the faithful. But the true theologian fears no evil in the works of nature or of natural reason, if only they are examined aright; for he knows that they bear within them the light of the Creator. Among the teachers of the Middle Ages, Albert stands out as the scholar who gave to the schools of his time the riches of the scientific culture of the ancients, which he delivered systematically and excellently arranged in his great encyclopedia, which begins from the simplest notions, and rises to the heights of theology. Small wonder, then, that he was hailed as one who was "ignorant of nothing and knew all that was knowable";[10] and could be said to be the wonder and miracle of his age.[11] Nor is it surprising that he was given the title of Universal Doctor and described of old as "the most resplendent sun of the philosophers of Christendom."[12]

Non-Catholics, too, in our own time have praised him as the greatest scientific investigator of the Middle Ages. One well-known writer calls Albert "the most enlightened pioneer of the study of science in the West. Albert was the first to assimilate to the Christian religion the wisdom of the Greeks; the first to reconcile natural history with the doctrine of the Church; the first to describe nature in terms of art; the first to attempt to reduce forms of created things to morphological notions; finally, he first and alone gave us the complete account of the whole of nature and explained it in all its details."[13]

To him belongs this great honor, that (excepting St. Thomas) there is scarcely another doctor of equal authority, whether in philosophy, theology, or the interpretation of Scripture. It would be an endless task to recount all that Albert has done for the increase of theological science. Indeed it was to theology that the whole trend of his mind was inevitably directed. The authority he had acquired in philosophy grew and increased, for, as we have said, he used philosophy and the scholastic method as a kind of implement for the explanation of theology. In fact, he is regarded as the author of that method of theology which has come down in the Church to our own time as the safe and sound norm and rule for clerical studies.

Albert's numerous theological works, and, above all, his commentaries on the Sacred Scriptures, bear the marks not only of an enlightened mind and a deep knowledge of Catholic teaching, but they are stamped with the spirit of piety and arouse in souls the desire to cleave to Christ; we readily discern therein the holy man discoursing of holy things. We need but call to mind his *Summa Theologica*, fragrant alike of piety and wisdom; his *Commentary on St. Luke's Gospel*, which bespeaks a skilled and sound interpreter of Holy Writ; his *Treatise on the*

---

[10] Pius II in his *Dogmatic Letter to the Emperor of the Turks*, 1464.

[11] Ulrich of Strasburg, *Summa de Bono*, lib. 4, tract. 3, Chap. 9.

[12] Henricus de Hervordia, *Chronicon* (Potthast: 1859), p. 196.

[13] C. Jessen.

Praises of Mary, in which he reveals his burning love and devotion toward the Mother of God; his incomparable work on the *Blessed Sacrament of the Altar,* in which appear his sincere faith and passionate devotion to the mystery of the Incarnation. Worthy of note, too, are his mystical writings, which show that he was favored by the Holy Ghost with the grace of infused contemplation: these writings provided an inspiration and a guide for the German mystics of the fourteenth century.

All the works of Albert are of monumental value and of imperishable authority. With our predecessor, Leo XIII, we venture to say: "Although time will bring its increase to every kind of science, still Albert's teachings, which served to form Thomas Aquinas and were regarded in his time as miraculous, can never really grow old."[14] Let what we have said suffice to suggest something of the excelling holiness of life and marvelous teaching of Albert the Great, who, after a life of labor in the Lord's vineyard and after having deserved so well of the entire Church, on the fifteenth of November, 1280, peacefully left this world for a blessed eternity. But since the setting of so great a luminary the glorious afterglow has never departed. Albert the Great still shines resplendent in the Church of Christ by the lofty fame of his science, the marvel of his holiness, the miracles he worked during life and after death—as trustworthy witnesses declare—hence, we can make our own the words of St. Peter Canisius, Doctor of the Church, who, besides calling Albert the "light of Germany," said of him: "He excelled in purity of life, in wisdom and science... God has witnessed to his greatness and holiness by many miracles."[15] No wonder, therefore, that after his death public ecclesiastical cultus was granted to Blessed Albert with all its attendant circumstances and privileges. And it is a matter for rejoicing that several of Our predecessors, "having due regard to the excelling merits of this holy man,"[16] have accorded special favors in order to extend his cultus. Innocent VIII, in 1484, granted to the Friar-Preachers of Cologne and Ratisbon the faculty to erect altars in his honor and to keep his Feast; such an authorization is equivalent

---

[14] Brief given on the tenth of December, 1889, to L. Vives, publisher of the works of Blessed Albert.

[15] The German Martyrology, under date of November 15.

[16] Clement X, in Decree of August 27, 1670.

to beatification. Gregory XV, in 1622, by word of mouth, granted the same privilege to the cathedral Chapter and clergy of Ratisbon. Urban VIII, in 1631, gave leave for the celebration of his Feast in the city of Lauingen, and in 1635, at the instance of the Emperor, extended the same right to all Friar-Preachers of Germany; Alexander VII, in 1664, granted the same favor to the Dominicans in the province of Constance; and, lastly, Clement X, in 1670, authorized the celebration of the Feast, with Office and Mass, throughout the entire Order of Preachers in perpetuity. Pius IX, in 1856, gave leave to the whole archdiocese of Cologne to keep the Feast as a semidouble, and later, in 1870, he raised it to the rank of a double. Three years later the same Pope, in the Church of St. Elizabeth, where a society of German Catholics had been formed, gave license to all priests celebrating there to say the Mass of Blessed Albert the Great. In more recent times other dioceses of Germany, and in France, the archdiocese of Paris, have obtained leave to keep Blessed Albert's Feast. A plenary indulgence has been granted at different times for his Feast in various places; and Leo XIII granted a plenary indulgence to all who visited the church dedicated to him at Riga. Wherefore it is not to be wondered at that a man of such excelling holiness and learning should be considered worthy of canonization and of the title of Doctor of the Church. In particular his cause was urged at the time of the solemn translation of his relics in 1483, and again with more energy at the beginning of the seventeenth century; but wars and the difficulty of access to the Roman Curia prevented this happy consummation.

During the Vatican Council the German bishops wished to realize the pious desire of the preceding centuries, and begged the Apostolic See to reopen the cause of Albert the Great; but the troubled times the Church was undergoing in Italy and Germany prevented the fulfillment of these hopes.

At last, in our own time and with due solemnity, cardinals, archbishops, bishops and prelates from all over the world, as well as abbots and religious superiors, and especially universities, faculties, seminaries and colleges, and learned societies, and personages of rank, fame, and learning all over Germany, have presented to Us earnest petitions to honor Blessed Albert with the aureola of the saints and the title of Doctor of the Church. We felt no reluctance in taking up a cause which was already so much in accord with Our own wishes, all the more because the present moment would seem to be the time when the glorification of Albert the Great was most calculated to win souls to submission to the sweet yoke of Christ. Albert is exactly the saint whose example should inspire this modern age, so ardently seeking for peace and so full of hope for its scientific discoveries. Everyone nowadays is looking eagerly for peace, but there is no agreement as to the best way of attaining it; indeed the very foundations of peace, namely, justice and charity, are cast aside.

Let all then look with confidence to St. Albert the Great; for he with all his heart adhered to God, and "God is not the God of dissension, but of peace,"[17] of that peace which "passeth all understanding and keeps the hearts and minds of the faithful."[18] Albert, who in his lifetime labored strenuously and successfully for peace between princes and peoples and individual men, is put before us now as the perfect model of peace. His power and authority as arbiter and peacemaker were derived from his holiness and learning, which men respected and esteemed; they reverenced, too, his innate dignity of person, which was further ennobled by his priestly character. He presented a living image of his Master, whom Scripture calls "the Prince of Peace."[19]

Learning is also most conducive to peace, provided it is obedient to reason and supernatural faith; indeed such obedience would seem to be necessary in order to assure to science its nobility, its security and its truth. But how often it happens, especially in our own times, that this subjection of science to reason and faith is neglected and despised in scientific research; indeed science is sometimes used against faith and reason, and "the Lord, the God of all knowledge,"[20] is set aside, and science, presuming upon its own all-sufficiency, leads to that deplorable state of materialism which is the cause of all those moral disorders and economic ills which have fallen as a bitter scourge upon the peoples of the whole world.

In Albert the Great the rays of human and divine science meet to form a shining splendor. His life is a standing proof that there is no

---

[17] 1 *Cor.* xiv. 33.

[18] Phil. iv. 7.

[19] Isa. ix. 6.

[20] I Kings ii. 3.

opposition, but rather the closest fellowship, between science and faith, between truth and goodness, and between learning and holiness. Like St. Jerome, Albert, as it were with powerful voice, declares and proves in his wonderful writings that science worthy of the name, and faith and a life lived according to the principles of faith, can, and indeed should, all flourish together in men, because supernatural faith is the crown and perfection of science. It is not true, as modern atheists assert, that the Christian life and the pursuit of Christian perfection destroy the human spirit, weaken the will, impede civil activity, and rob men's minds of their native nobility; on the contrary, grace perfects nature, develops, improves, and ennobles it.

Having maturely considered all Albert's titles and claims to saintship and to the worship of all the faithful, and with the desire that he should shine more brilliantly before the Universal Church, and in order to make up that which seemed to be still lacking to complete his glory, We have decided at length to fulfill Our daily growing desire in his regard by equipollent canonization. Since, therefore, the time seems opportune, and since none of the conditions required by the most ancient custom and law of the Church in such matters are lacking, We have decided to follow a way of procedure which several of Our predecessors have at times thought fit to use in the canonization of the servants of God. Therefore, We intrusted the whole matter to the Sacred Congregation of Rites. Thereupon Our dear sons, the Cardinals of the Sacred Congregation, met in ordinary assembly to hear the report of Our beloved son, Francis Cardinal Ehrle, the Promoter of the Cause; and when the historical investigation had been officially made into the sanctity of Blessed Albert's life and into the legitimacy of his cultus, and when the official written verdict upon his doctrine had been given by two learned men, well versed in his works; and after taking the votes of the official prelates of the same Congregation of Rites, and all points maturely weighed and discussed, the large assembly unanimously agreed that We should be well advised to grant the favor. We therefore on the following day—that is, today—having attentively heard a report of all these matters from Our beloved son, Salvator Natucci, Promoter Fidei, and in full agreement, most willingly approved the decision of the Sacred Congregation. Therefore, in virtue of Our Sovereign Apostolic Authority, We order that the Feast of St. Albert the Great be celebrated by the Universal Church on the fifteenth of November each year as a minor double, with the Office and the Mass of a Confessor and Pontiff, with the addition of the title of Doctor.

Let abundant thanksgiving be offered to God, who in the marvelous designs of His providence has, through our lowliness, deigned to perfect the glory of Albert in the sight of all the Church, and has revealed him in our age as a "shining light and morning star illuminating by his fecundity the whole body of the Church,"[21] and as one who truly labored not for himself alone, "but for all who seek out the truth."[22] May, then, St. Albert the Great be our intercessor, he who sought after wisdom and virtue from his earliest youth and bore the Lord's yoke cheerfully even as St. Paul the Apostle, who thought nothing could be more desirable than to bring into captivity every understanding unto the obedience of Christ.[23]

Therefore, having well considered everything that had to be examined, with full knowledge and with the fullness of Our Apostolic Authority, We confirm, ratify, and again declare and order all that We have said above; We publish it to the whole Catholic Church; and We command that all copies, transcripts, or impressions of this present Letter, provided they are signed and sealed by a Notary Apostolic, shall be given the same reverence and acceptance as this Our Letter, wherever it shall be necessary for it to be exhibited and shown. If, however, anyone shall presume to infringe or rashly attempt to contradict this Letter of declaration, decree, command, and will, let him know that he shall incur the anger of Almighty God and His blessed Apostles, Peter and Paul.

Given at Rome, in St. Peter's, in the year one thousand nine hundred and thirty-one, on the sixteenth day of the month of December, the tenth year of Our Pontificate.

P. PIUS,

Bishop of the Catholic Church.

---

21 Anon. O.P. Saec., XIV.

22 Sirach xxiv. 47.

23 II Cor. x. 5.

www.ingramcontent.com/pod-product-compliance
Lightning Source LLC
Chambersburg PA
CBHW010347170726
48284CB00011B/2817

* 9 7 8 1 9 5 3 7 4 6 0 4 7 *